IMAGES
of America

MARION COUNTY

On the Cover: Exuberant crowds line Main Street to experience a Christmas parade. This early-1950s image of scenic Main Street in downtown Columbia captures the optimism of a Southern town that has maintained its sense of place. The annual Christmas parade has been a holiday season tradition for many decades. (Courtesy of Bates Bullock.)

IMAGES *of America*

MARION COUNTY

Marion County Historical Society

ARCADIA
PUBLISHING

ISBN 978-0-7385-9193-3

Published by Arcadia Publishing
Charleston, South Carolina

Printed in the United States of America

Library of Congress Control Number: 2012930855

For all general information, please contact Arcadia Publishing:
Telephone 843-853-2070
Fax 843-853-0044
E-mail sales@arcadiapublishing.com
For customer service and orders:
Toll-Free 1-888-313-2665

Visit us on the Internet at www.arcadiapublishing.com

This is dedicated to the charter members of the Marion County Historical Society in appreciation and gratitude for their efforts to preserve and pass along the rich history of Marion County and South Mississippi.

Contents

ACKNOWLEDGMENTS

The Marion County Historical Society wishes to express heartfelt gratitude to all who have assisted in the preparation and completion of this volume. Were it not for those who were willing to share their stories, memories, and photographs, this book would not be a reality. Thanks again!

INTRODUCTION

The first pioneers had already staked their claims to rich lands in the lower Pearl River valley when a new county was established in the Mississippi Territory on December 9, 1811. This county, located in the heavily forested Pine Belt region, was named Marion in honor of Francis Marion of South Carolina. He gained renown for his unconventional methods of warfare and relentless pursuit of the British forces as an officer during the Revolutionary War and was highly esteemed by the many South Carolinians who settled in South Mississippi.

Large numbers of settlers continued to arrive over the next two decades with most coming from the Carolinas and Georgia. Some traveled overland on horses and wagons through the wilderness that lay between western Georgia and the Mississippi River, while others came by way of Tennessee and the Natchez Trace. Many made their journey down the Mississippi River on flatboats, beginning on the Tennessee River or Ohio River and ending at Natchez, Fort Adams, or other towns along the lower Mississippi River. From there, they traveled overland to reach their destination in Marion County. They arrived with the hope of creating a more prosperous life for themselves and their families on what was then the Western Frontier. A few large-scale antebellum plantations thrived along the Pearl River supported by the labor of large numbers of slaves. To the enslaved, their new home in the Mississippi Territory offered no hope of anything other than a continuation of a lifetime of servitude. Most residents worked their land without extensive use of slave labor. They lived modestly on small farms and relied on their own agricultural produce and wild game as primary means of sustenance. Descendants of the earliest settlers, both free and enslaved, have continued as residents of the county since its founding.

Indian mounds near the Pearl River a few miles south of Columbia stand as a monument to the presence of Native American Indians. The settlers generally lived peacefully with the Indians who inhabited the area, and some Native Americans even fought for the defense of the United States during the War of 1812. Yet, in 1814, Gov. David Holmes ordered that a stockade be built in Marion County at the home of John Ford to offer protection to the settlers—an indication of the violence that sometimes erupted from conflicting cultural values that ultimately led to the removal of the original inhabitants.

John Ford's home, a three-story, wood framed structure, was near one of the most frequently traveled roads through the county. In 1814, Andrew Jackson stayed at Ford's while en route to Louisiana shortly before the Battle of New Orleans. The Ford home was also the site of the first Mississippi Methodist Conference in 1814. The Pearl River Convention was held there in 1816 to debate whether the Mississippi Territory, which, at that time, included the present-day state of Alabama, should be divided or if it should remain one territory.

Columbia, the seat of local government, was formally established by act of the legislature on January 13, 1818, making it one of the first towns to be incorporated in the lower Pearl River valley. The townsite, originally known as Lott's Bluff, is centrally located on the east bank of Pearl River. A political struggle between the wealthy and influential residents of the more densely populated counties along the Mississippi River and the residents of the sparsely populated interior counties led to the selection of Columbia as the temporary capital of Mississippi in 1821. The state legislature met at Columbia Springs, a renowned resort hotel a short distance north of Columbia, owned by the Stovall family. The hotel was situated on Buckhorn Creek near the Pearl River and was a popular summer retreat for the elite of Mississippi, New Orleans, and elsewhere. Here, the Poindexter Code, the first uniform code of law of Mississippi, was adopted in 1822. Columbia was one of several landings on the Pearl River where steamboats arrived laden with supplies from New Orleans. Boats plying the waters of the Pearl were a vital means of transport for cotton and other produce and stock to the markets of New Orleans. Commercial traffic on the river rapidly declined after the arrival of the railroad near the turn of the 20th century. From its earliest days as a frontier village with dirt streets and a few wooden structures to its growth into a modest city with handsome brick buildings constructed in the early 1900s, Columbia has the distinction of being the only incorporated city in the county.

Though no battles were fought within the boundaries of Marion County, the Civil War brought turmoil to its residents. Most able-bodied men were engaged in military service for the Confederacy and were absent from their farms. In their absence, their families struggled to grow crops necessary to meet their most basic needs. A Columbia resident wrote Gov. John J. Pettus in 1862 informing him that merchants in the city were preying upon the community by demanding exorbitant prices for their goods, and many families were destitute of the means to feed and clothe themselves. December 1864 saw the arrival of more than 4,000 Federal troops led by Gen. John W. Davidson on a march from Baton Rouge to Pascagoula. During their two-day passage through the county, they plundered grain bins and smoke houses, slaughtered or confiscated livestock, and destroyed crops.

The end of the war heralded freedom for the slaves and the end of the Old South culture, but political, economic, and social turmoil lingered for years afterwards. The struggle between the mostly republican supporters of Reconstruction and the Old South democrats is evident in a series of letters addressed to Gov. James Alcorn from Columbia. The letters, written by local officials and a carpetbagger attorney, reveal that by the end of 1871 most officials in the county—including the clerk of the courts, treasurer, tax assessor, superintendent of education, all justices of the peace, and all members of the board of supervisors—had resigned or been removed from office. Their recommended replacements were aligned with the Reconstruction effort.

The White Caps, an organization of white men that enforced appropriate standards of behavior on all citizens, developed a strong following in South Mississippi. They delivered stern warnings or whippings to those who violated the accepted code of conduct without regard for the law and often under cloak of darkness. Over time, their actions became more violent and were frequently directed against those of African descent. A blast from a shotgun ended the life of a white Marion County farmer named Will Buckley in 1893, and whitecapping activities in Marion County captured national attention. Will Purvis, a young man affiliated with the White Caps, was convicted of the murder and sentenced to death. A large crowd gathered on the grounds of the courthouse to witness his execution, but when the door of the gallows opened beneath his feet, the noose slipped, and Purvis fell to the ground unharmed. Legal proceedings against Purvis continued for several years until Gov. John Stone pardoned him in 1898. A series of trials were held in Columbia in the 1890s, and several men were convicted of whitecapping offenses. Some served sentences in the state penitentiary, and the severity of their punishment effectively ended whitecapping in the county. Two decades later, a deathbed statement by another man exonerated Purvis of the murder for which he was convicted, and the state compensated him for the injustices he endured.

Although the agrarian-based Southern economy had collapsed after the war, a substantial economic boost eventually came from a vast natural resource that had been substantially untouched. Beginning in the 1880s, representatives of Northern lumber companies purchased thousands of acres of red clay hills covered in vast forests of virgin pine timber. The largest early logging company in Marion County was likely S.A. Jones & Bros., which was, in time, followed by J.J. White and Great Southern Lumber Companies, among others. In fact, to date, the oldest continually operating business in Marion County is the sawmill of W.F. Foxworth & Son on Silver Creek.

Throughout the era of the timber boom, bustling logging and sawmill villages, with names such as Kokomo, Pickwick, and White Bluff, sprang up, only to become a mere shadow of their former selves once the hills had been stripped bare of the majestic forests that gave the Pine Belt its name.

By 1931, with most of the trees gone, the J.J. White Lumber Company ended its operations. The mill was at the time the largest employer in Columbia, and the loss of jobs soon brought the grim realities of the Great Depression. To combat the economic downturn in the era, Columbia mayor Hugh White advocated an economic development strategy that became known as "Balance Agriculture with Industry." The policy proved to be successful in attracting business and industry to Columbia and was, in time, copied by many communities nationwide. White went on to serve two terms as governor of Mississippi. As of 1965, local employment in the industrial sector was, for the first time, equal to that of the agricultural. In 1935, cowboy Earl Bascom organized Mississippi's first rodeo, which was held in the Columbia City Park. This famous event is today remembered as the first rodeo ever held at night in a lighted arena.

Heavily involved in the war effort, by 1942, Marion County had mobilized and became the land of war bond drives, victory baby contests, and patriotic displays in the picture windows of the downtown businesses. In fact, Pioneer Manufacturing in Columbia was the largest producer of parachutes in the nation during the war. Before the war ended, some 1,700 residents of Marion County had served in uniform. Marion County has always responded to the nation's call to arms, from the War of 1812 all the way up through the current campaigns in Iraq and Afghanistan.

The winds of social change blew once more through the county during the turbulent 1960s. As activists demanded equality, voting rights, and school integration, a multiracial group of community leaders, led by Mayor E.D. "Buddy" McLean, took steps to avoid the racial violence that had erupted in the surrounding communities. Ultimately, businesses and schools were peacefully desegregated, with the Columbia School System the first in the state to completely desegregate schools and buses.

The progressive county has been home to its share of prominent politicians, scientists, and sportsmen. Notable among those who called the county home are two-term Mississippi governor Hugh White; Earl Bascom, the father of modern rodeo; musician Jeff Bates; and Dr. Charles Bass, the father of preventive dentistry. Sylvester Magee, thought to have been the last surviving slave in America, is buried in Foxworth. Numerous distinguished athletes have hailed from Marion County, perhaps most notably Walter Payton, easily one of the most prolific running backs in the history of American football.

Well into the 21st century, Marion County has remained an idyllic picture of the rural American South at its best, always maintaining its historic character, atmosphere, and sense of place. The images presented in this brief collection portray only a small fraction of the people, places, and events that have helped shape the past two centuries of Marion County, Mississippi.

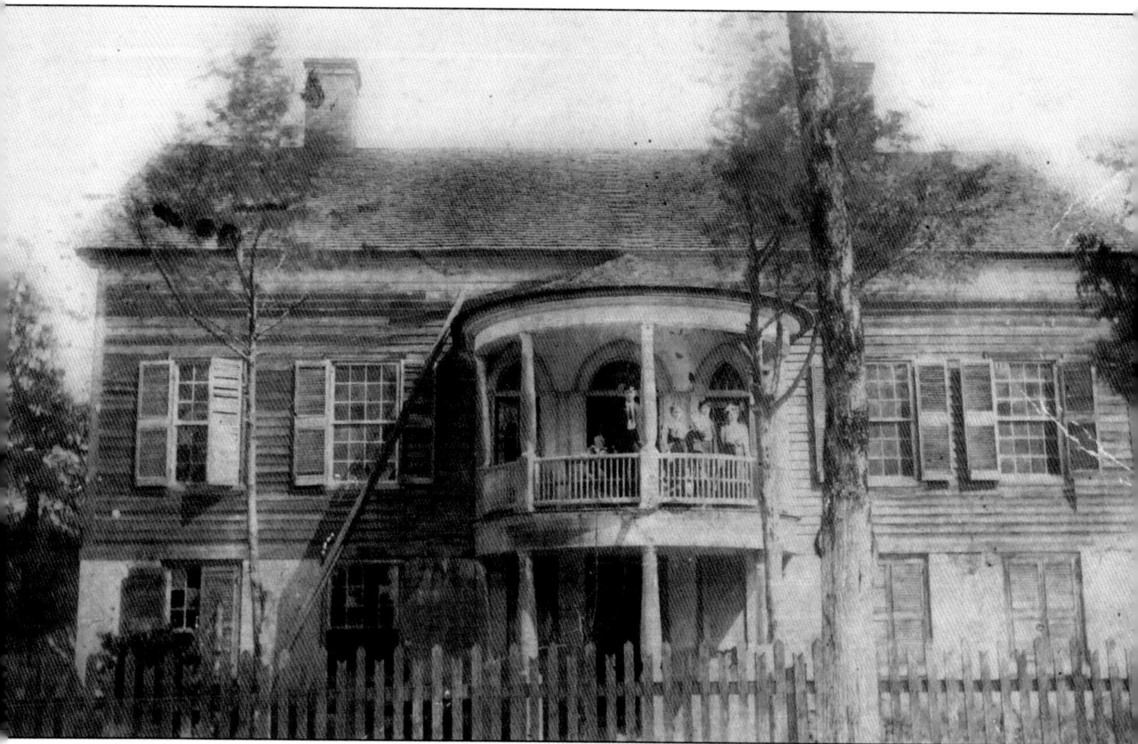

A working plantation prior to the Civil War, the LeNoir Plantation operated on the banks of Pearl River in what is now Morgantown. Occupied by 1818, the house was built for the family of William T. LeNoir. William's brother Hope Hull LeNoir had a home located nearby at White Bluff, while his first cousin Francis Barnes LeNoir was the state representative for Marion County in 1820–1821. This photograph was made in 1905 when Louis N. and Hollie Morgan owned the house. The LeNoir home is widely considered one of the finest examples of the antebellum plantation homes that existed along the Pearl River. The renowned old home burned in 1924, but a family cemetery still exists and is maintained by residents of Morgantown. (Louis F. Morgan collection.)

One

When Agriculture was a Way of Life

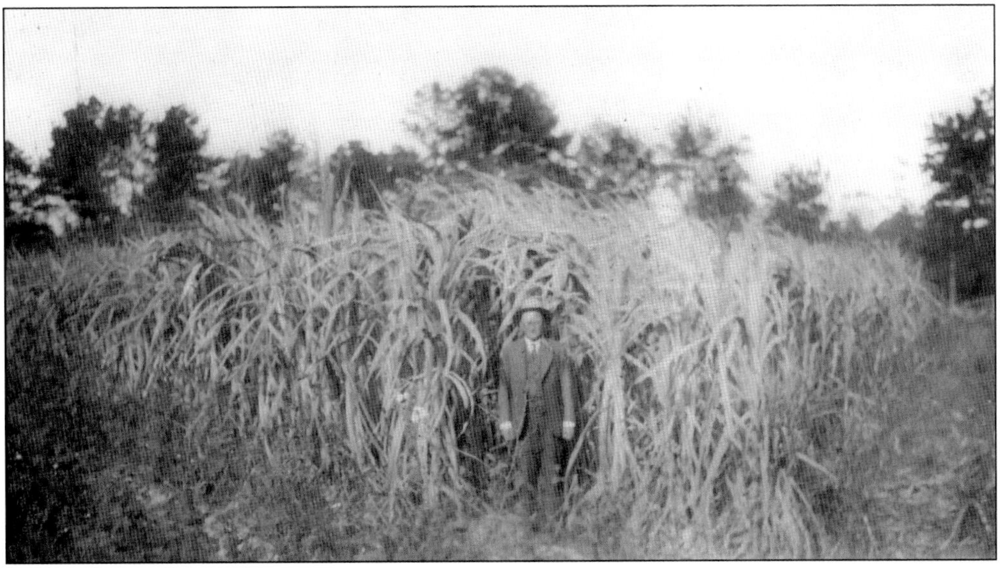

Sugar cane was cultivated early on in Marion County agriculture. In fact, geologist Benjamin Wailes notes that there were at least 20 functional sugar mills in Marion County as early as 1854 and that "many of the most substantial planters make all the sugar and molasses required for their own use, and some to spare to their neighbors." (Courtesy of Marion County Development Partnership.)

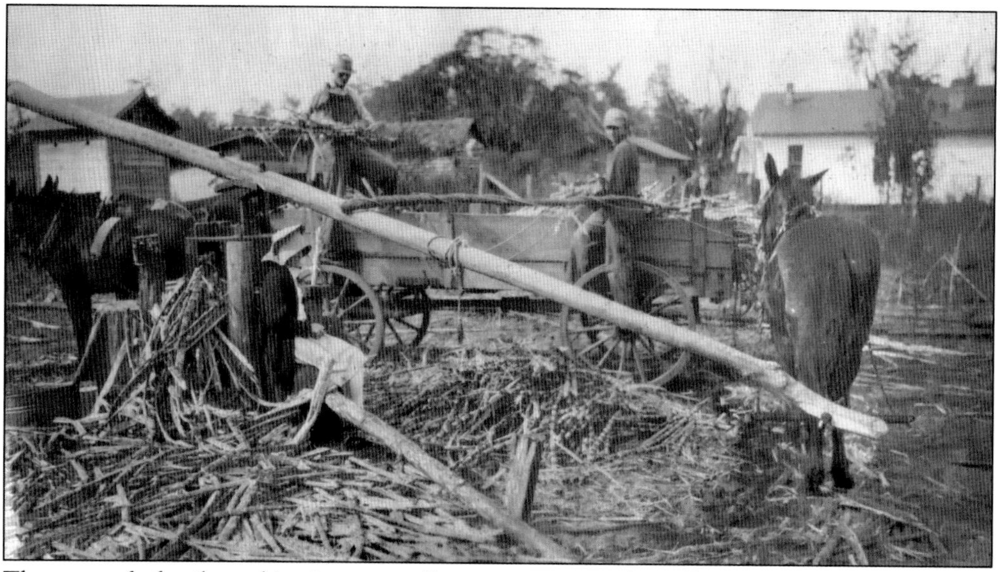

The scene of a family working its cane mill was a common sight well into the 20th century. Sugar cane was crushed in the mill to extract the juice, which was then cooked into syrup. (Courtesy of Marion County Development Partnership.)

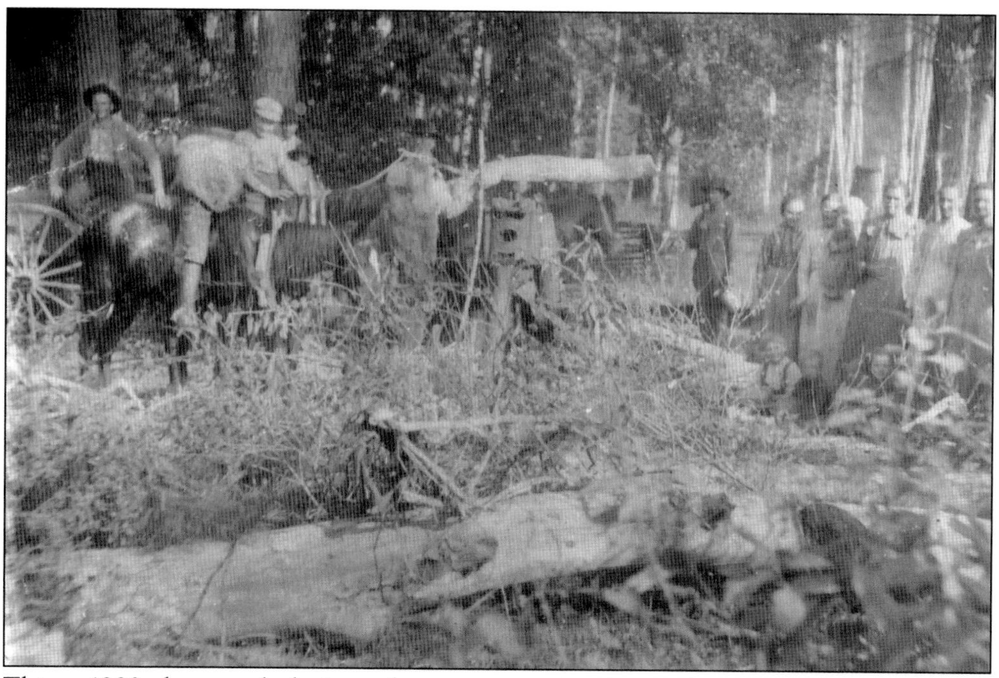

This c. 1900 photograph depicts a large group engaged in making syrup from sugar cane near Morgantown. Note the ladies and children posing on the ground at right. (Louis F. Morgan collection.)

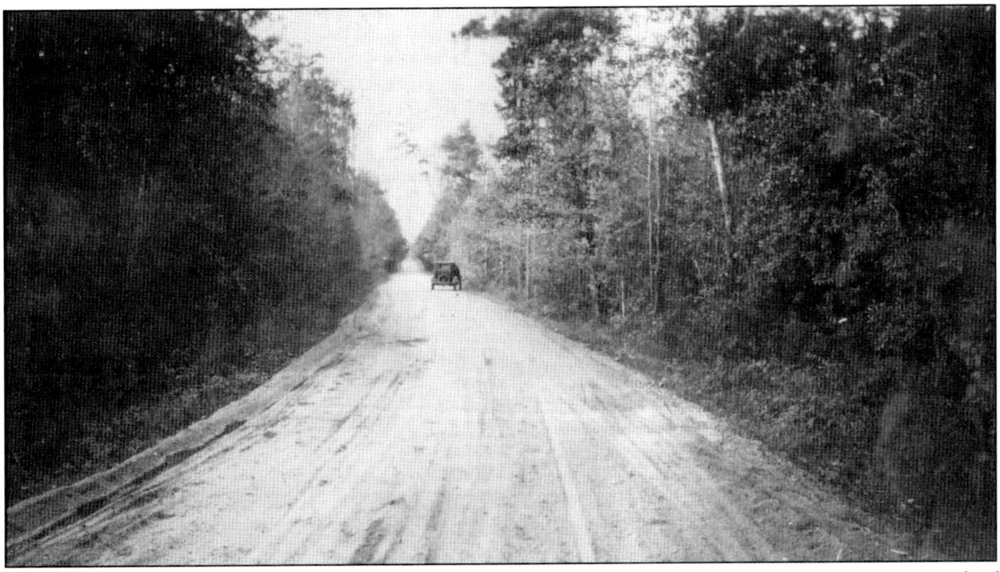

This gravel highway, located somewhere in the rural sections of Marion County, is typical of early-20th-century roadways that were in use throughout the expanses of the county. (Courtesy of Marion County Development Partnership.)

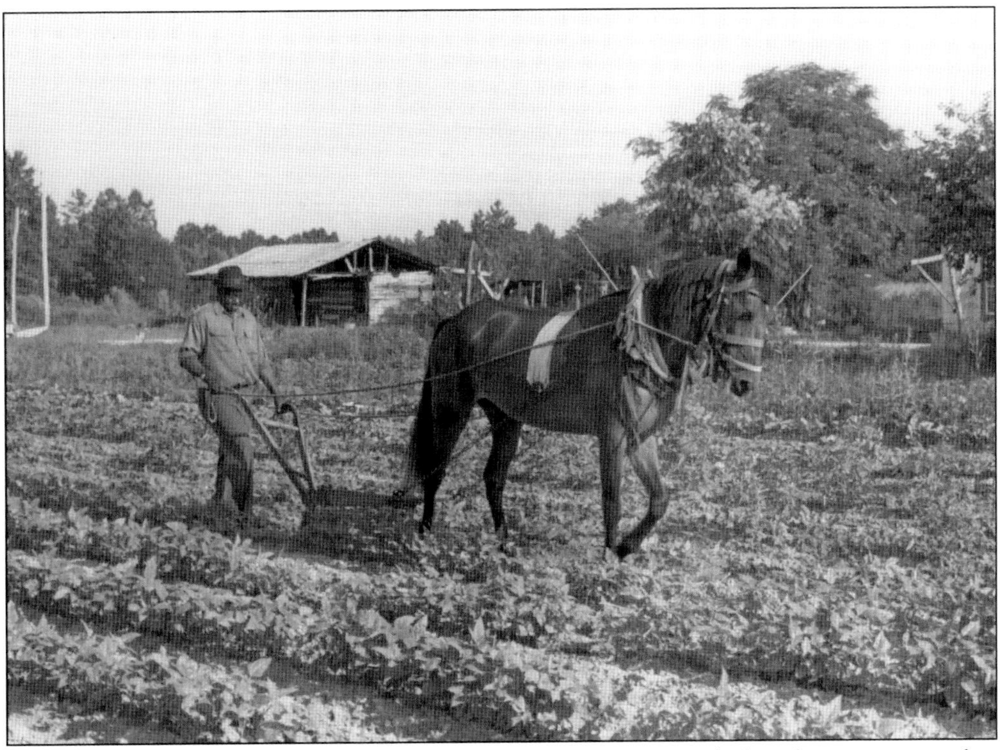

The sight of Harrison Jefferson plowing his fields with a horse and plow depicts a scene that was common in the rural areas of Marion County for well over a century. Photographer Bret B. Bradley most likely made this image in the Lampton community. (Courtesy of Marion County Historical Society.)

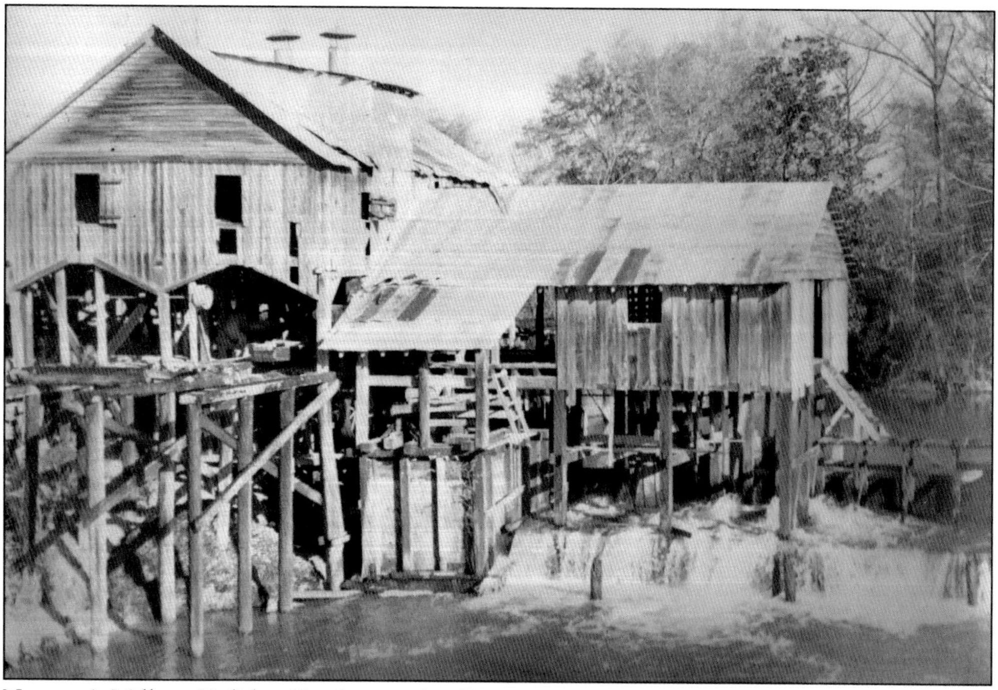

Newsom's Mill on Holiday Creek near the Goss community was a county landmark for many years. The mill had many functions, including grinding corn, ginning cotton, and even sawing lumber. (Courtesy of Charlotte Yarborough.)

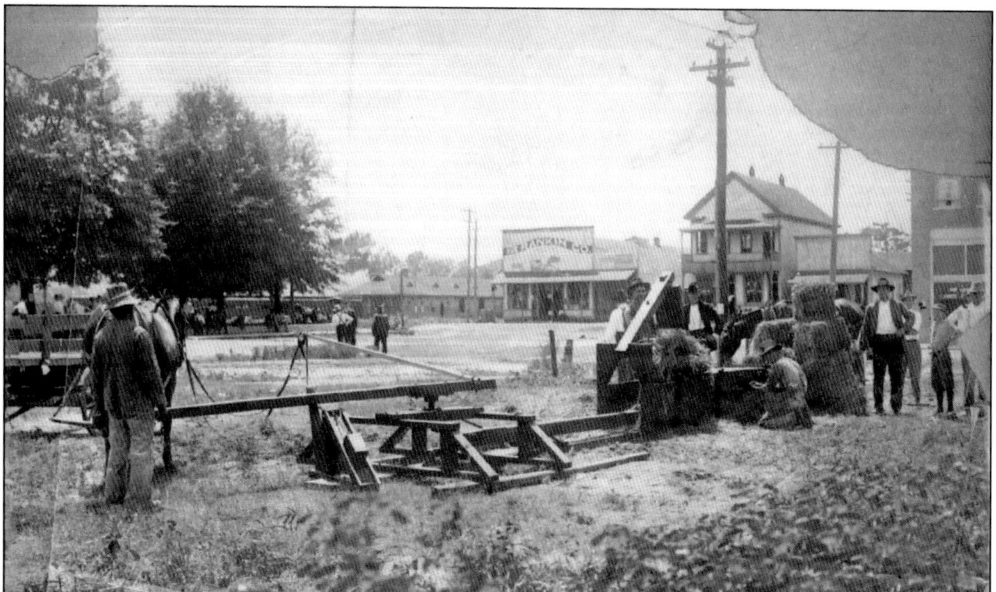

In the foreground, Zach W. Roper (kneeling) demonstrates the workings of his mule-powered hay baler near Courthouse Square. In the background, the New Orleans & Great Northern Depot can be seen, as well as an early Rankin Company Building and a two-story boardinghouse. The Courthouse Square has long been a favored location for citizens to visit with one another, as evident in this early photograph. (Courtesy of Bates Bullock.)

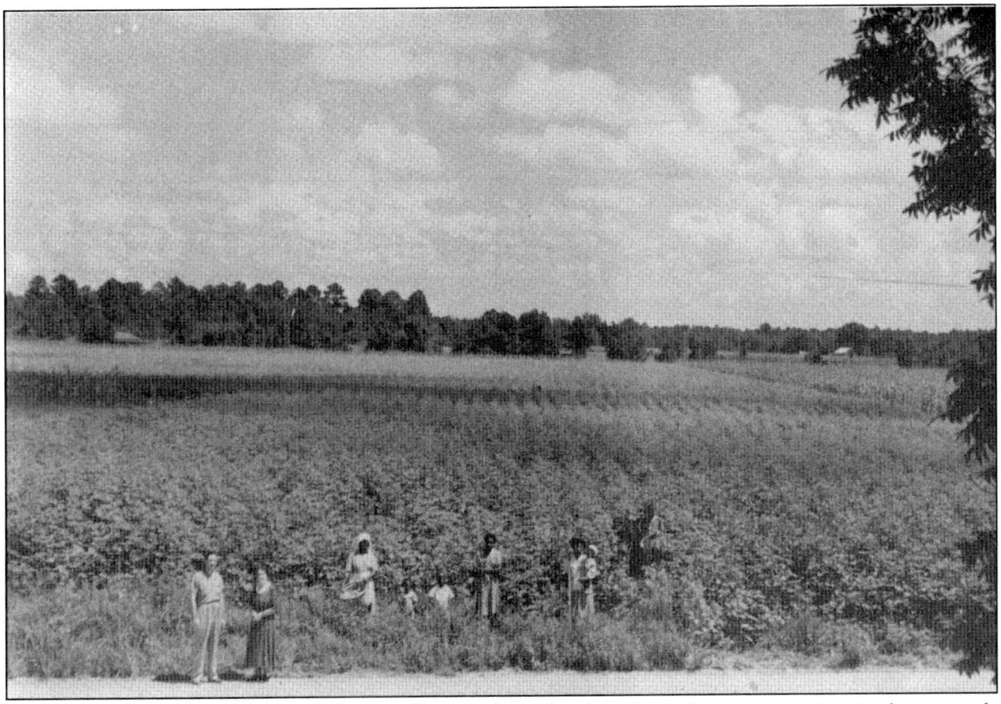

Although the identity of the farmer who produced it has been lost, this c. 1940 photograph captured what was then the longest row of cotton in Marion County. Cotton culture took root in the county early on as numerous plantations lined the Pearl River and outlying areas. Well into the 20th century, the Columbia cotton warehouse and compress churned out thousands of bales annually. (Courtesy of Marion County Historical Society.)

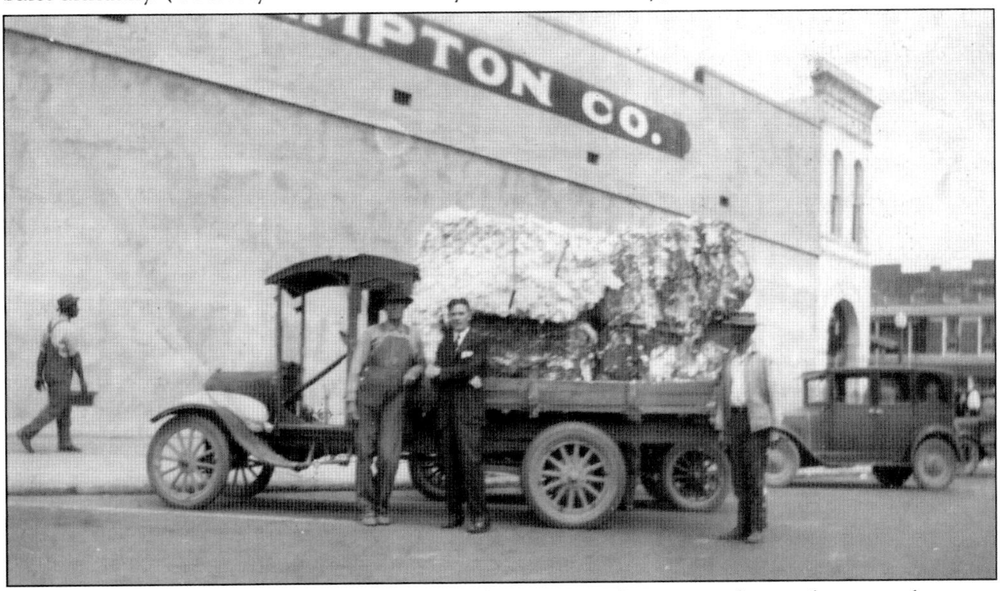

Merchant George Ben Lampton (center, in business suit) poses with two farmers who were the first of the picking season to bring in a load of cotton to sell to the Lampton Company. Photographing the first sale of the season became an annual practice for the business. (Courtesy of Fran Ginn.)

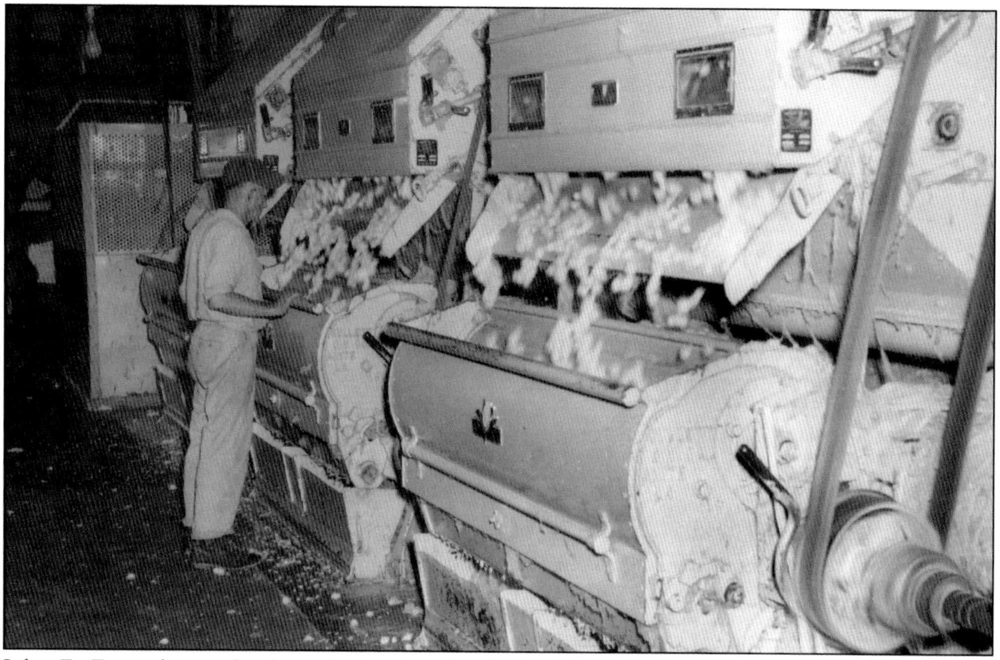

John D. Fortenberry checks a gin head at Rankin's Gin in the Lampton community. The first cotton gin in the county was water powered and operated by the Rev. John Ford at Sandy Hook. At the height of cotton cultivation, at least 19 gins, most with long lines, operated in Marion County. (Courtesy of Marion County Historical Society.)

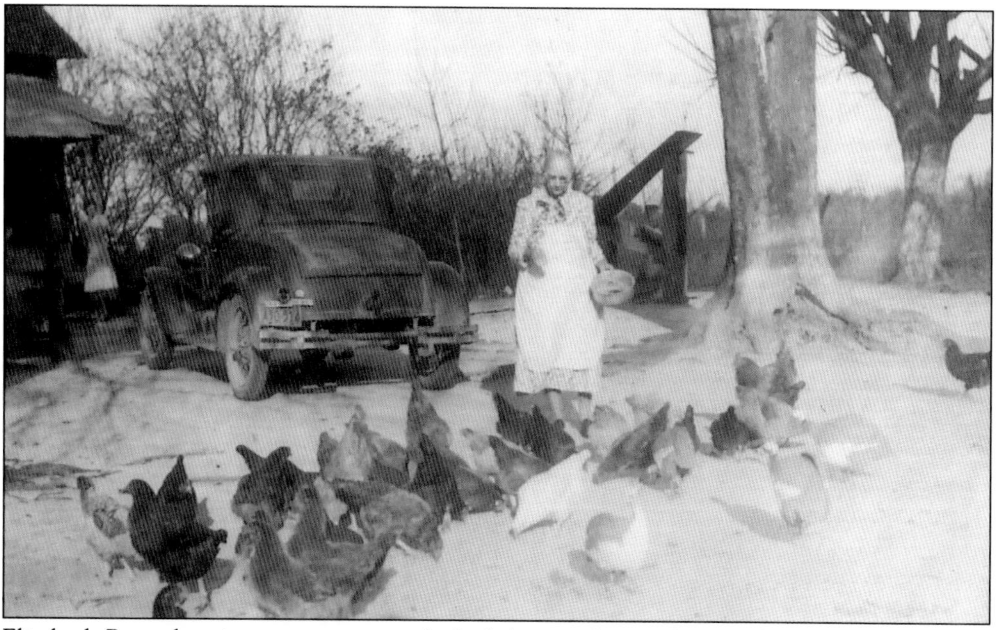

Elizabeth Burt, donning an apron, quietly feeds her poultry on her rural farm. No stranger to hardships, her son Jay was captured at Corregidor and held in Japanese death camps for some 40 months during World War II. As the war drew to a close, Jay was eventually released and returned home. Her community credited Elizabeth Burt, a noted woman of faith, with literally "praying her son back home." (Courtesy of Damon Watts.)

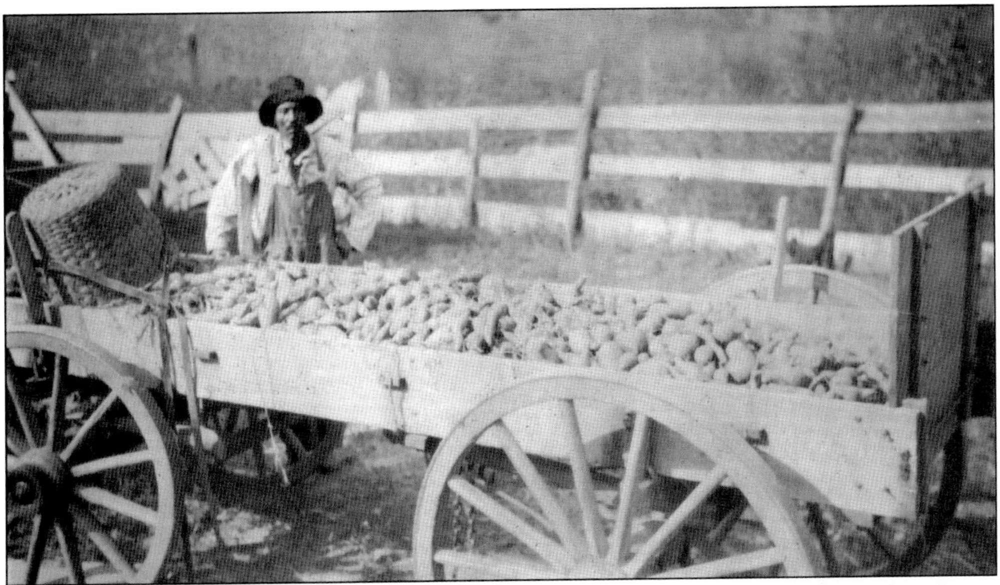

Sweet potatoes have been a local staple crop from at least the early settlement period. In fact, a raiding Yankee soldier noted wryly that South Mississippi was "too poor to raise anything except sweet potatoes, which grow so long that we could (sit) on one end and roast the other (in the campfires)." So plentiful were the potatoes that were stolen from Marion County farmers in the winter of 1864 that Union veterans involved in the raid forevermore referred to their campaign as the "Great Sweet Potato Raid." (Courtesy of Marion County Development Partnership.)

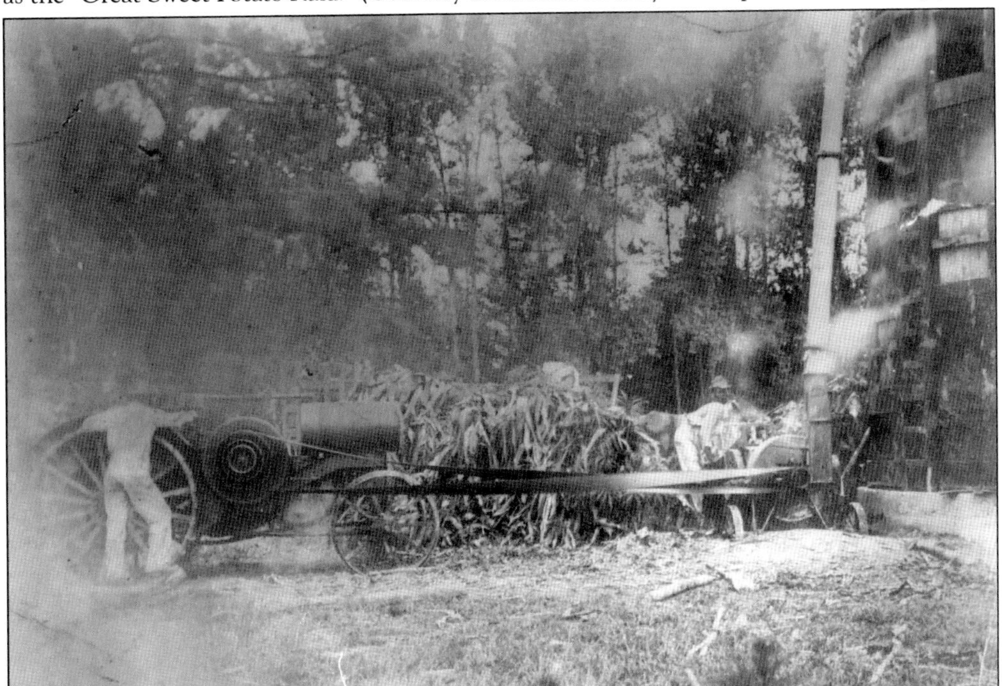

Farmers fill a silo with silage with the use of a steam-powered tractor around 1920. Bret B. Bradley and J.L. Rankin shared this equipment for a number of years. (Courtesy of Marion County Historical Society.)

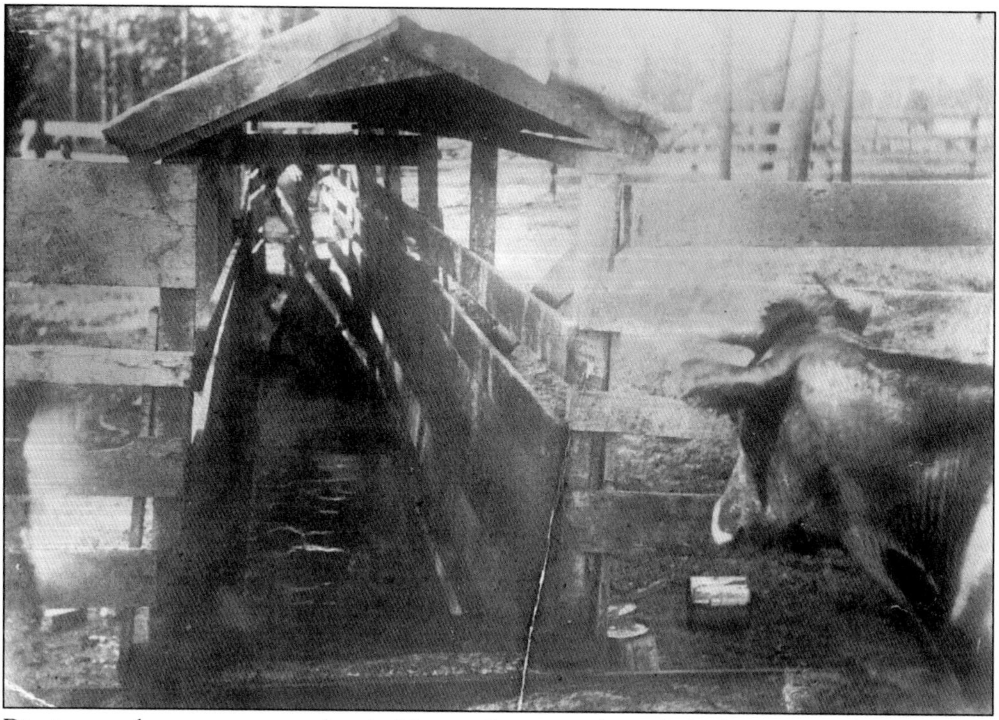

Dipping vats became commonplace in Marion County in the early 20th century and were used to eliminate disease-causing ticks from farm livestock. This dipping vat was photographed, along with a wary cow, in 1917 on Beechwood Farm, located five miles south of Columbia. The photograph is attributed to B.B. Bradley. (Courtesy of Marion County Historical Society.)

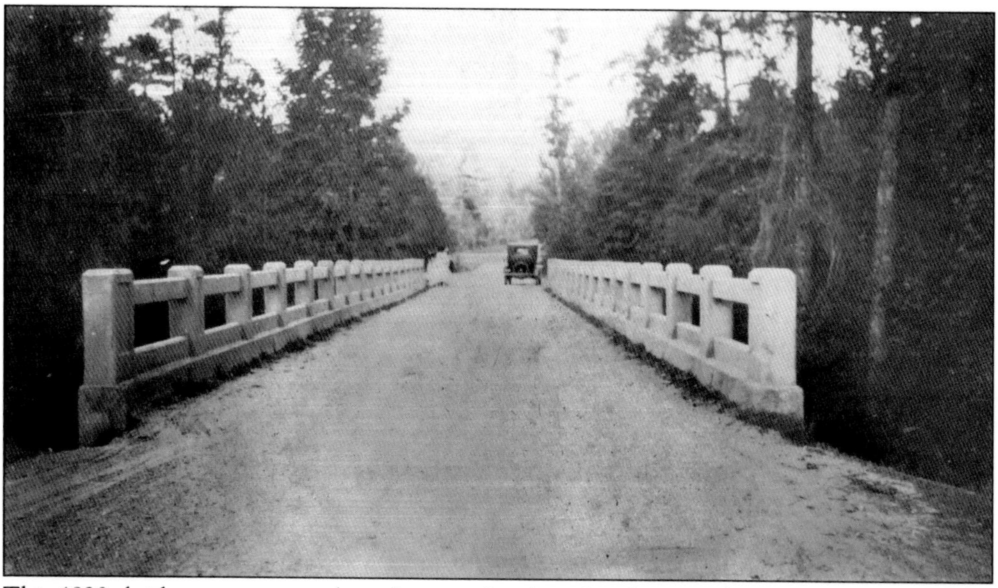

This 1920s bridge was apparently such a novelty that the photographer captured an image of it, complete with his car and passengers posed in the background. (Courtesy of Marion County Development Partnership.)

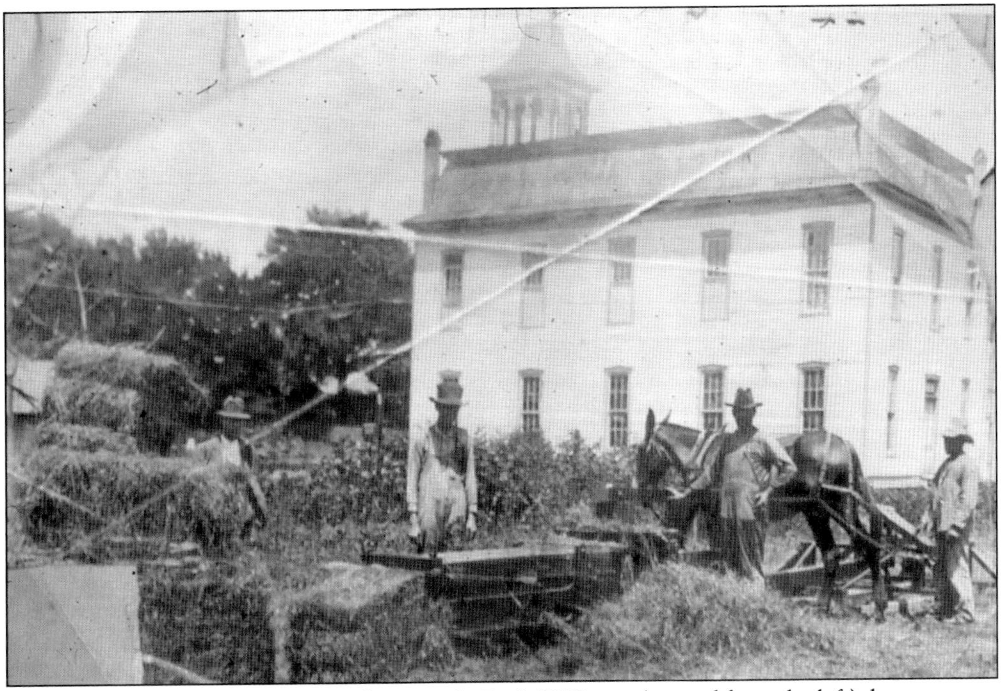

In the foreground of this pre-1905 photograph, Zach W. Roper (second from the left) demonstrates his new hay baler on the west side of the Marion County Courthouse. Roper, a blacksmith, built the baler in his shop on Pearl Street. (Courtesy of Marion County Historical Society.)

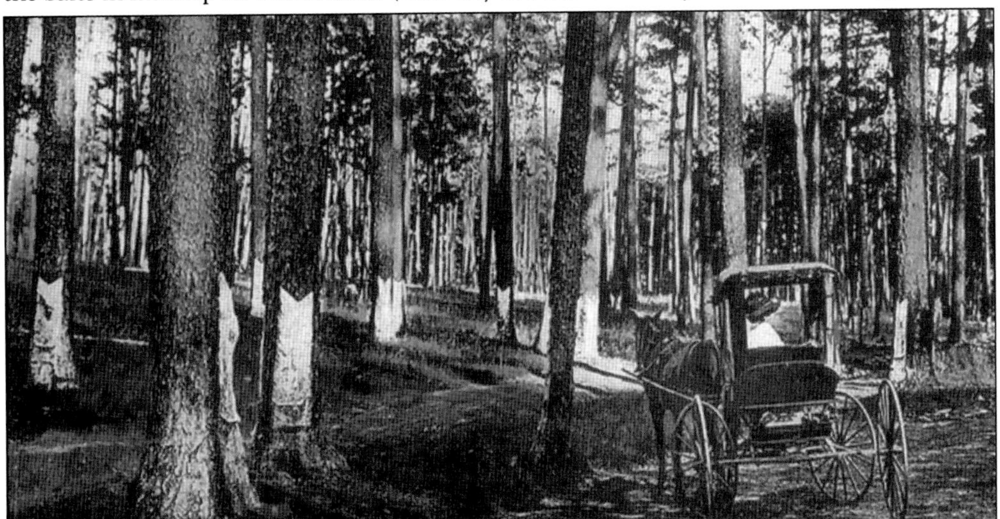

Turpentine production was a growing industry in Marion County well into the 20th century. As turpentine was beneficial to the Southern war effort, Davidson's cavalry destroyed all local orchards they encountered during the winter of 1864. One New York cavalryman remarked, "We passed through magnificent forests of pine trees . . . We fired these forests as we went through . . . to prevent our enemies from utilizing this resin in their war against our Government . . . the fires from the resin of thousands of trees in this great turpentine orchard, gave to the marching columns a weird appearance." The image is from a postcard sold by Berry's Pharmacy. (Courtesy of Mississippi Department of Archives and History.)

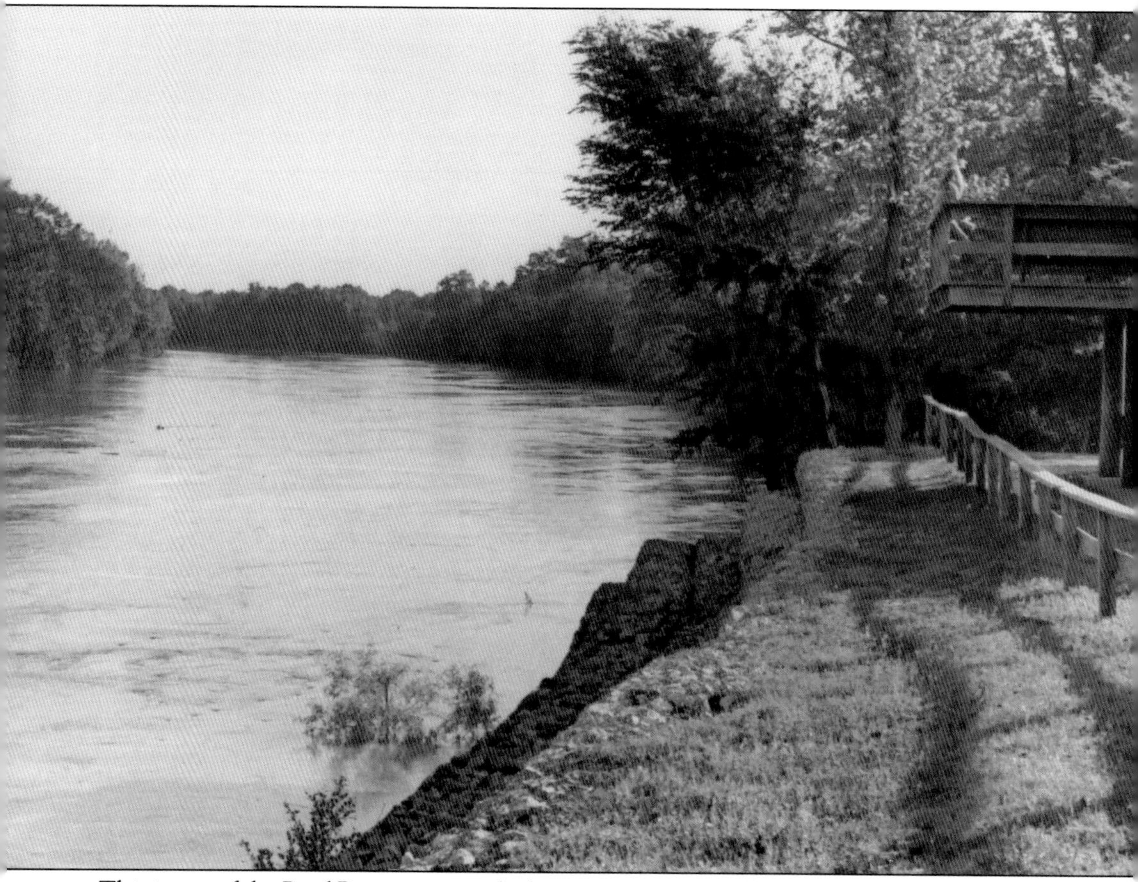

This image of the Pearl River captures the historic waterway well after the end of its romantic era. First surveyed by the French in 1732, at one time rustic plantations, steamboats, and ferries were all fixtures along the river throughout the 19th century. Raiding Federal soldiers were forced to build a pontoon bridge to span the river in both 1864 and 1865, and fought a brief skirmish along the banks. Even the likes of Anthony Butler and Stephen Douglas once called the banks of the Pearl River home. Douglas, who famously debated Abraham Lincoln during the 1860 presidential elections, at one time lived on a 1,700-acre plantation just upriver in adjoining Lawrence County. In fact, in 1852, Douglas was involved in a lawsuit with the Pearl River Navigation Company over the spoilage of 64 bales of his cotton. Butler was appointed US Ambassador to Mexico by Pres, Andrew Jackson in 1829. (Courtesy of Marion County Historical Society.)

Two

Of Education and Worship

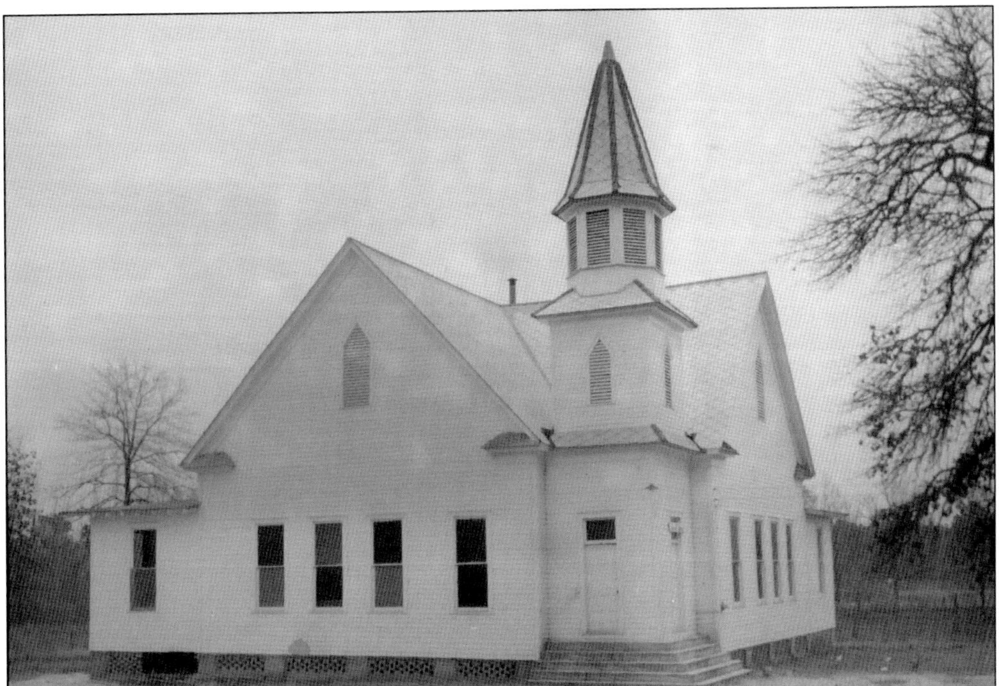

Kokomo Methodist Church was built in 1911. A logging company owned by the Enoch family donated the lumber used to construct the church. One early church organizer was Dr. Henry Carruth, who was once the mill doctor for the Fernwood, Columbia & Gulf Railroad. (Courtesy of Marion County Historical Society.)

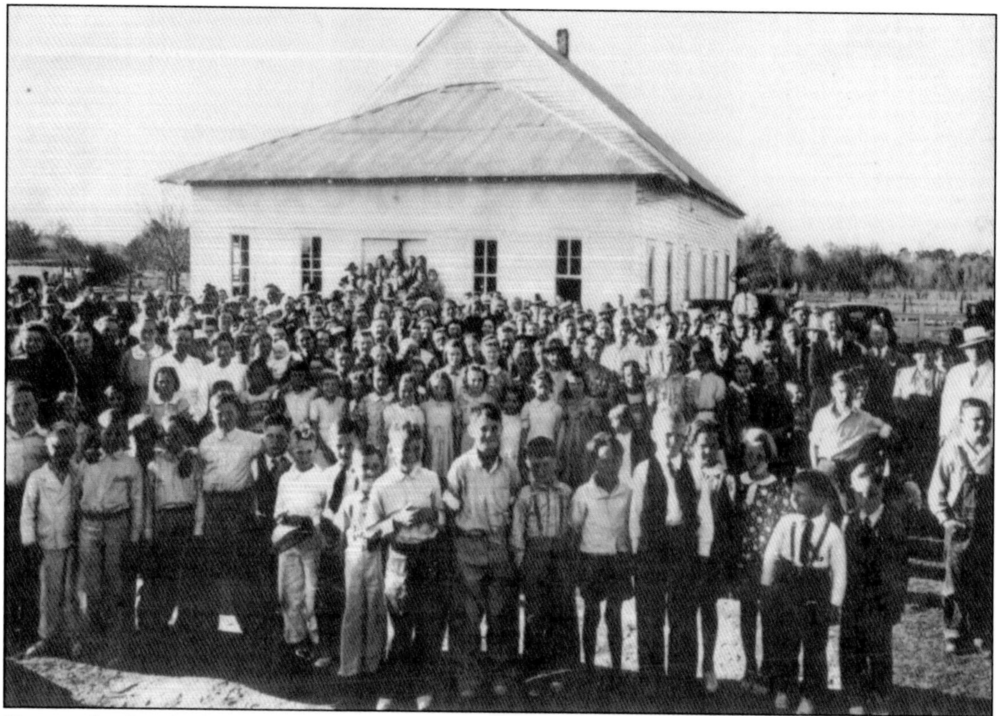

Here is the first building of the Morgantown Church of God as it appeared on a typical Sunday in 1939 when Rev. DeWitt Sharp was pastor. In those days, it was common for the overflow crowds to stand outside near the open windows to participate in the church services. It was in this building that Morgantown School principal and area pastor R.R. Walker united with the Church of God in 1933, becoming the first Church of God minister with a college degree. (Louis F. Morgan collection.)

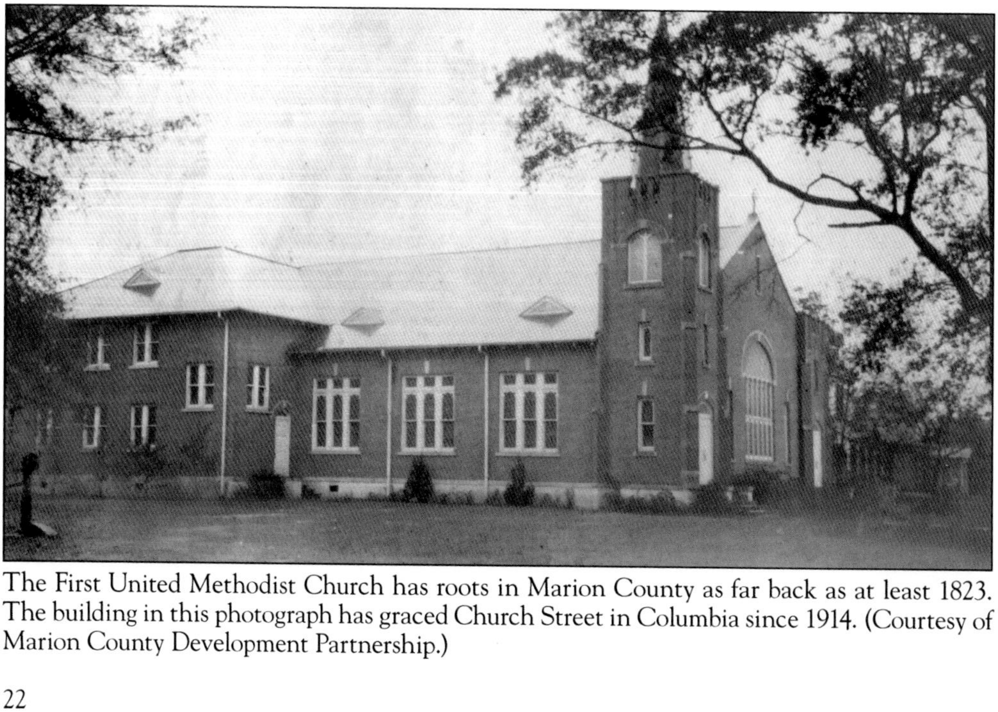

The First United Methodist Church has roots in Marion County as far back as at least 1823. The building in this photograph has graced Church Street in Columbia since 1914. (Courtesy of Marion County Development Partnership.)

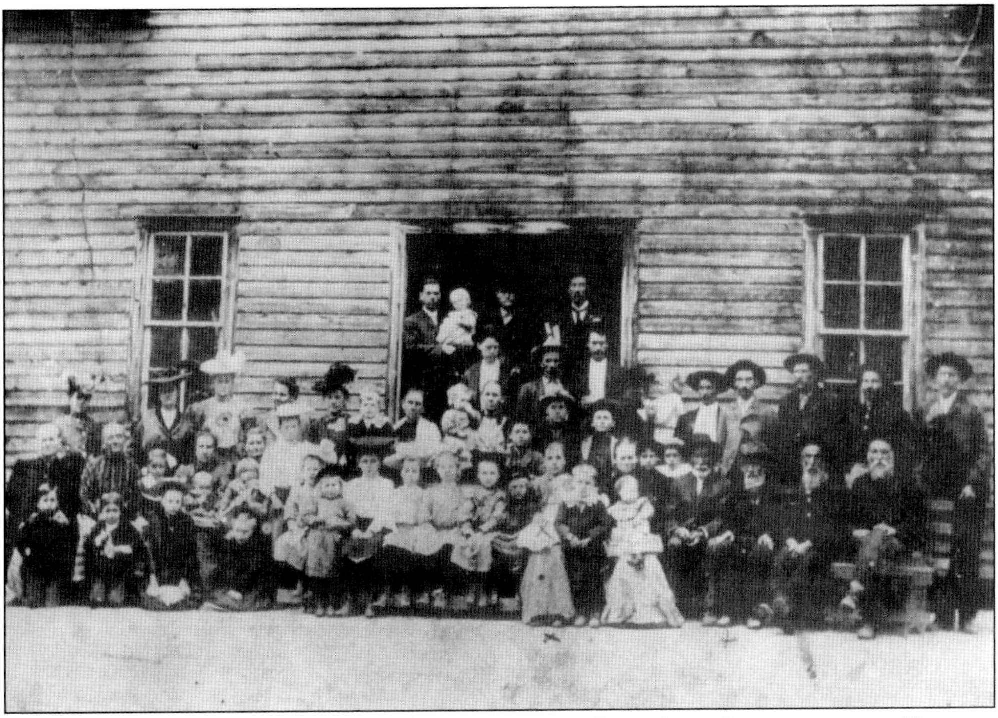

Organized during the summer of 1902, this c. 1907 image shows the early congregation of Improve Baptist Church posed in front of the first church building. (Courtesy of Damon Watts.)

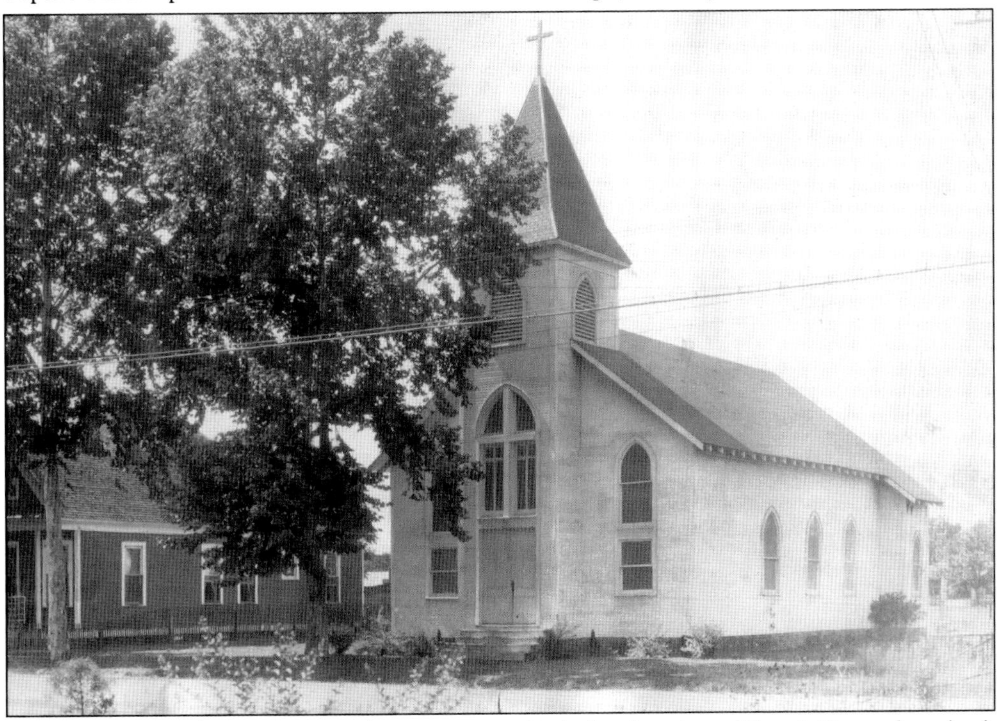

Although its steeple is now gone, the picturesque Catholic church on Church Street dates back to about 1900. (Courtesy of Marion County Development Partnership.)

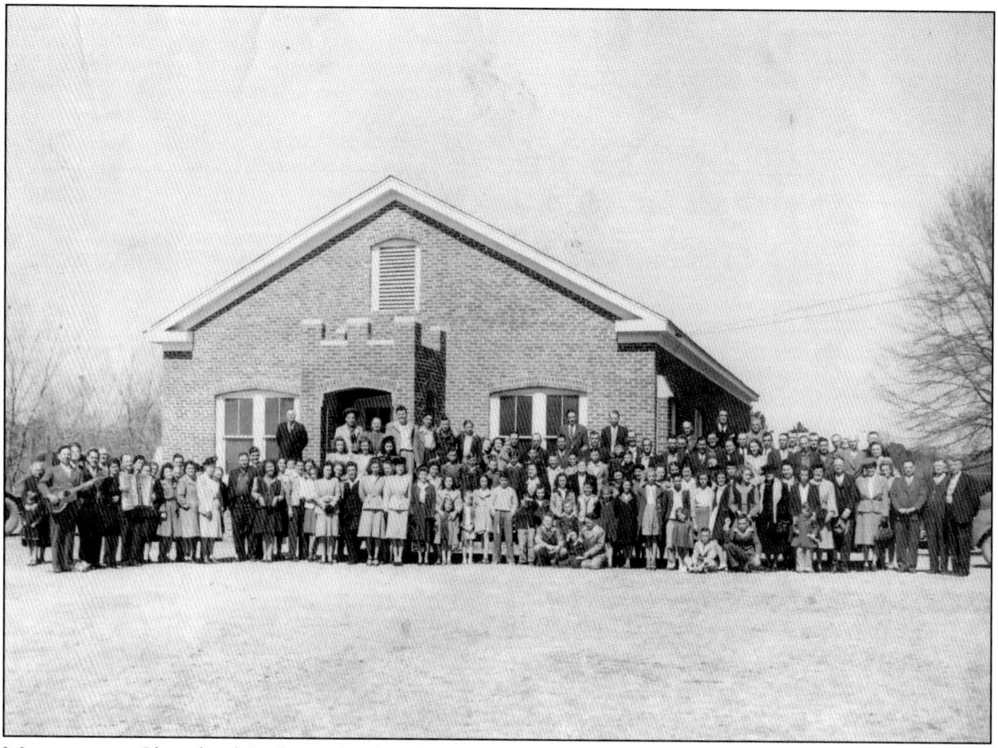

Morgantown Church of God was the first brick Church of God sanctuary constructed in Mississippi. The structure was built in 1945 following a nine-week revival when W.R. Messer was pastor. Morgantown is where the Pentecostal message was introduced into Marion County in 1915. (Louis F. Morgan collection.)

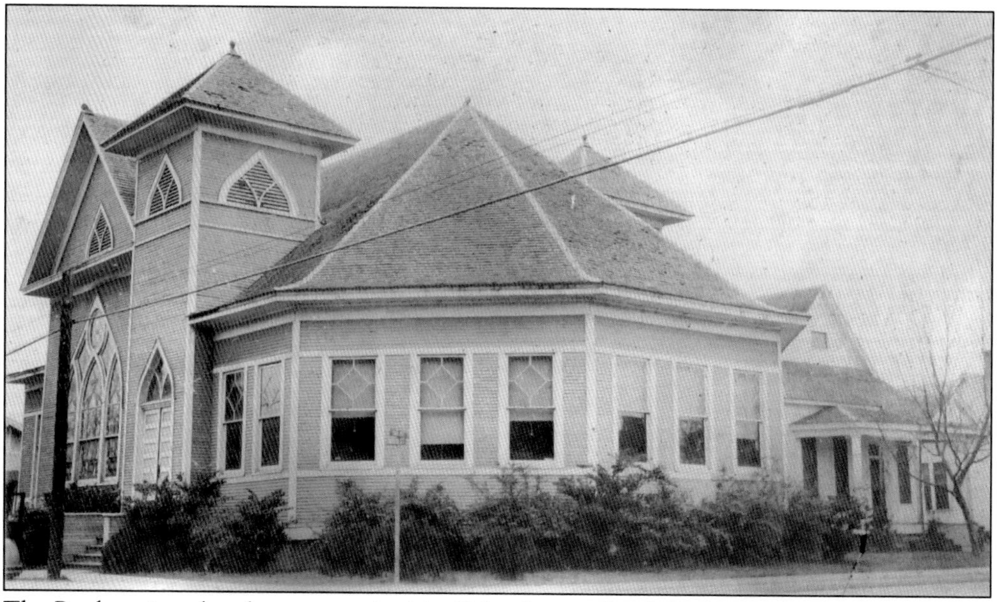

The Presbyterian church was organized in Columbia on April 20, 1910. This handsome wood framed building served the congregation on Church Street for many years. (Courtesy of Marion County Development Partnership.)

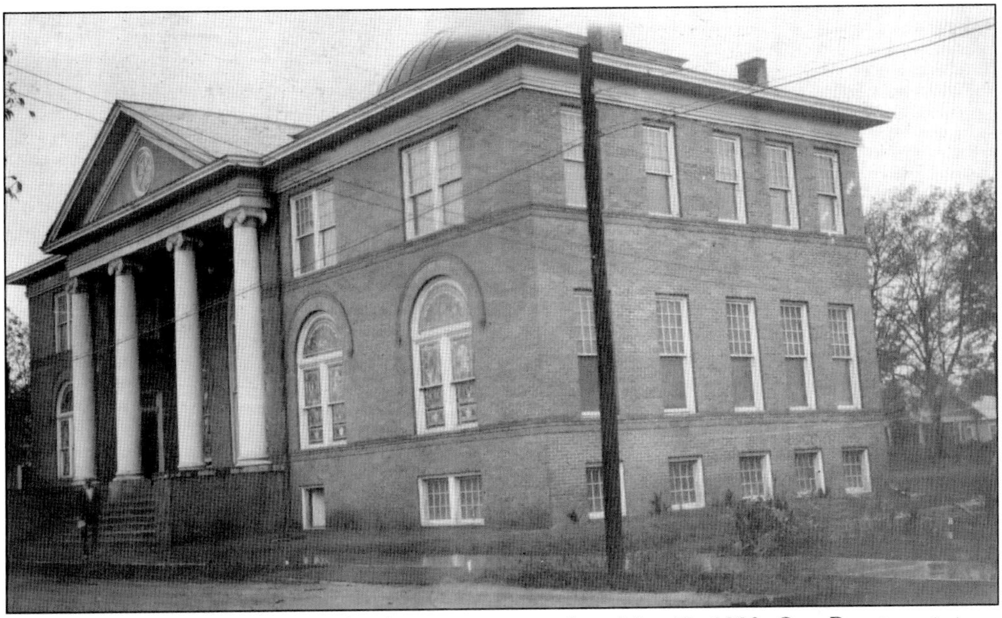

The First Baptist Church of Columbia was organized on May 12, 1883. One Baptist minister stated that a Baptist church was sorely needed in Columbia due to wickedness in the town and because of the three saloons that were flourishing along Columbia's Main Street during the period. (Courtesy of Marion County Development Partnership.)

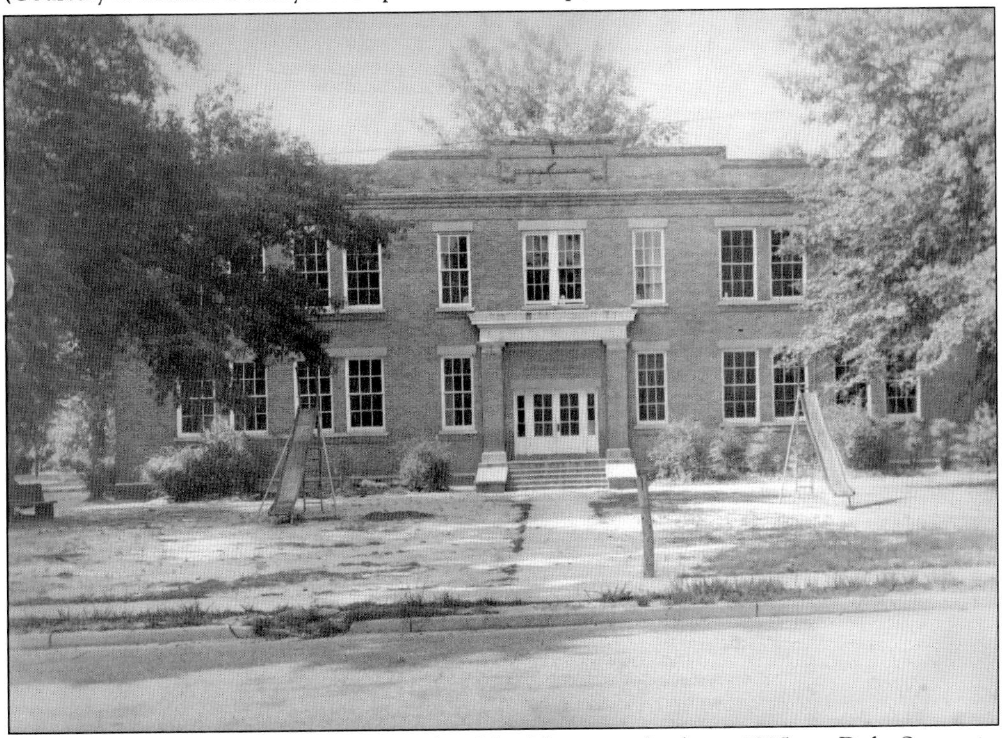

The handsome Columbia Primary School building was built in 1915 on Dale Street in Columbia and served the city students until the building was torn down in 1951. (Courtesy of Glenda Shivers.)

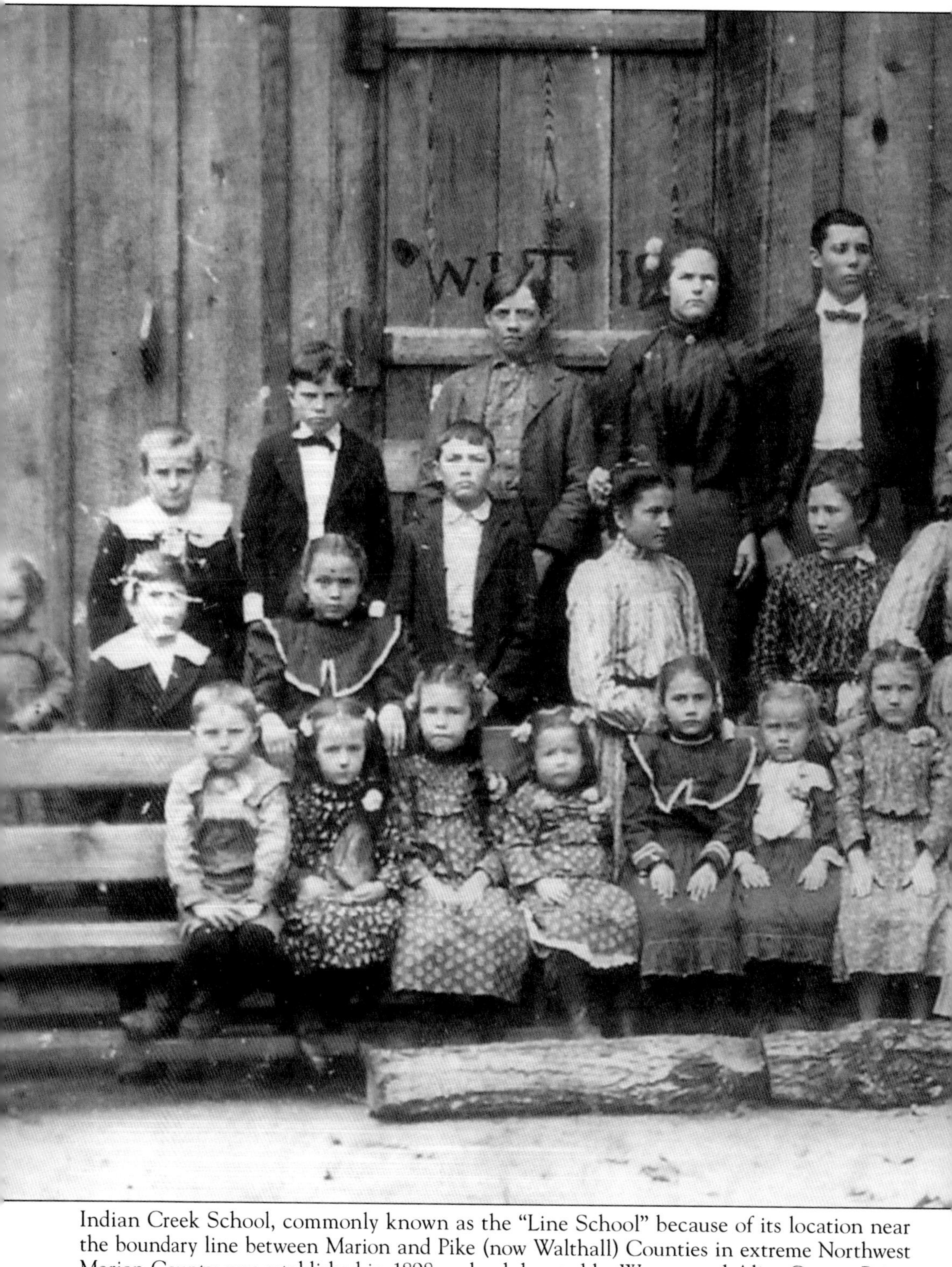

Indian Creek School, commonly known as the "Line School" because of its location near the boundary line between Marion and Pike (now Walthall) Counties in extreme Northwest Marion County, was established in 1898 on land donated by Warren and Alice Cooper Price. The building was constructed by men in the neighborhood, and though partially obscured by

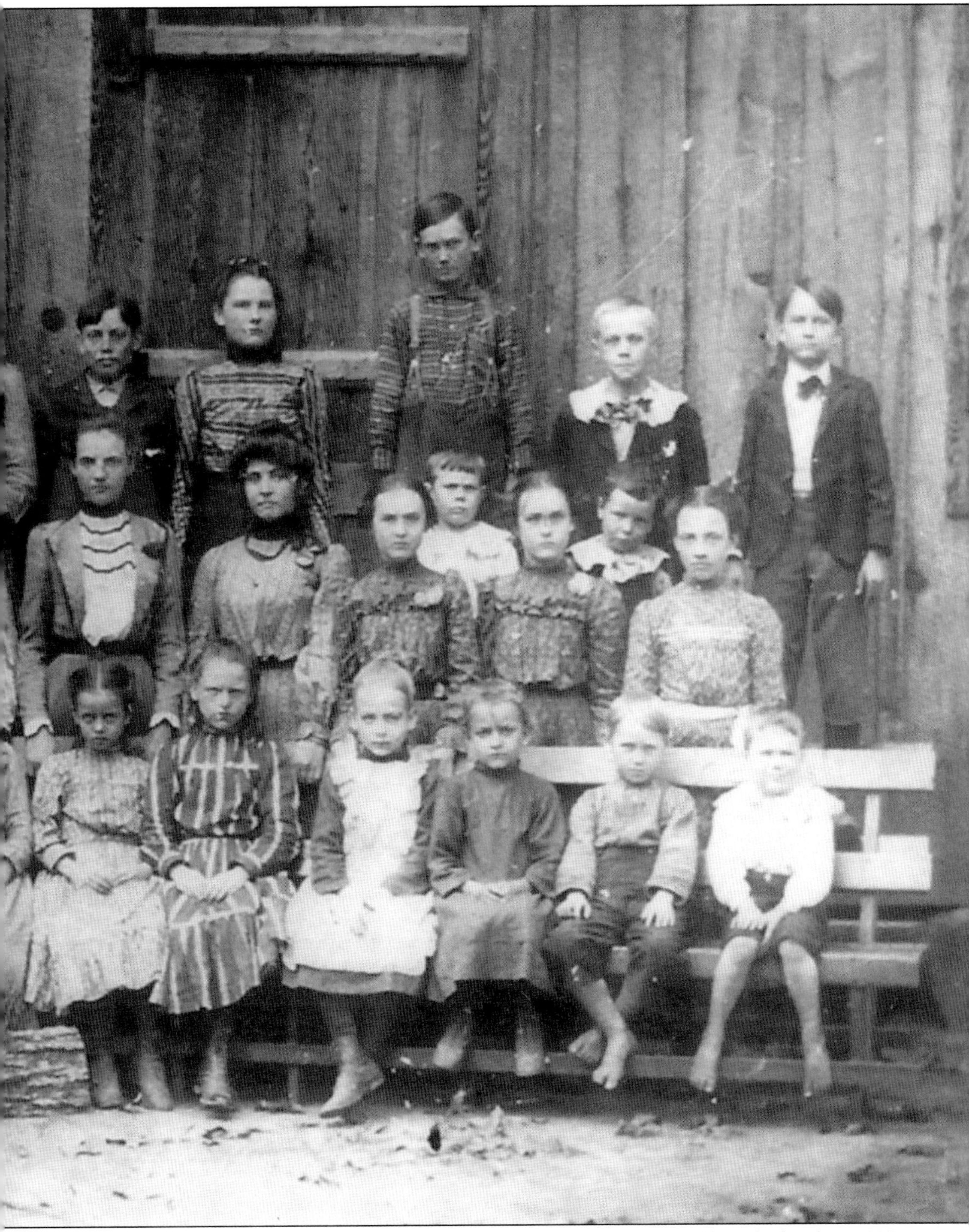

one of the students, the initials of one of them, William Louis Thornhill, with the date 1898 can be seen burned into one of the wooden shutters. This photograph was taken around 1900. (Courtesy of Annette Reid.)

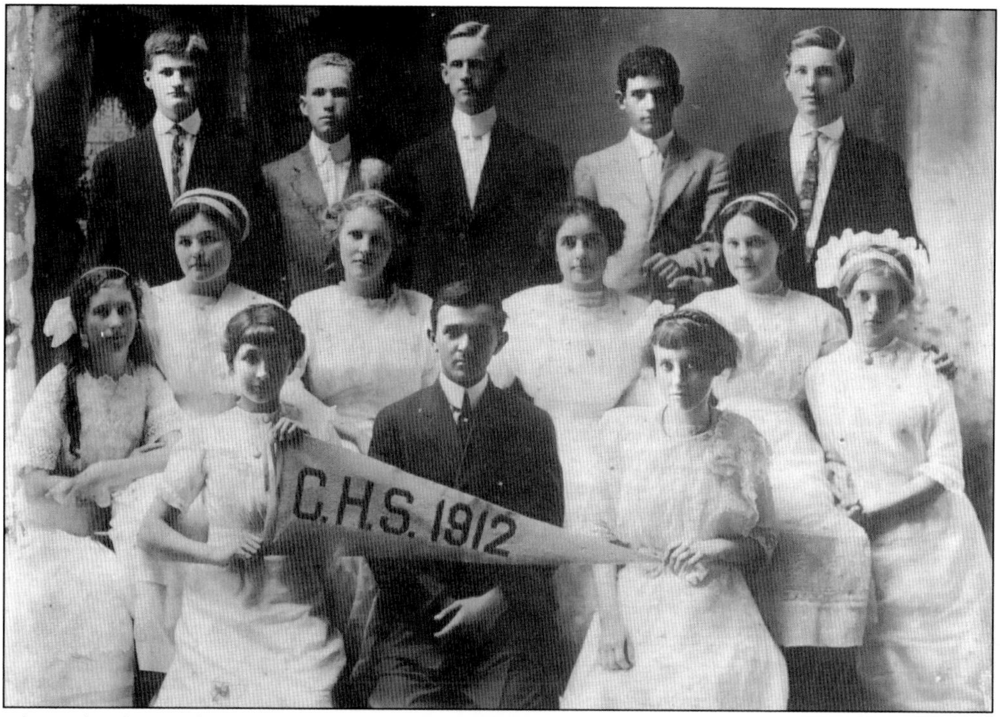

The Columbia High School graduating class of 1912 poses for a formal studio portrait. (Courtesy of Marion County Historical Society.)

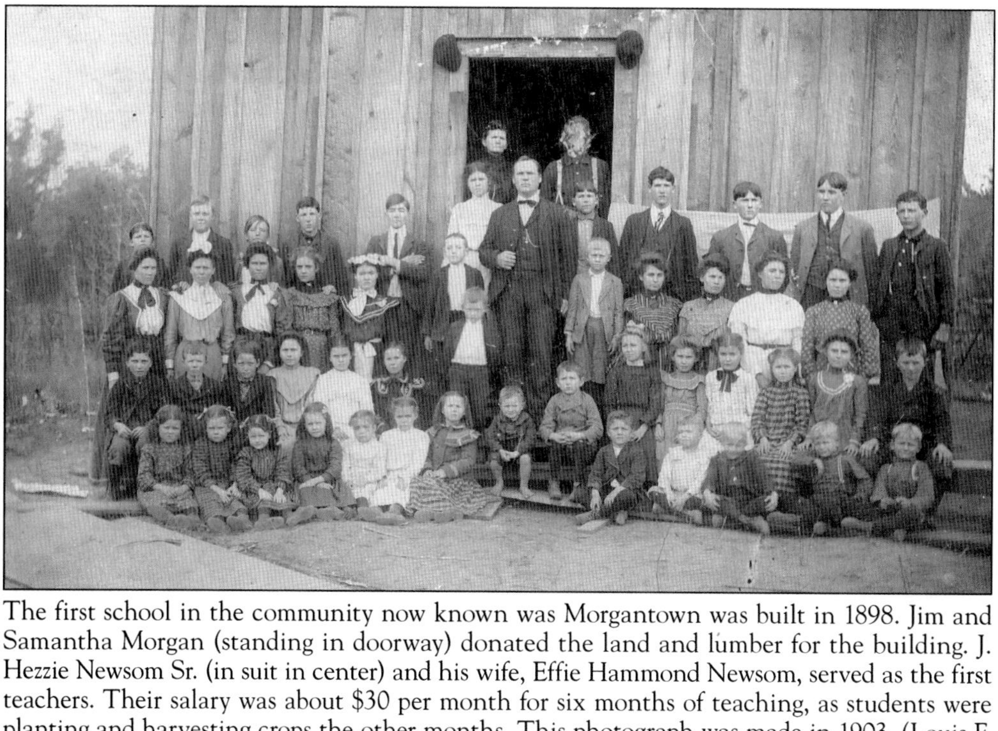

The first school in the community now known was Morgantown was built in 1898. Jim and Samantha Morgan (standing in doorway) donated the land and lumber for the building. J. Hezzie Newsom Sr. (in suit in center) and his wife, Effie Hammond Newsom, served as the first teachers. Their salary was about $30 per month for six months of teaching, as students were planting and harvesting crops the other months. This photograph was made in 1903. (Louis F. Morgan collection.)

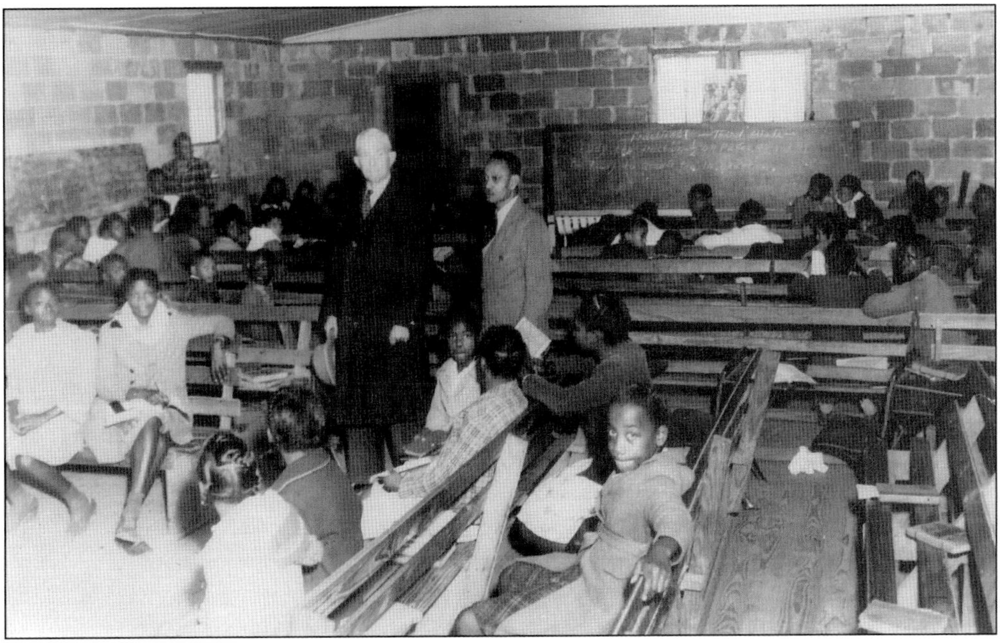

Although the name of this school is not known, the men in the photograph have been tentatively identified as P.H. Easom (left) and L.F. Bowles (right). Common for the time, different grades were taught in the same makeshift school building. This particular school has rough-hewn benches in lieu of desks. (Courtesy of Marion County Historical Society.)

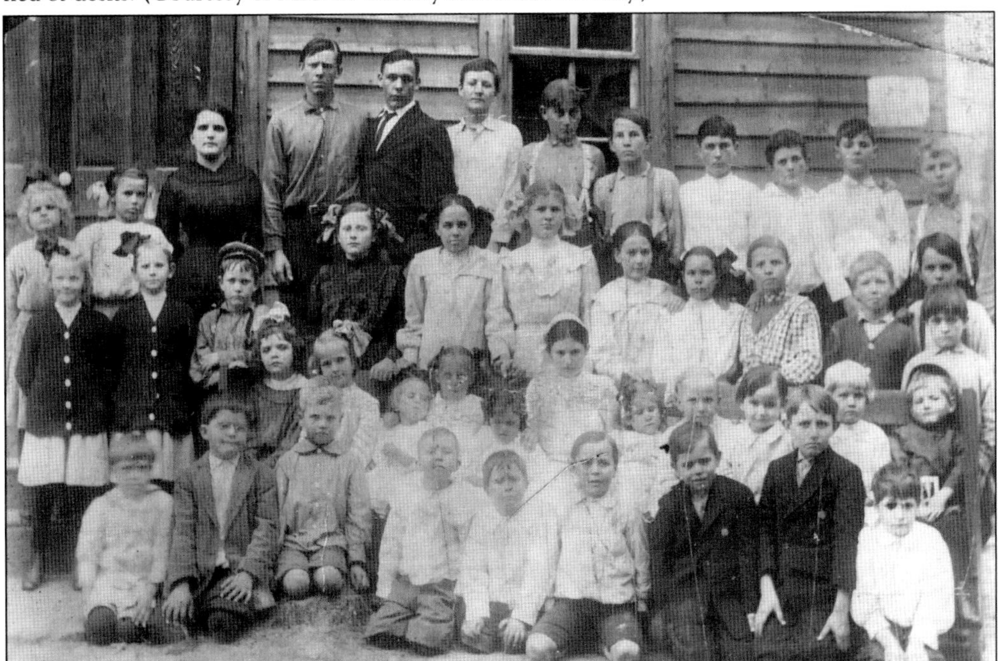

An early school for the Kokomo community was the Lewis School, named after one of the prominent families who were among the first to settle that section of the county. This photograph was made in 1912 when Ilene Foxworth (standing in doorway) was the teacher. (Louis F. Morgan collection.)

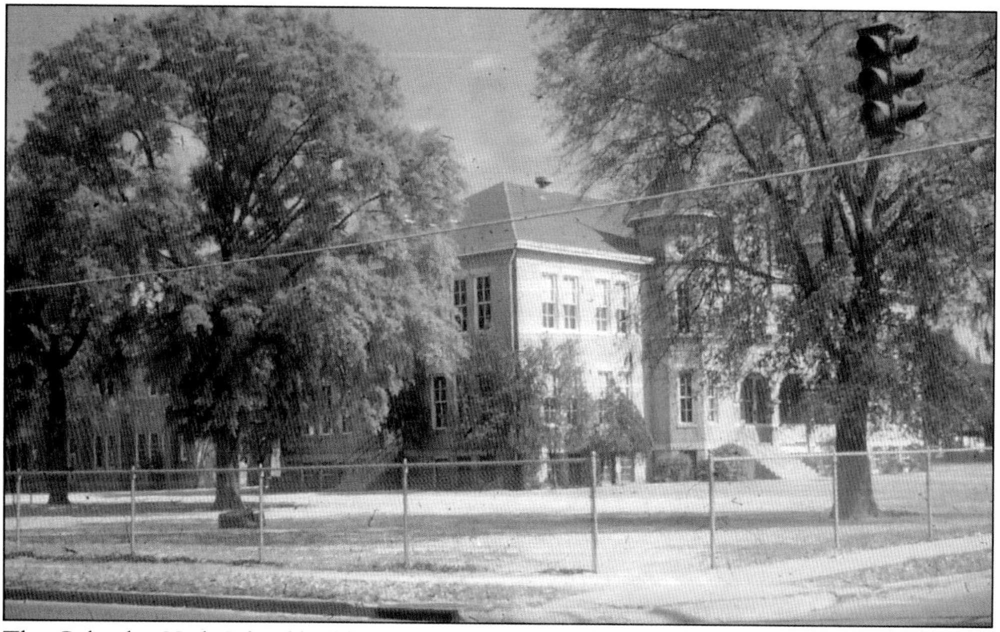

This Columbia High School building was constructed in 1905, with its cornerstone being laid in the afternoon of the same day as that of the courthouse. In May 1915, about 700 people crowded the building to hear US vice president Thomas Marshall deliver a speech titled "The Tendencies of the Times." The school is the namesake for High School Avenue in Columbia. (Courtesy of Bates Bullock.)

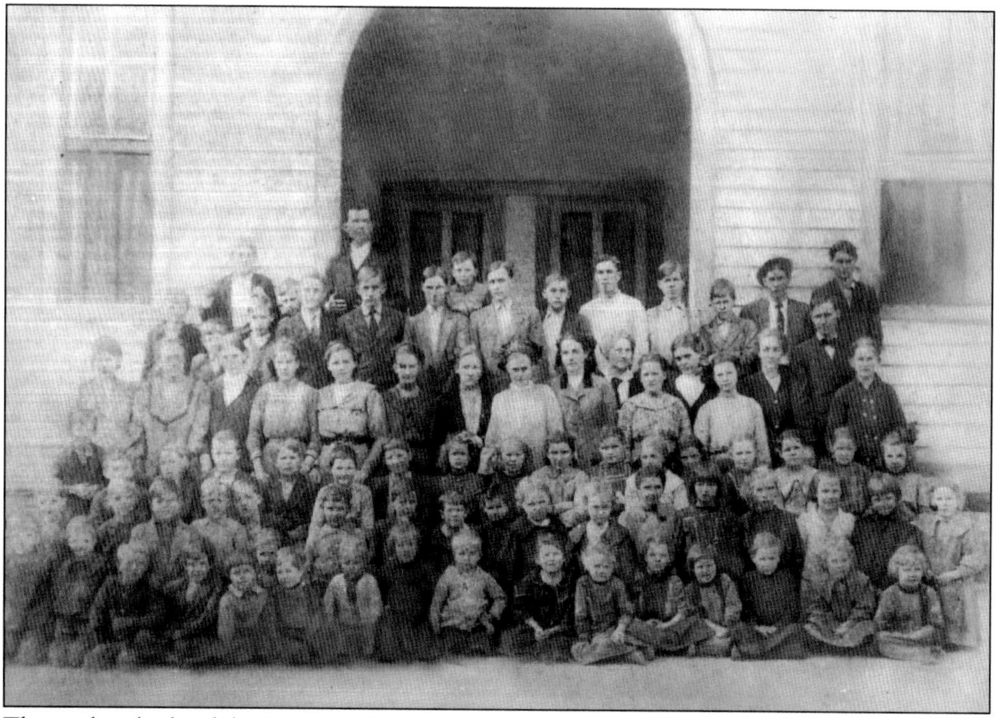

The student body of the Morris School poses for a formal photograph around 1900. (Courtesy of Damon Watts.)

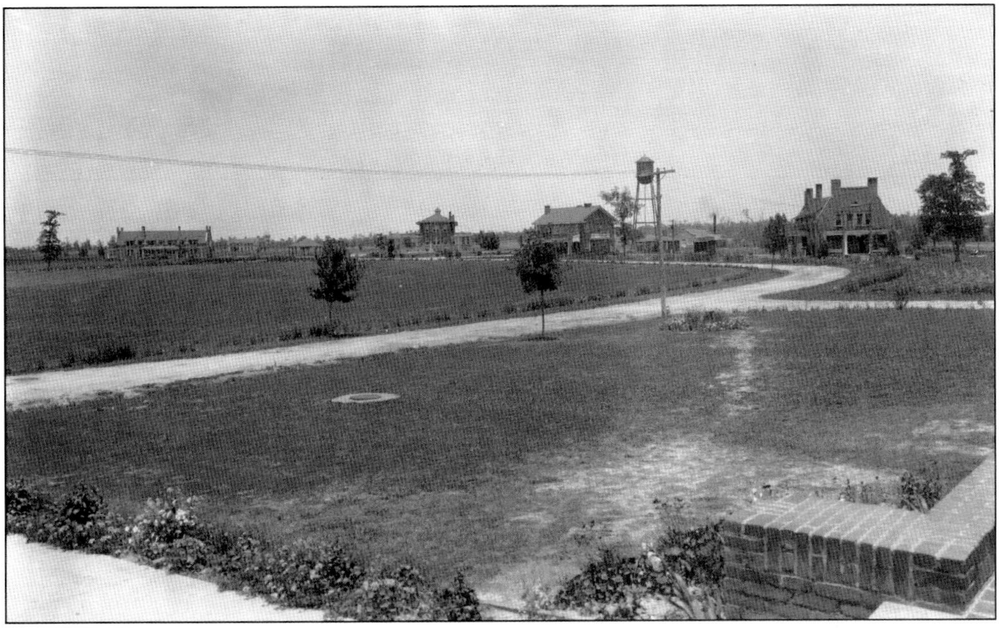

A plume of smoke rises from the laundry on the campus of the Mississippi Industrial Training School around 1925. The school was established near Columbia as the state school for indigent and delinquent children and was the only one of its kind in Mississippi and one of only a few in the South in its time. This photograph of structures on campus, taken from the vantage point of Burrow Cottage, shows, from left to right, Jacob Cottage, Rouse Cottage, Singley Cottage, the administrator's mansion, laundry building, and Hammond Hall. (Courtesy of Marion County Development Partnership.)

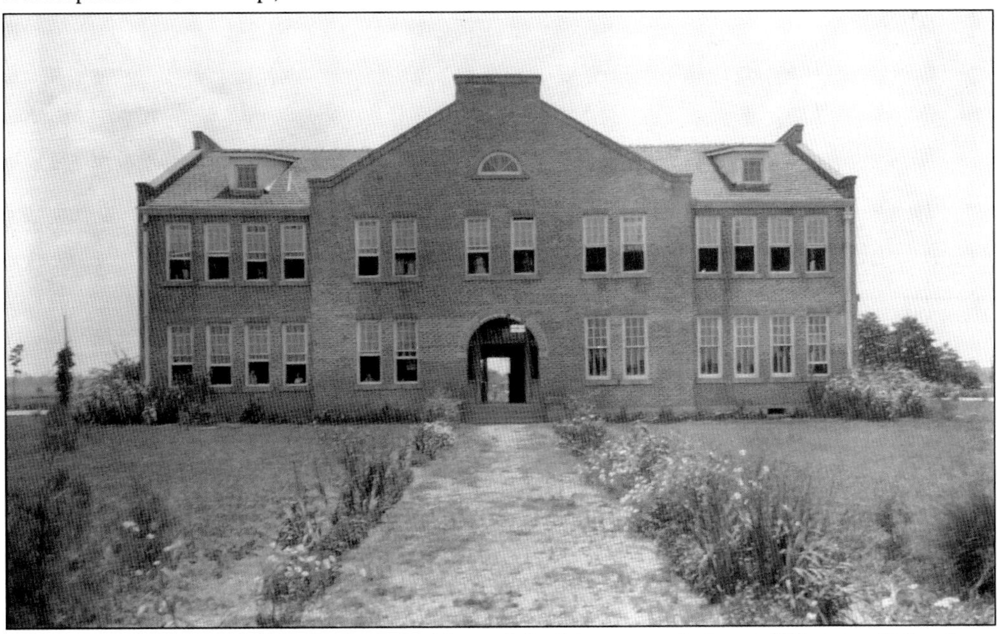

The impressive brick Administration Building of the Mississippi Industrial Training School was constructed about 1917. Note the number of people who are peering out the windows at the photographer. (Courtesy of Marion County Development Partnership.)

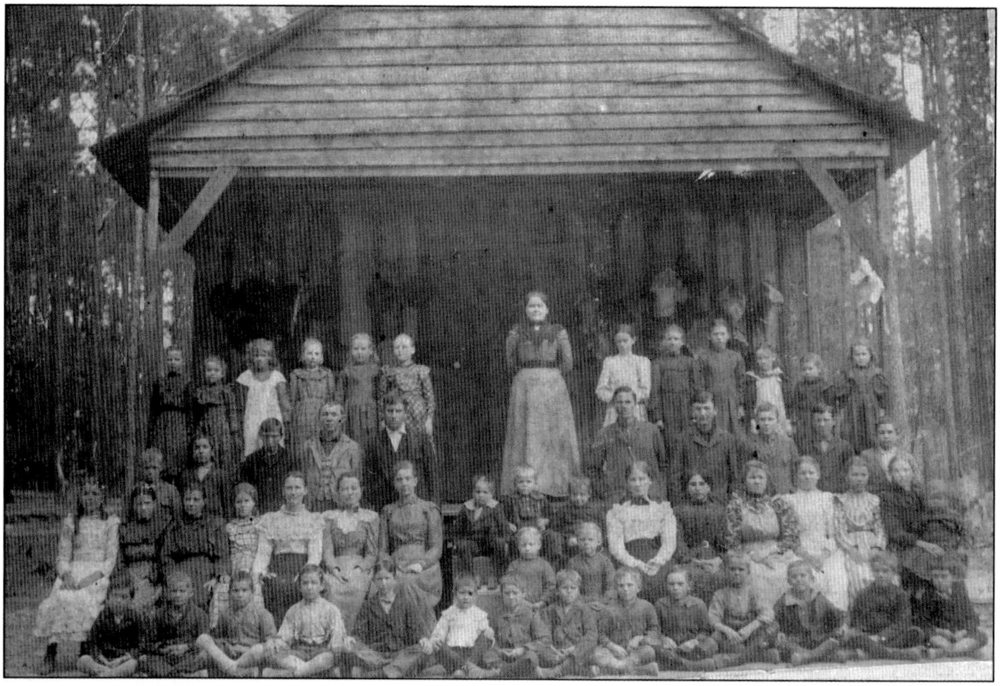

It was in this building that Shiloh Baptist Church was organized and first met for services. In this c. 1892 photograph, boys' hats and girls' bonnets hang on opposite sides of the doorway. (Louis F. Morgan collection.)

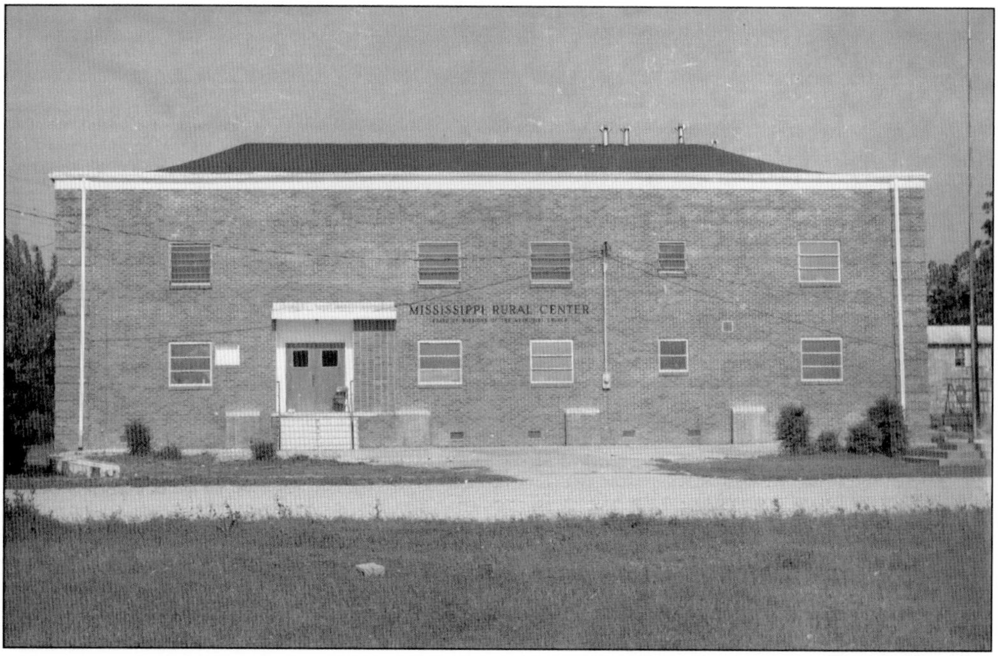

The Mississippi Rural Center, located in the Lampton community, was dedicated on February 9, 1949, and served the community for the 60 years. The project was begun by the Woman's Division of Christian Service of the Methodist church through its board of missions. (Courtesy of Marion County Historical Society.)

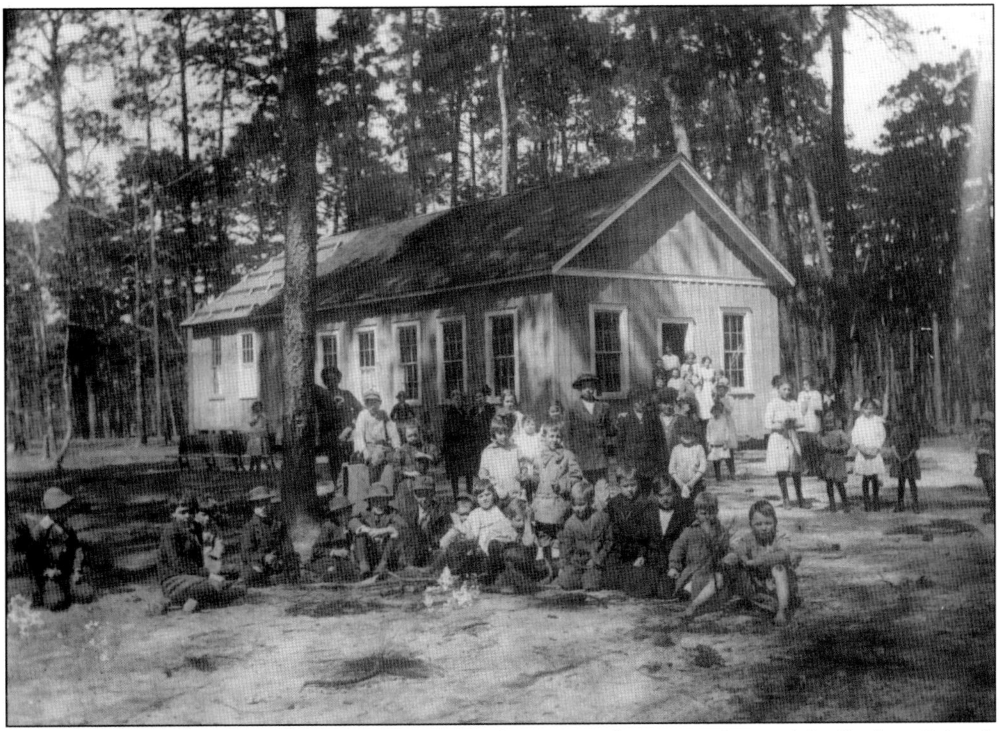

In this c. 1925 photograph, Mamie Hathorn's students casually pose in front of the Darbun School. (Courtesy of Marion County Public Library.)

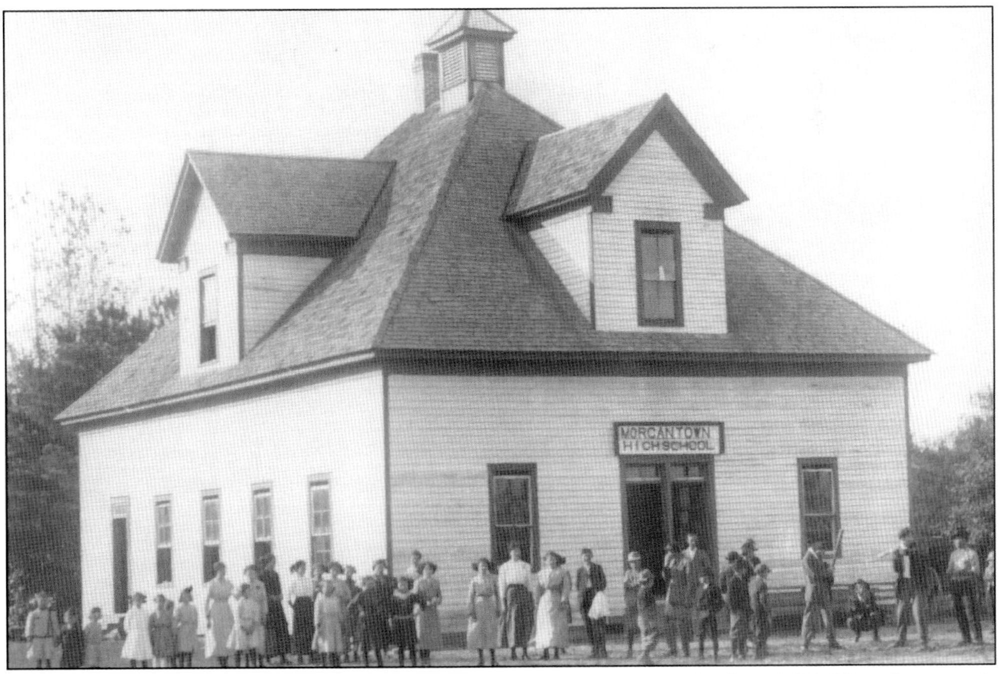

The second school building located in what is now Morgantown was built in 1914. This photograph was made in 1915. (Louis F. Morgan collection.)

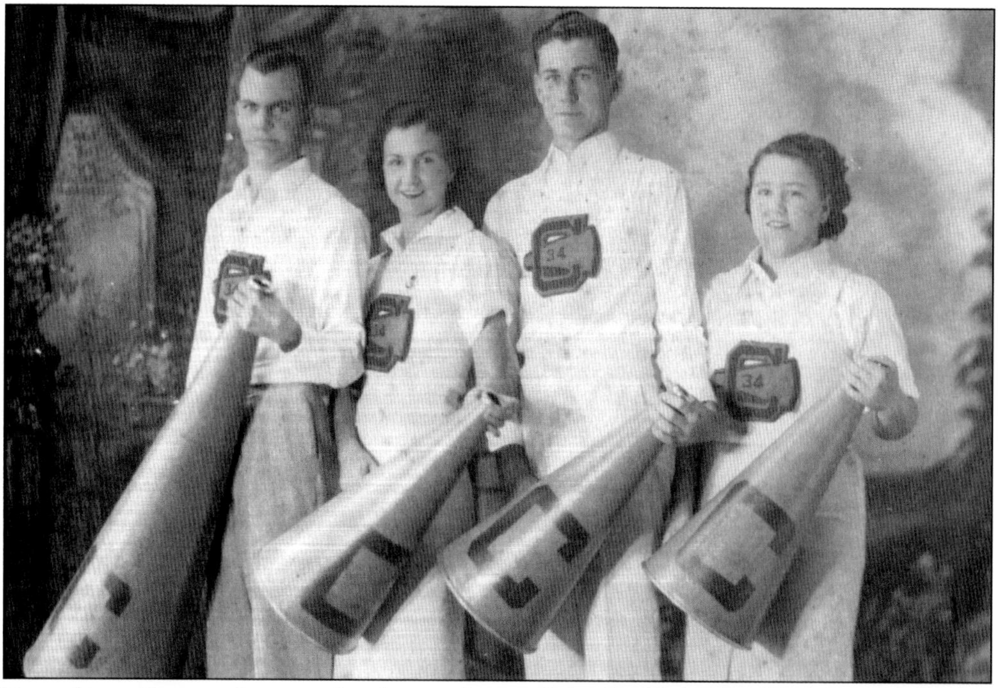

Dressed in uniforms and equipped with megaphones, Columbia High School had four cheerleaders in 1934. Although two are unidentified, the two at left are W.B. "Buster" Barnes and Lucy Barnes Burkett. This photograph was made at Columbia Studios. (Courtesy of Fran Ginn.)

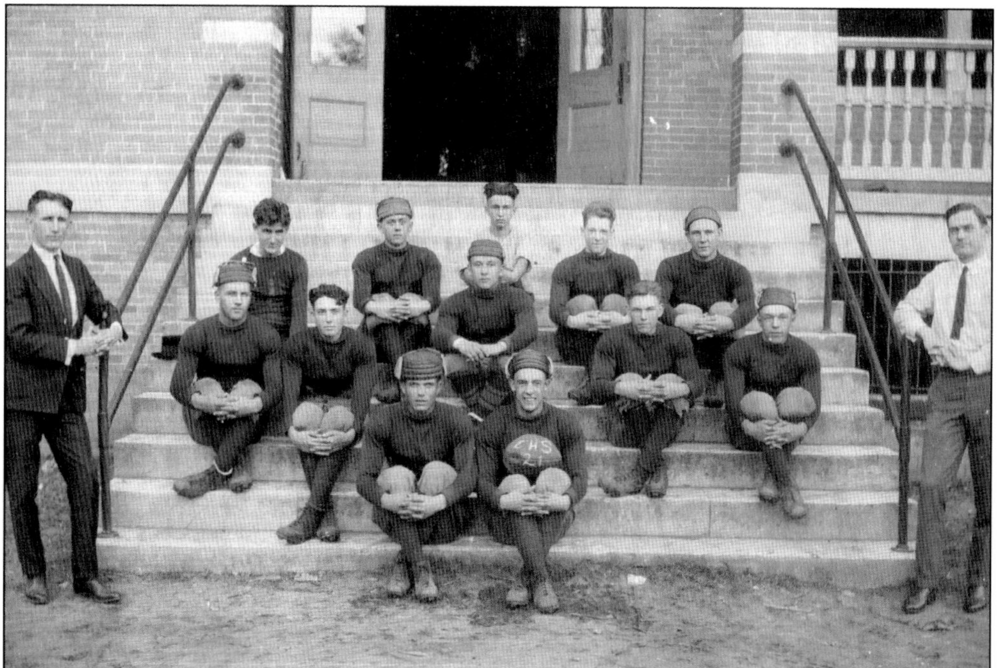

Twelve players of Columbia High School's first football team pose on the front steps of the high school in 1921. Note the period's football helmets. (Courtesy of Marion County Historical Society.)

Three

EVENTS AND GATHERINGS

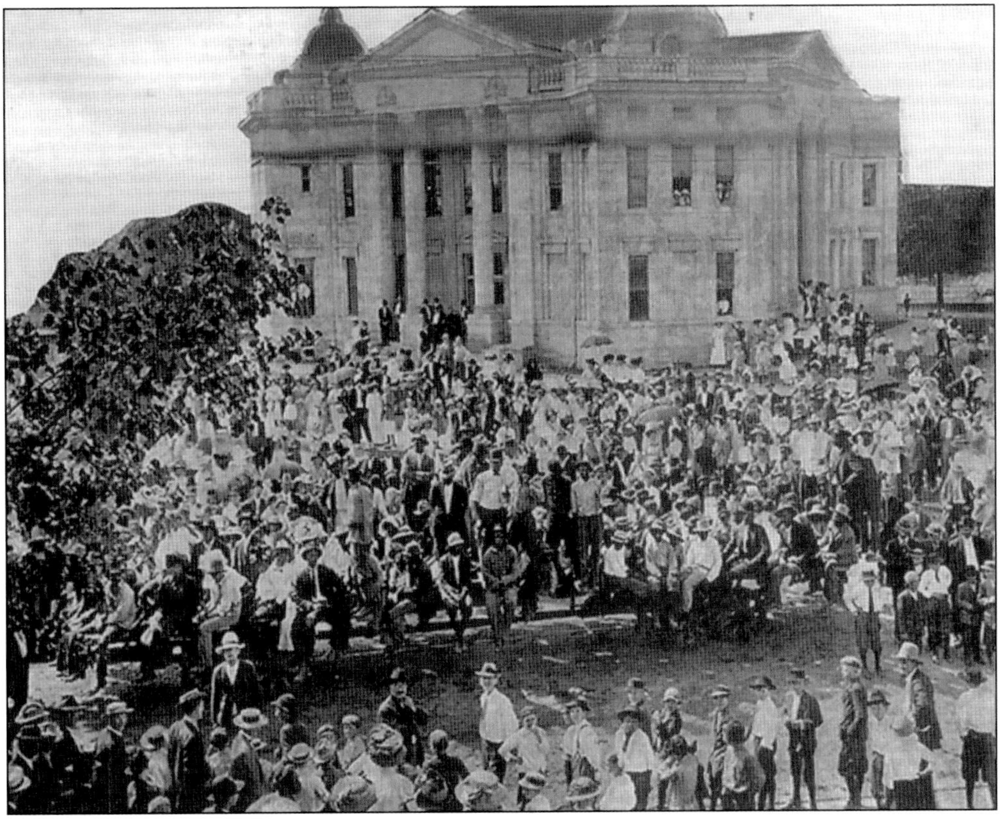

Although the occasion is unknown, this early scene depicts the Marion County Courthouse among a throng of citizens, many of whom have their attention on the photographer. Note the numerous riders on the log wagon and the revelers in the open windows of the courthouse. This image is from a postcard. (Courtesy of Mississippi Department of Archives and History.)

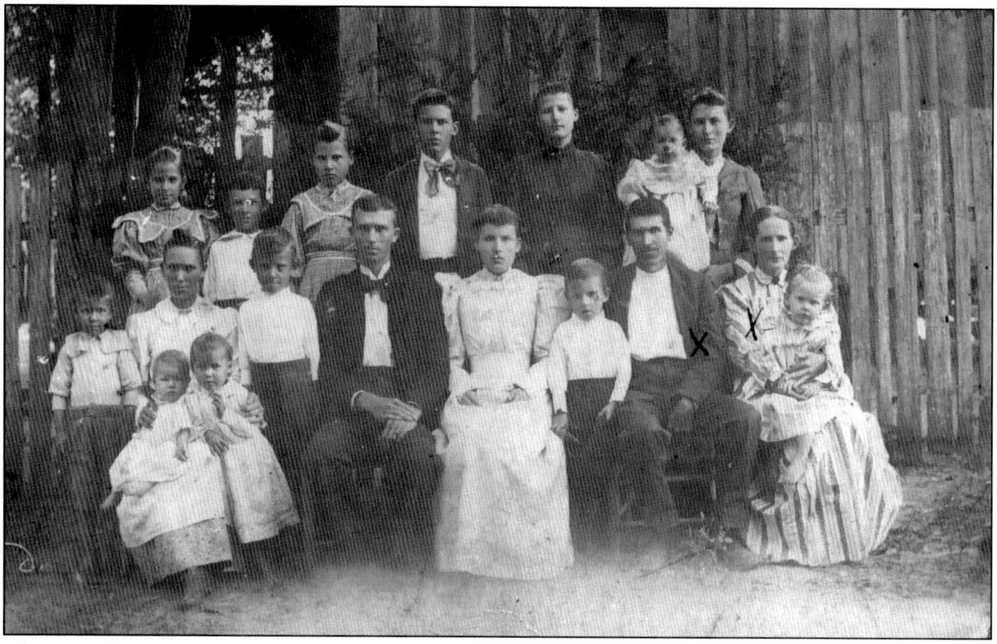

The Beard family settled in Marion County at an early date and prospered as educators and farmers. This photograph was made on December 6, 1895, at the wedding of Louis N. and Hollie Beard Morgan. (Louis F. Morgan collection.)

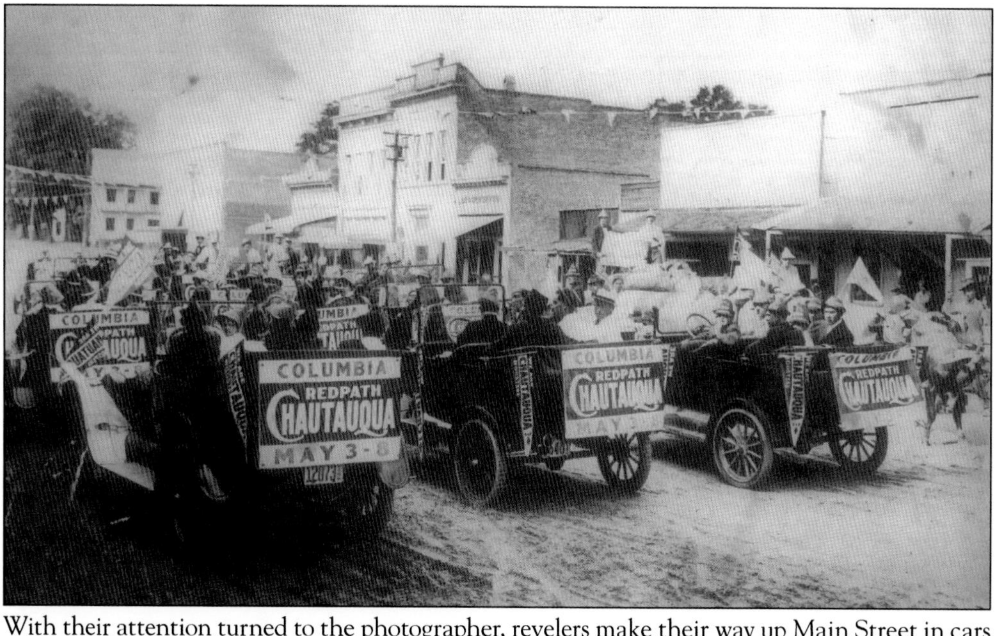

With their attention turned to the photographer, revelers make their way up Main Street in cars advertising the Redpath Chatauqua Celebration. Chatauqua was a national movement designed to bring learning and culture to pre-radio rural America. A World War I-era festival held on the grounds of Columbia High School had sideshow acts, including a magician named the "Great Reno," as well as a show titled the "Marvelous Torpedo with Ears." Theodore Roosevelt once stated that Chatauqua was "the most American thing in America." (Courtesy of Marion County Historical Society.)

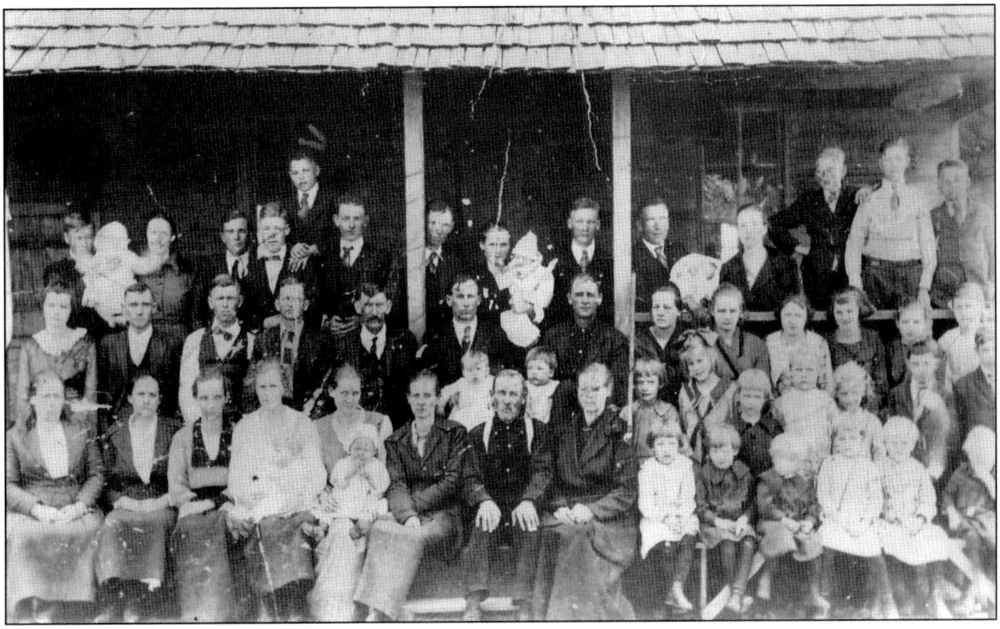

Members of the Morris family gathered on Martha Kendrick's back porch on February 17, 1921, for this photograph celebrating the 71st birthday of Nathan Lott Morris (in the center of the first row). Ollin Hutson (on the far left of the second row) is wearing her wedding dress made for her by Ida Morris. Note that only three people feel it necessary to smile! (Courtesy of Eula Morris Watts.)

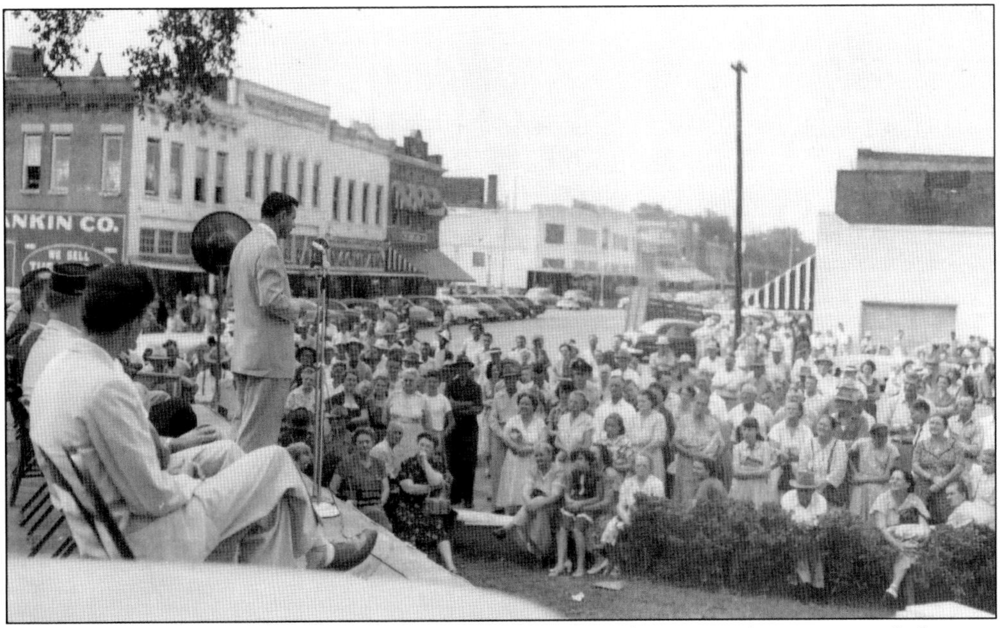

Crowds gather on Courthouse Square in August 1953 to take part in the ceremony dedicating Marion County's War Memorial. While many took part, the featured speaker of the day was Lt. Gov. Carroll Gartin, who can be seen standing at the microphone. District attorney Vernon Broom, who acted as the master of ceremonies, can be seen sitting directly behind Gartin. (Courtesy of Damon Watts.)

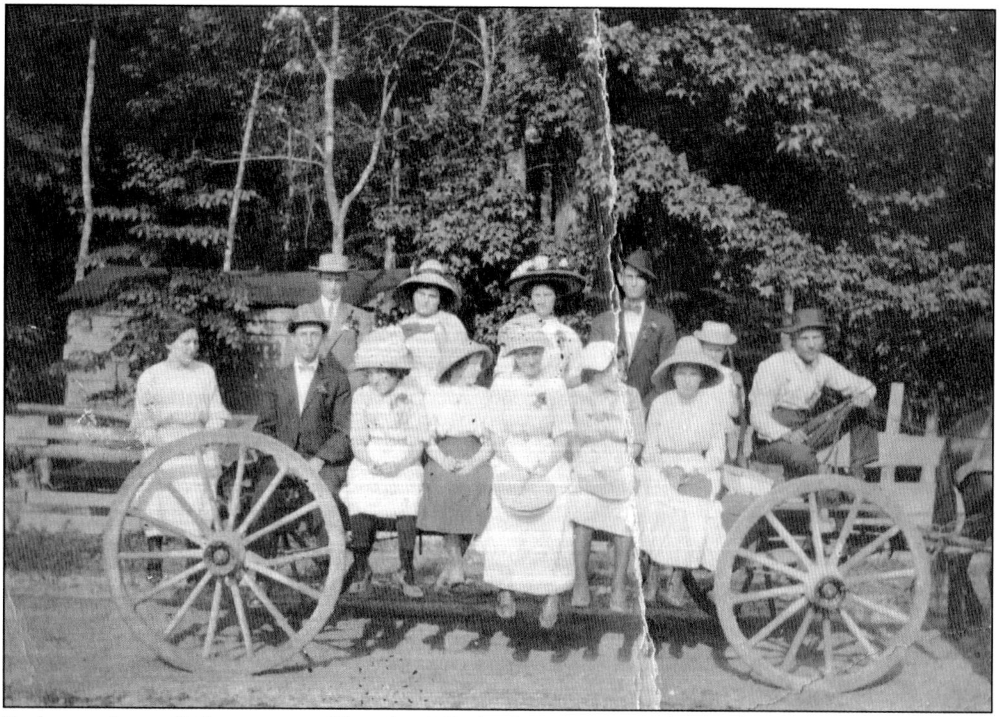

Early members of Morgantown Church of God ride a wagon to the Darbun community to share a Sunday picnic with members of the Mount Sinai Church of God. This photograph was made around 1917. (Louis F. Morgan collection.)

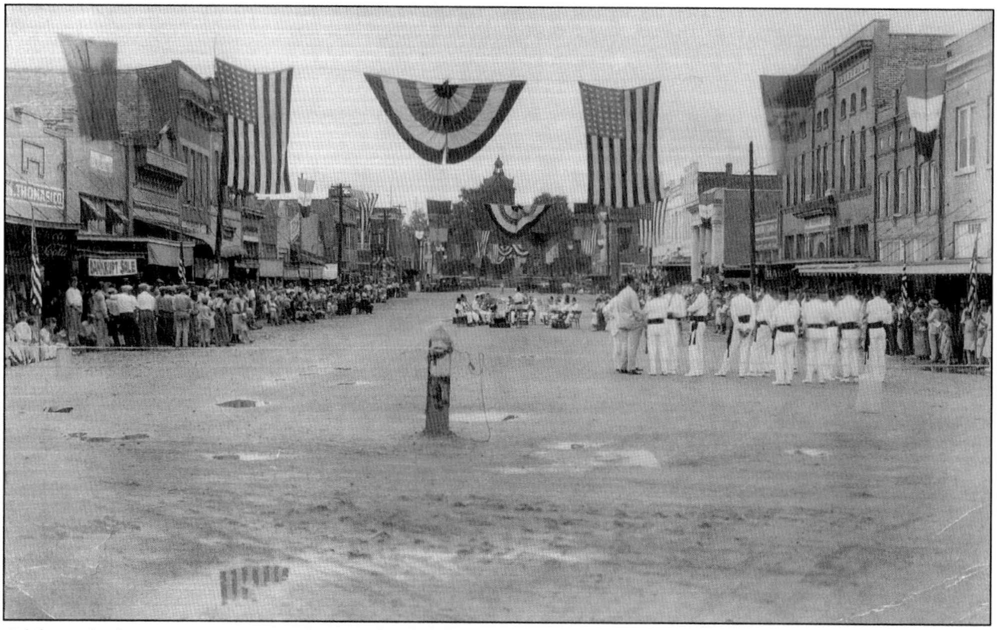

Although the occasion is unclear, colorful flags and patriotic bunting decorate Main Street on a rainy day in this c. 1920 scene. Excited crowds line the muddy, yet unpaved street, while a brass band plays near the center. Though much has changed in Columbia, the downtown skyline is not that much different than it was on this day. (Courtesy of Marion County Historical Society.)

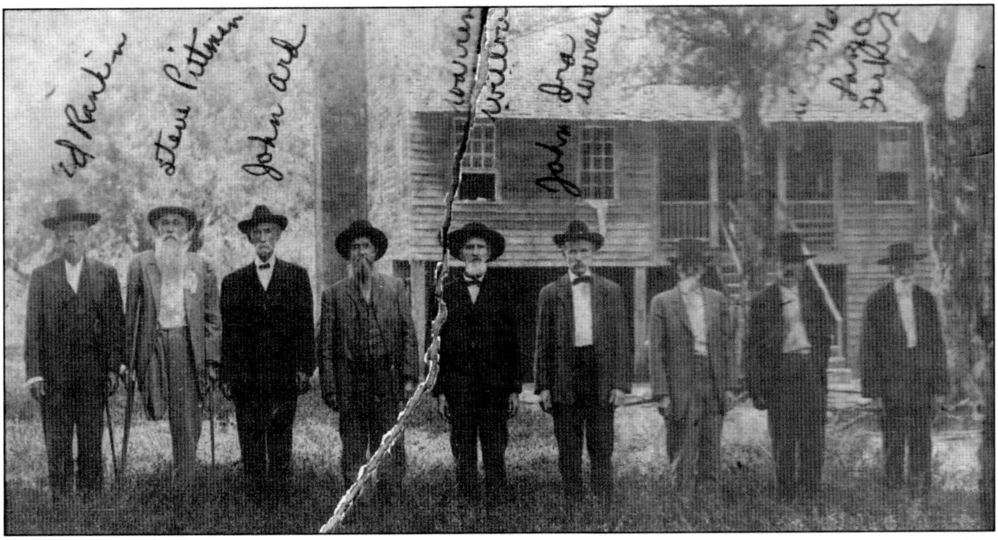

For many years, the remaining Confederate veterans of the county gathered for reunions. In this c. 1906 photograph, what was likely the last nine pose for a photograph at the rear of the Ford home. Although the identities of most of those pictured are unclear, the man on the far left is Samuel Edward Rankin (wearing his sword), and the man on crutches is Stephen Pittman. The other seven are thought to be (from left to right) John Ard, unidentified, Warren Willoughby, John Ira Warren, William G. Holmes, William Magee, and Lance Forbes. Pittman was seriously wounded in Jonesboro, Georgia, which necessitated the amputation of his right leg. (Courtesy of Virginia Chain.)

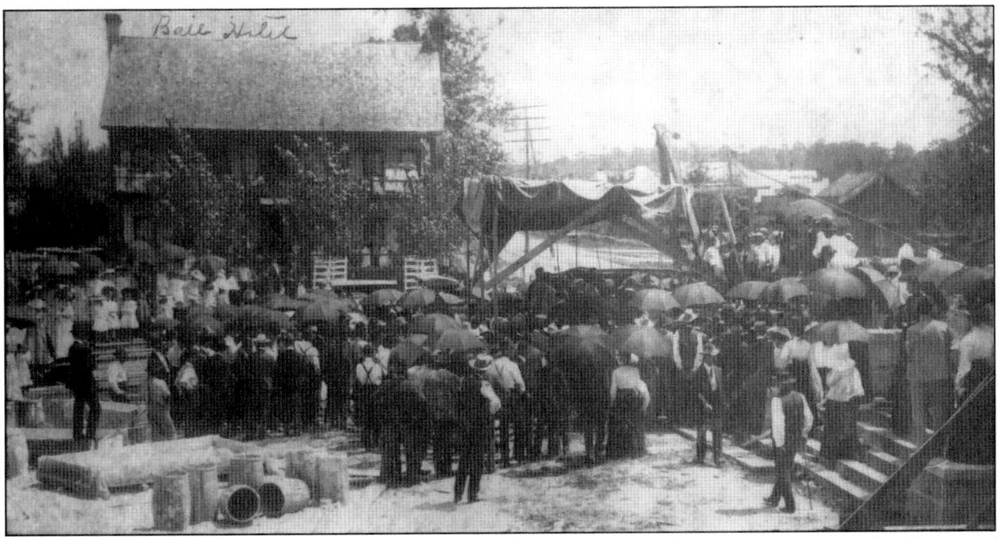

On Thursday, August 31, 1905, citizens of the surrounding area gathered to witness the laying of the cornerstone for the new courthouse. The ceremony was preceded by a marching band, which played as some 60 members of the Stalbon's Masonic Lodge filed in line to the site. Several items were placed inside the cornerstone, including a synopsis of the county's history, a Bible, and period newspapers. This view is from the west looking east at the Ball Hotel across the street. What became a portion of Broad Street, then known as "Purvis Road," can be seen to the right of the hotel. Note the large number of umbrellas being used as shade from the summer sun. (Courtesy of Marion County Historical Society.)

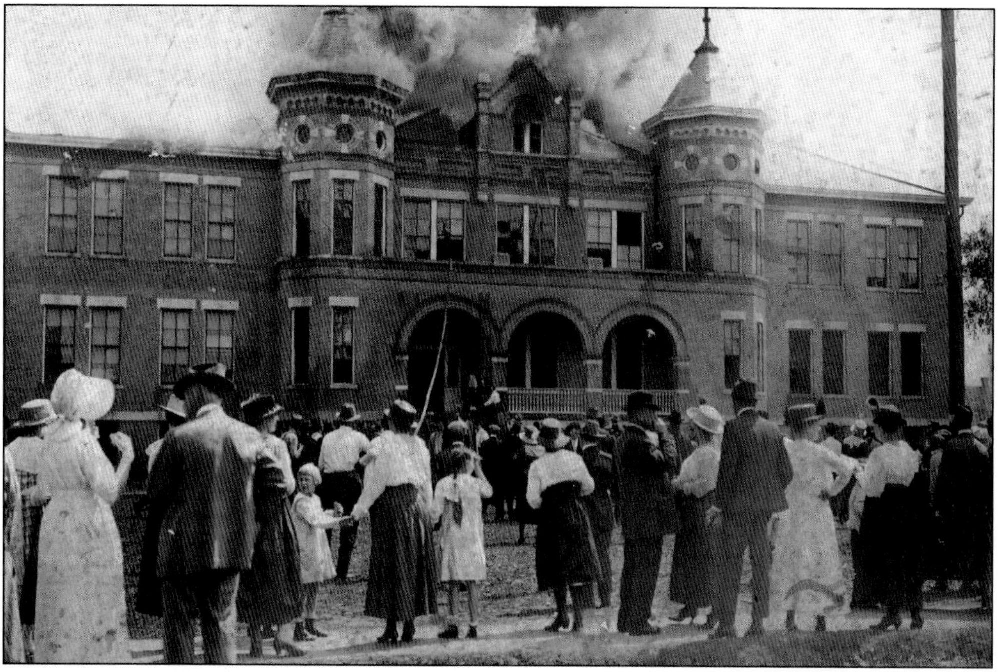

On Sunday morning, March 24, 1918, the grand Columbia High School building caught fire. Church parishioners fled their Sunday schools to find smoke billowing from the school's roof. Arson was strongly suspected, evident when Sheriff Ball offered a $100 reward for information concerning the guilty party. In time the school was repaired, and in the meantime, classes resumed in area churches, the Masonic Hall, and the courthouse. (Courtesy of Marion County Historical Society.)

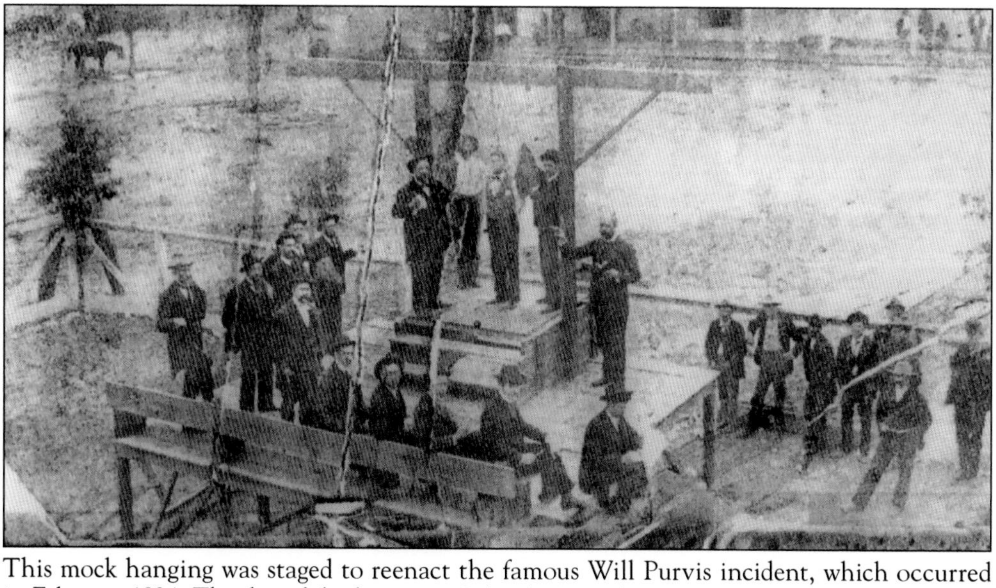

This mock hanging was staged to reenact the famous Will Purvis incident, which occurred in February 1894. The day of the hanging, Columbia's roads were guarded while a huge crowd gathered to such degree that Purvis himself stated, "South Mississippi had declared a holiday to witness the hanging. Schools turned out, crowds assembled and picnic dinners were eaten on the courthouse lawn." The famous Will Purvis hanging was nationally known and still the subject of conversation over a century later. (Courtesy of Marion County Historical Society.)

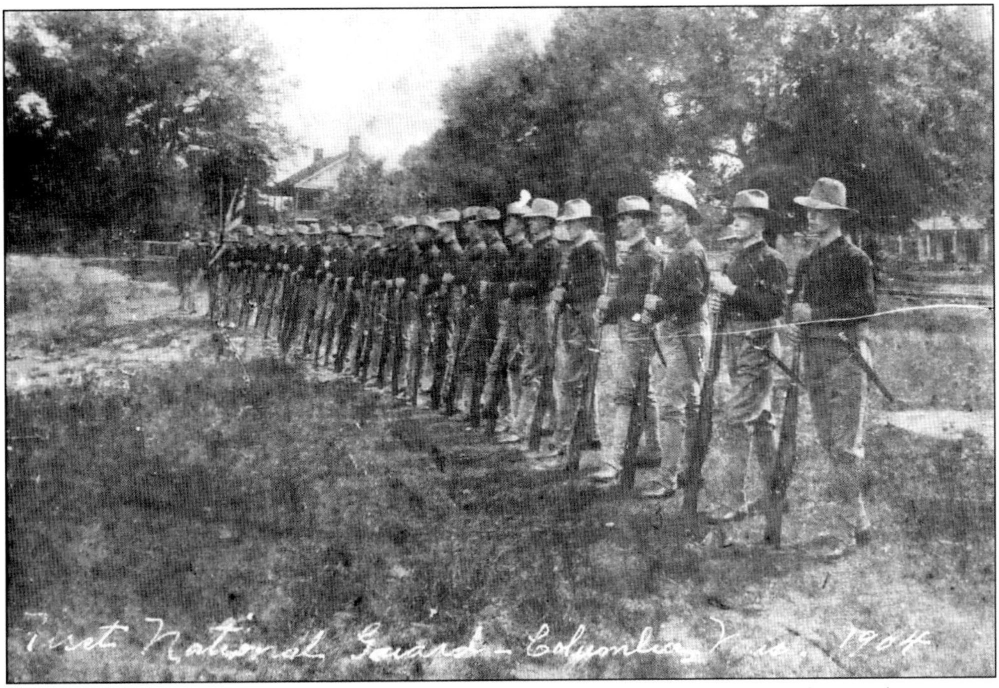

A total of 28 National Guardsmen, armed with Krag-Jorgensen rifles, drill near the Marion County Courthouse in 1904. At the far right, railroad tracks are visible, most likely part of the Gulf & Ship Island line. (Courtesy of Marion County Historical Society.)

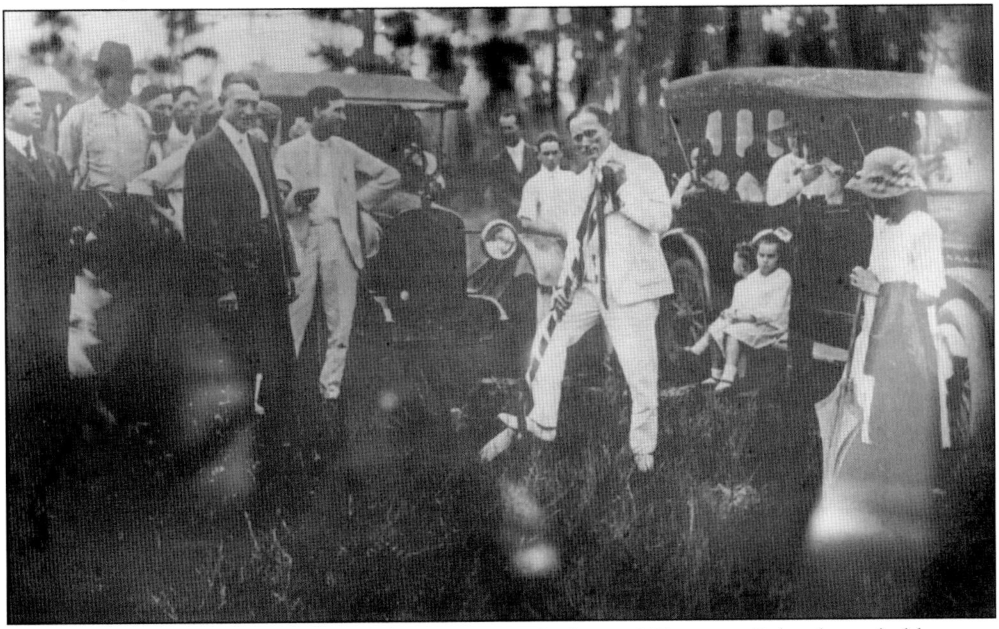

The ground-breaking ceremony of the Mississippi Industrial Training School was held at two o'clock in the afternoon on Saturday, September 15, 1918. While the Columbia Band played, Gov. Theodore Bilbo ceremonially turns over the first shovel full of soil to start the construction. The Marion County Board of Trade put up 3,300 acres of land and 50,000 in the successful effort to have the institution located in Marion County. (Courtesy of Marion County Historical Society.)

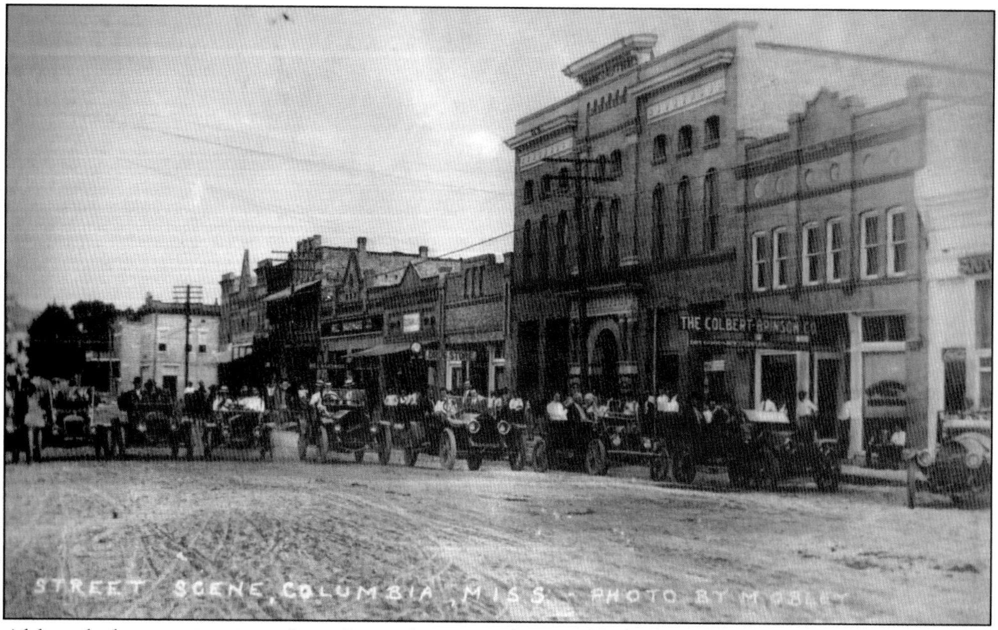

Although the occasion is unclear, this early postcard image likely depicts the majority of automobiles owned in Marion County at the time. Experiencing the sight and sound of a "motor car" must have made an impression on locals. An antiquated wagon and a man on horseback can be seen in the background. This image was made by early photographer Benjamin Franklin Mobley. (Courtesy of Marion County Historical Society.)

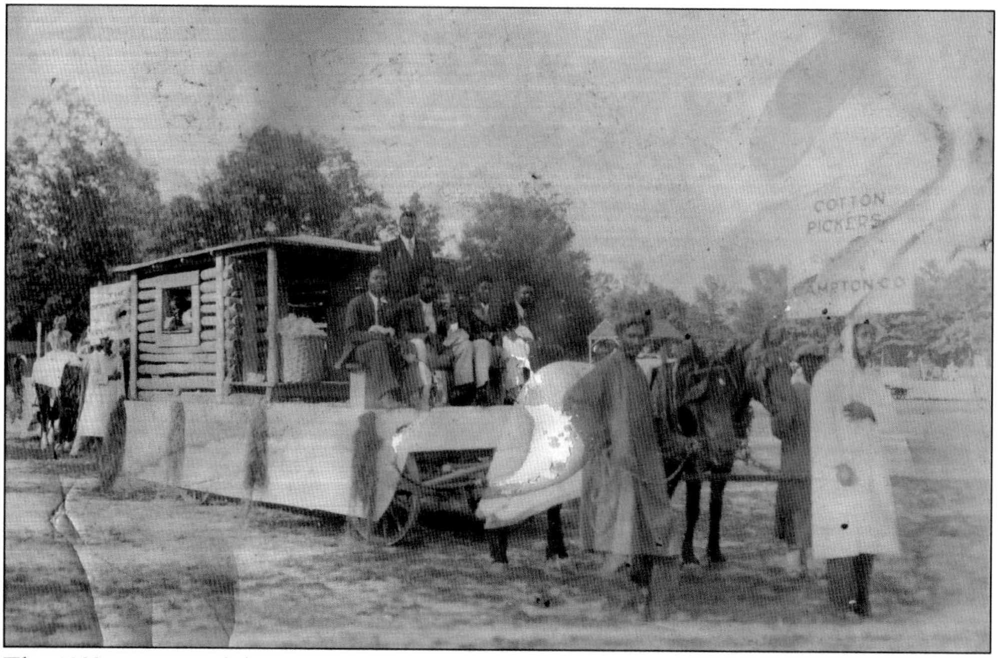

The 1933 opening of the Reliance Manufacturing plant in Columbia was the cause of such celebration that a parade was held. The Lampton Company float was a visual recreation of *Uncle Tom's Cabin*; the lead man is carrying a sign that reads, "Cotton pickers courtesy of the Lampton Company." Note the young boy peeking out the cabin's window. (Courtesy of Fran Ginn.)

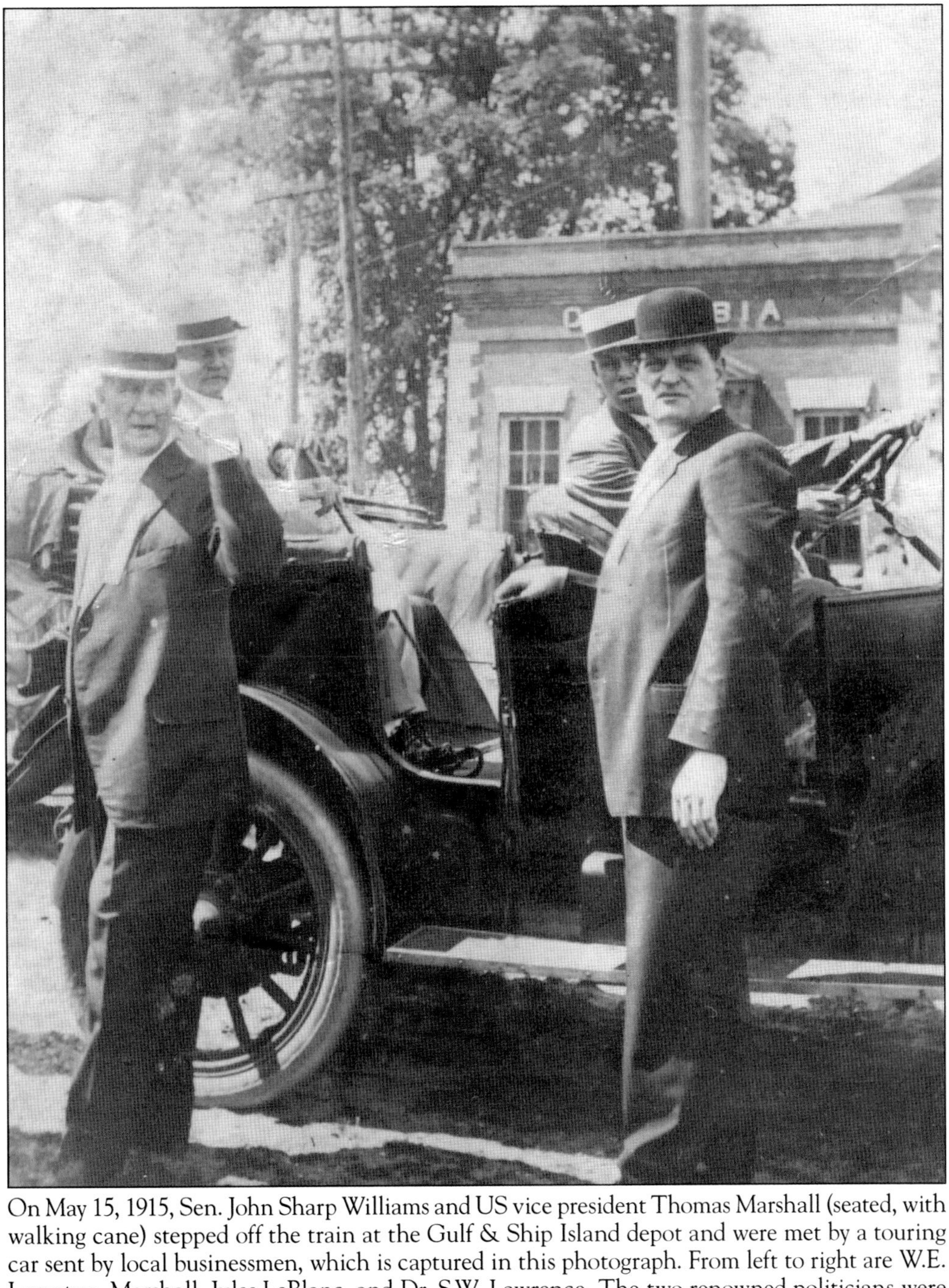

On May 15, 1915, Sen. John Sharp Williams and US vice president Thomas Marshall (seated, with walking cane) stepped off the train at the Gulf & Ship Island depot and were met by a touring car sent by local businessmen, which is captured in this photograph. From left to right are W.E. Lampton, Marshall, Jules LeBlanc, and Dr. S.W. Lawrence. The two renowned politicians were escorted to the Columbia High School auditorium. District attorney Toxey Hall introduced the speakers. About 700 people crowded the auditorium and loitered outside. Marshall's speech, titled "The Tendencies of the Times," addressed the recent *Lusitania* incident and had a tone of antiwar sentiment. In his speech, Marshall stated, "If there are those here tonight that want to go to war, why just remember that there are recruiting stations open day and night at London, Berlin and Paris, and they will be glad to enroll you." (Courtesy of Fran Ginn.)

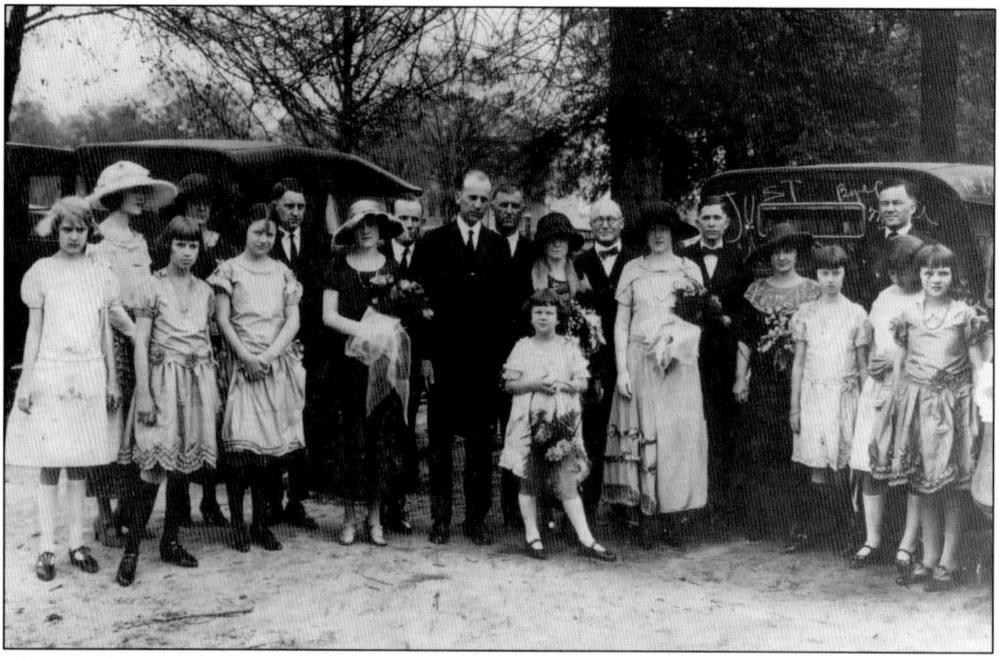

The Kingsberry-Baylis wedding party poses for a photograph on the wedding day, March 23, 1923. Apparently, even as early as the 1920s, it was traditional to decorate the groom's car before the couple left for their honeymoon. (Courtesy of Marion County Historical Society.)

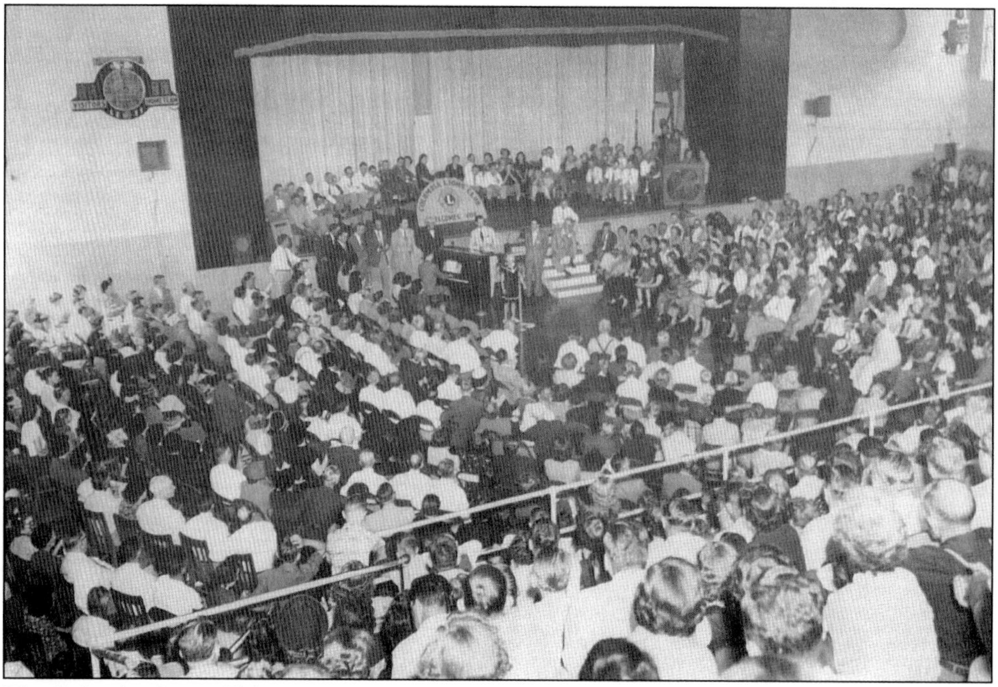

The Columbia Lions Club singing convention was held at the Columbia High School auditorium, attracting crowds from the region. The performances were broadcast over loud speakers set up outside the auditorium and simultaneously broadcast over WCJU radio. B.B. Bradley took this photograph. (Courtesy of Marion County Historical Society.)

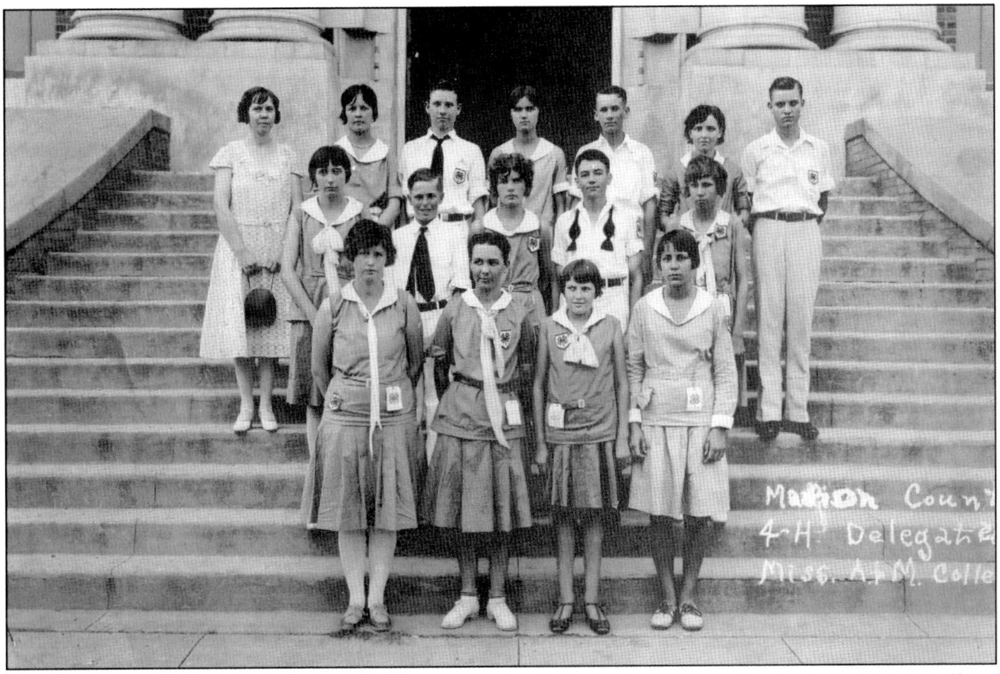

Marion County students are seen attending a 4-H Club conference at Mississippi A&M College prior to 1930. Among the participants were sisters Lavada Morgan (first row, far left) and Mava Jean Morgan (second row, far right). (Louis F. Morgan collection.)

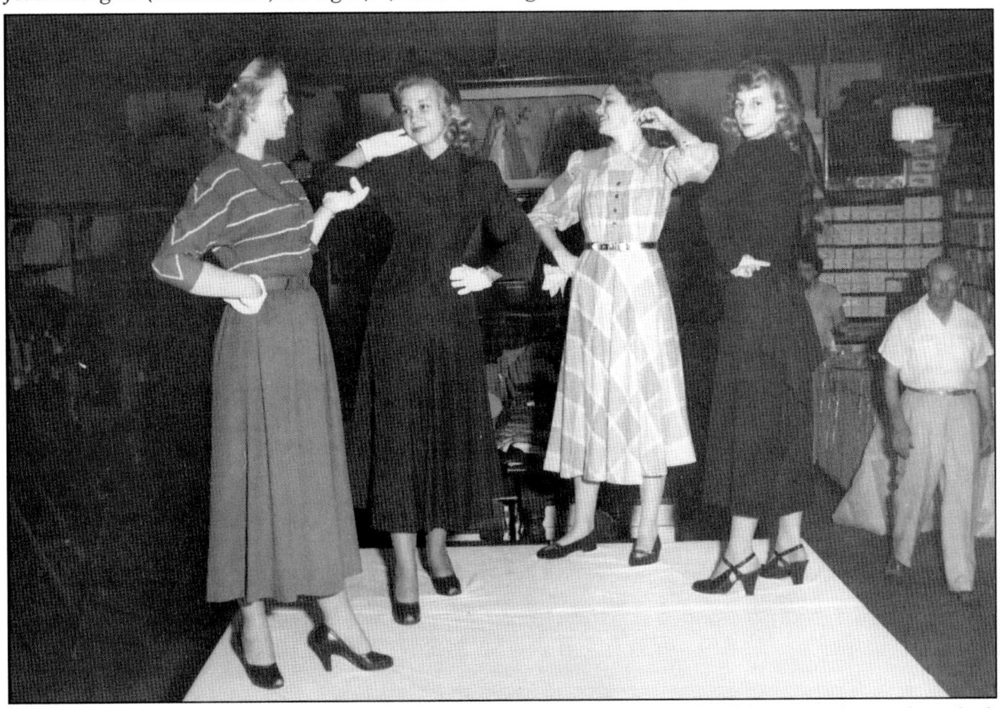

Models pose at a fashion show held at the Watts Company. Although all have not been identified, on the far left is Mary Francis Barnes Watts, and next to her is Charlotte Yarborough. (Courtesy of Fran Ginn.)

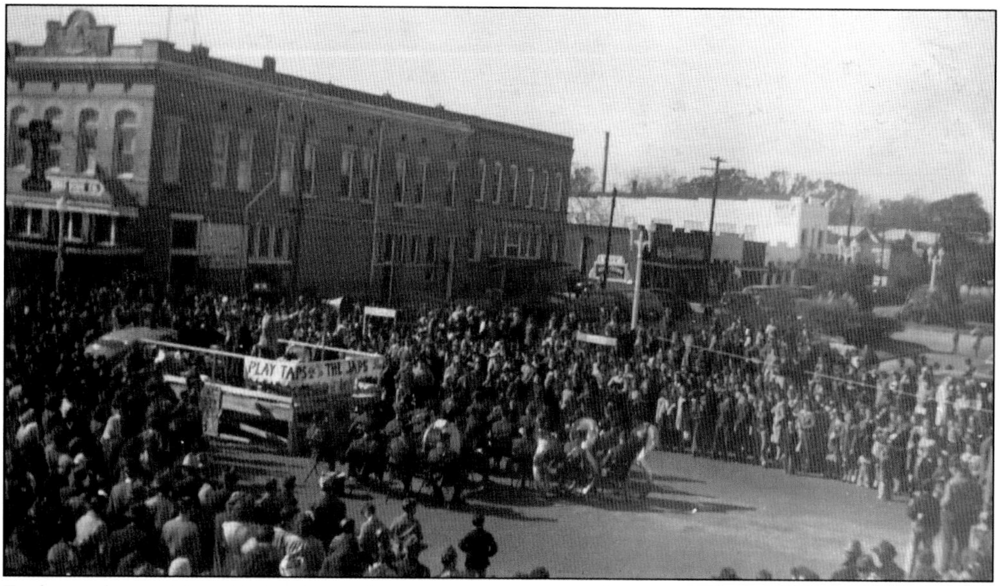

Early on during World War II, war bonds and stamps could be purchased nearly everywhere in Columbia, including the box offices of the local theaters. In fact, in July 1944, the Ritz Theater (visible farther down Second Street) began selling war bonds in lieu of tickets for admittance to the theater. In the foreground, crowds gather to attend a "Play Taps for the Japs" rally on Main Street, most likely a drive to increase the sale of war bonds. (Courtesy of Fran Ginn.)

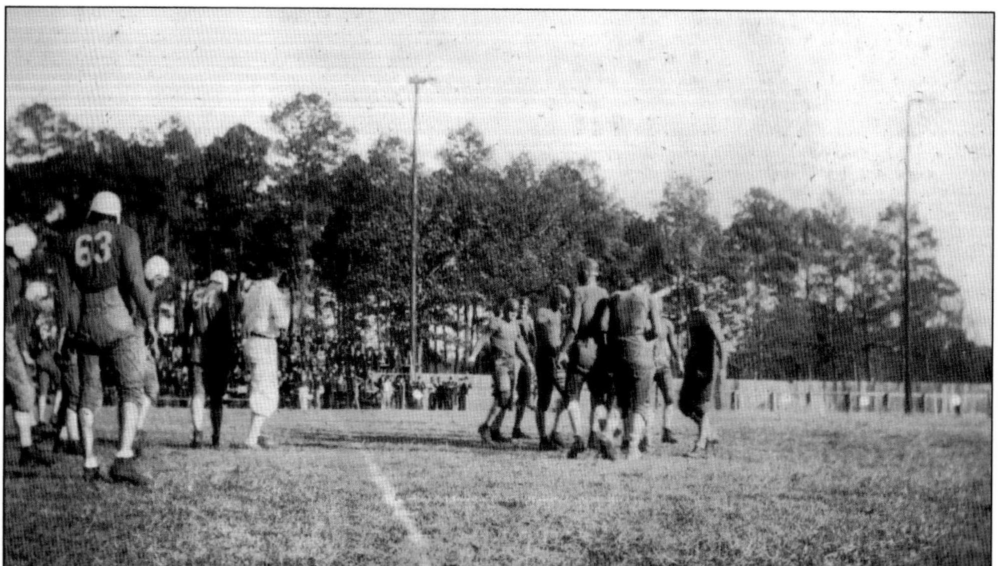

In a rare action shot, the Columbia High School football team takes on Mount Olive in the fall of 1936. Marion County schools have long produced superior athletes, most famously the late Walter Payton of Chicago Bears fame who also played on this same field. (Courtesy of Bates Bullock.)

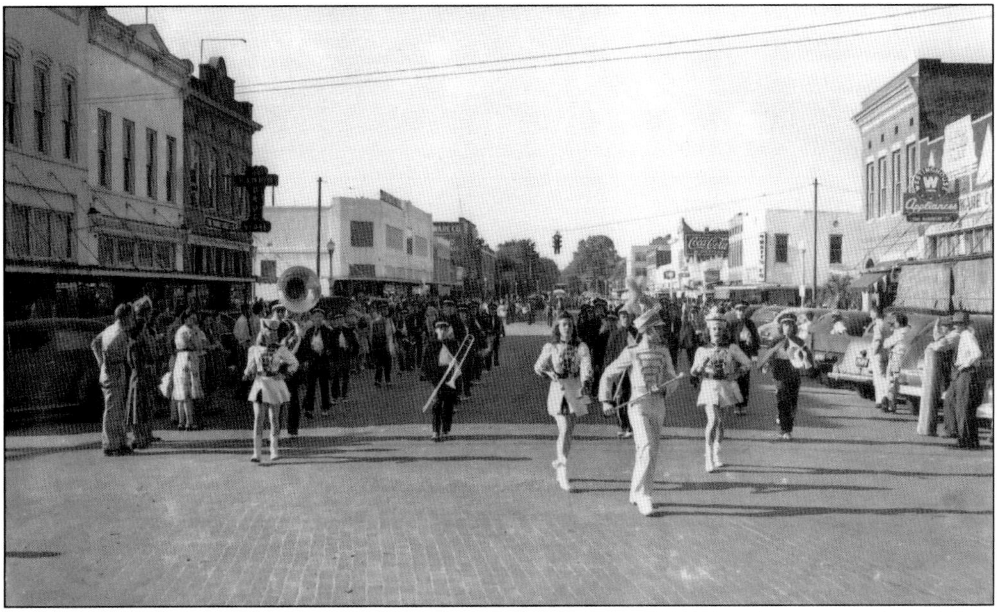

Likely taken during the late 1940s, the Columbia High School Band makes its way down Main Street. Sims Hardware can be seen at right. (Courtesy of Bates Bullock.)

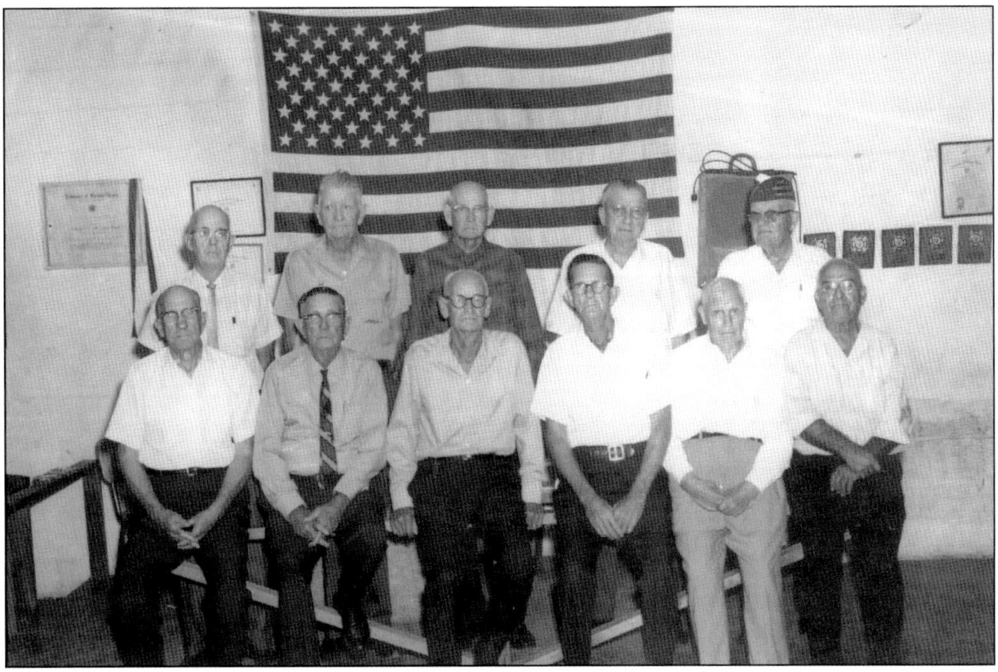

In the summer of 1917, more than 100 young men "joined up" at the courthouse, courageously volunteering for service in World War I. The company became Troop G, 2nd Separate Cavalry Squadron, Mississippi Cavalry, with Capt. A.L. Yates in command. It saw service in various places throughout Europe. The troop included two cooks, two horseshoers, and a saddler. Judge Sebe Dale was the first to volunteer, and Ott C. Lowe was the first casualty, dying at camp in Louisiana. B.B. Bradley took this 1969 photograph at a reunion of the old soldiers. (Courtesy of Marion County Historical Society.)

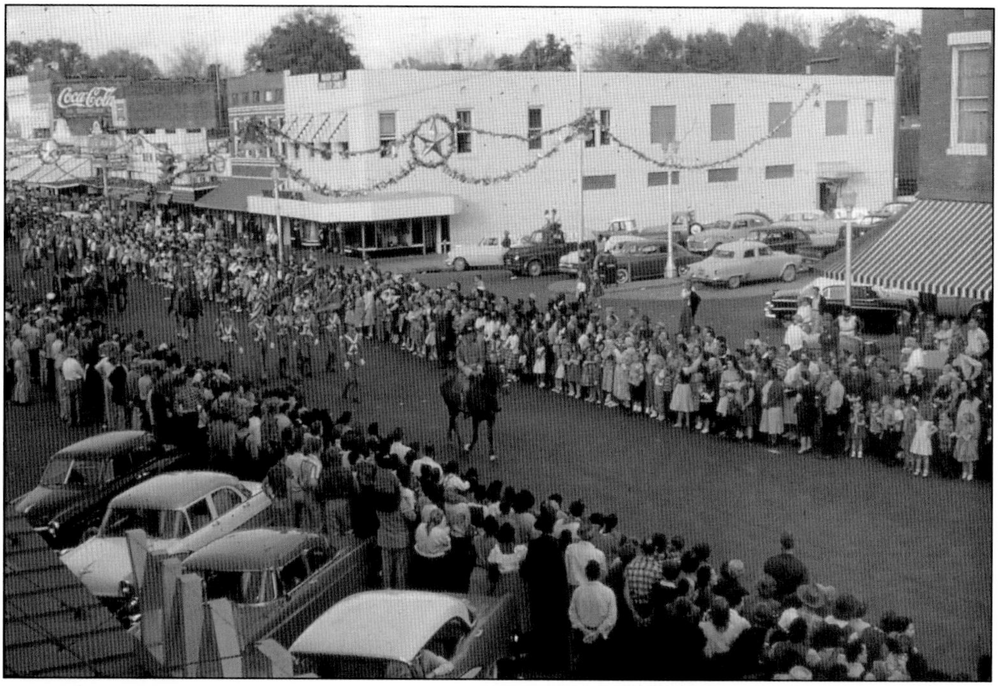

Throngs of Columbians gather along Main Street in this nostalgic mid-1950s parade scene. Confederate reenactors make their way south toward Courthouse Square, even with what appears to be a Civil War–period artillery caisson. (Courtesy of Bates Bullock.)

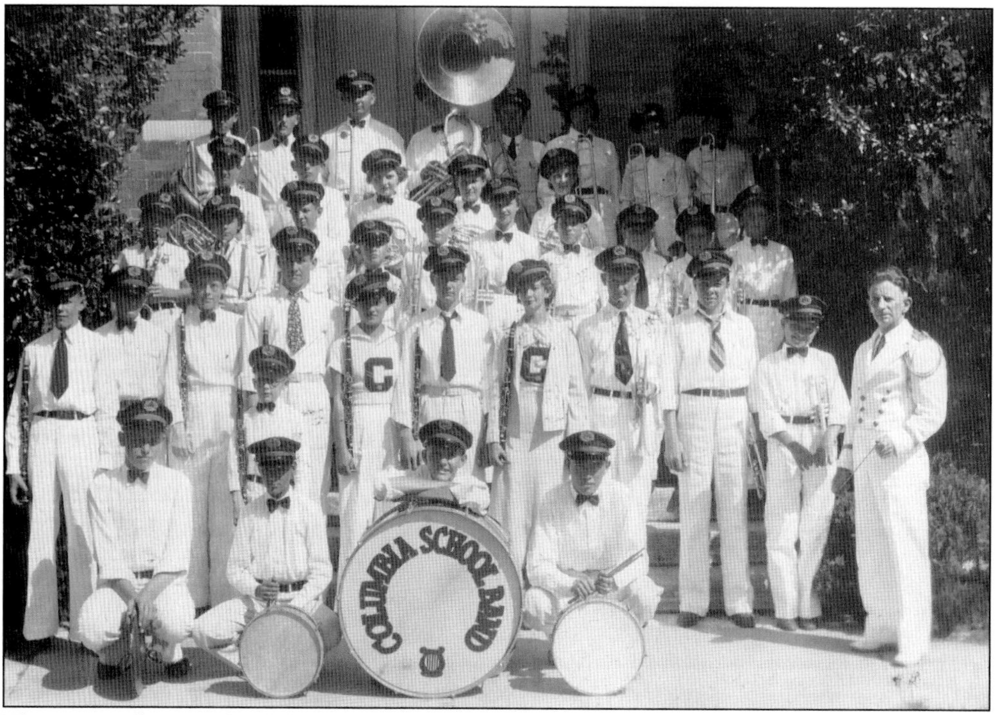

This group photograph of the Columbia High School Band was taken on September 29, 1935, on the steps the school. (Courtesy of Bates Bullock.)

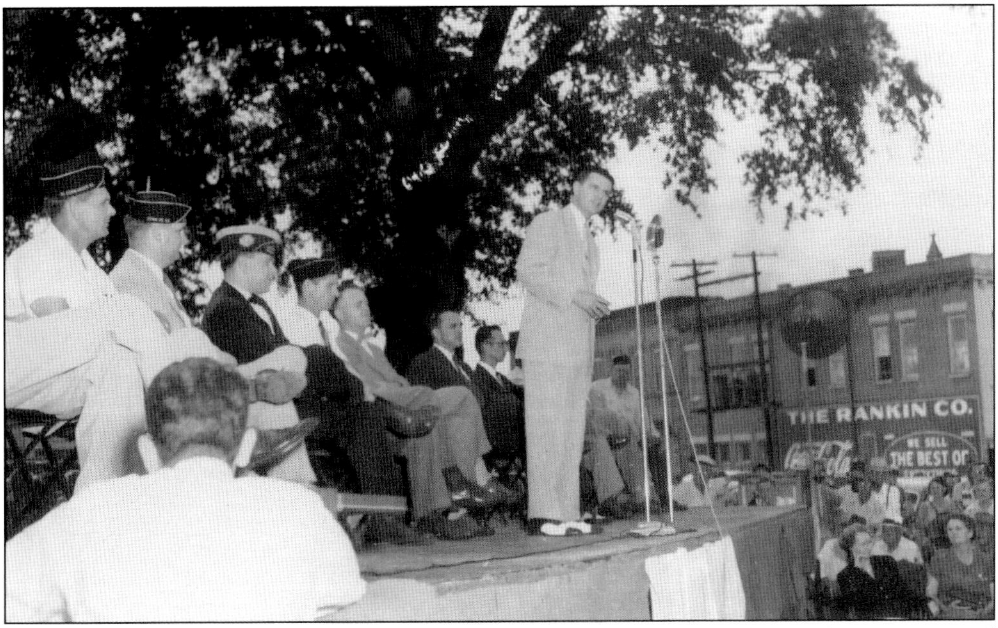

Lt. Gov. Carroll Gartin speaks to the crowd gathered at the courthouse during the war memorial dedication on August 1953. Note the attractive period advertisement on the Rankin Co. building. This photograph was taken by former POW Larkin J. Burt. (Courtesy of Damon Watts.)

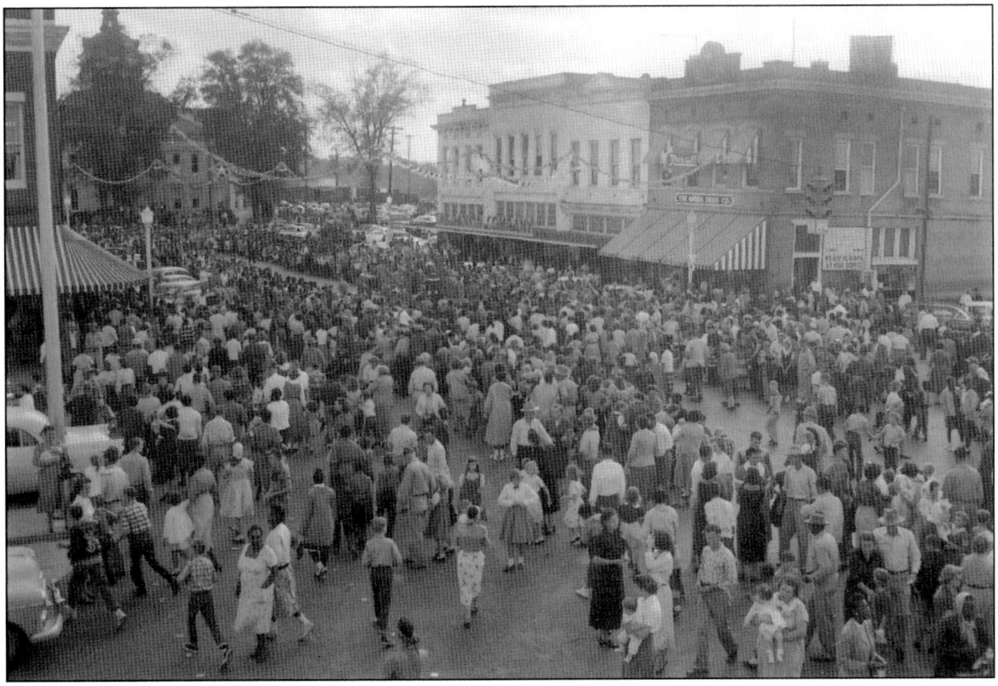

This 1950s parade scene is seen from the vantage point of the Columbia Chamber of Commerce Office on the second floor of the Watts Company Building. Harris Drug Company's sign promises "we are always at your service." Note the period awnings on the buildings. (Courtesy of Bates Bullock.)

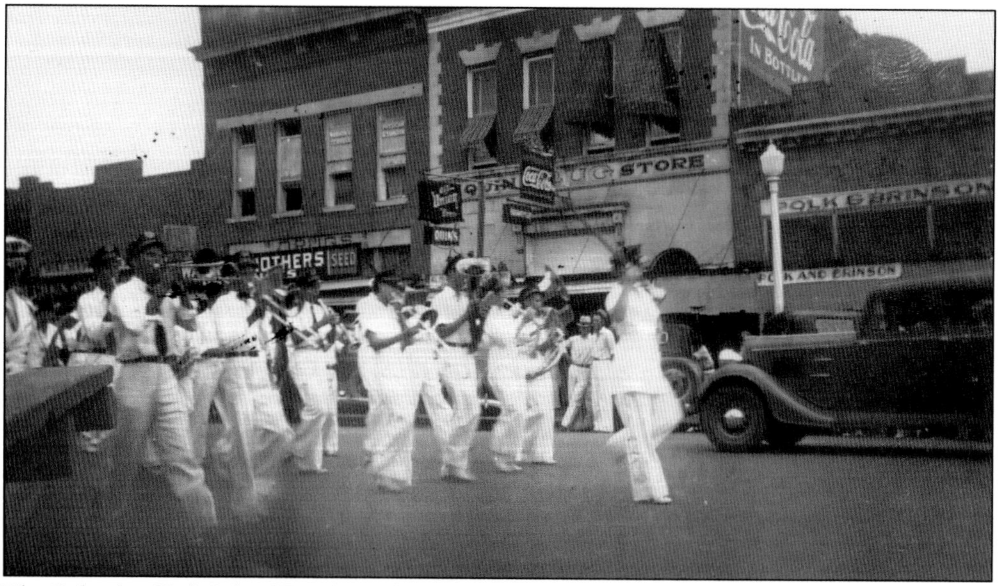

The Columbia High School Band parades past Quin's Drugstore and the Polk & Brinson Company. The landmark Coca-Cola sign, painted directly onto the bricks of Quin's Drugstore, can still be seen today. The building was erected around 1900 and originally housed the Pearl River Bank and Trust Company. (Courtesy of Bates Bullock.)

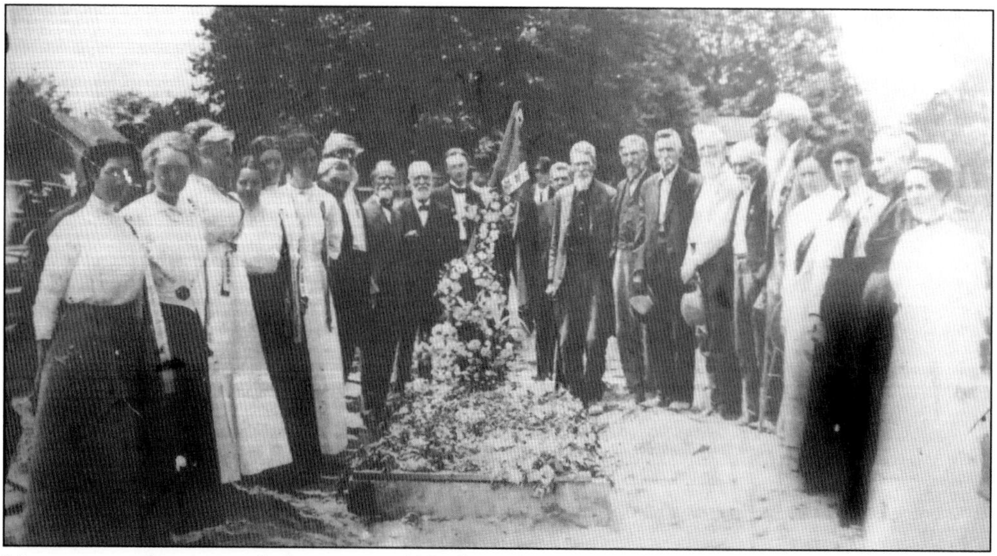

Mourners gather around the grave of Nathan A. Lott at the Columbia City Cemetery on Dale Street. The ladies on the right are likely the family of the deceased, while the ladies on the left are members of the Zeno Goss Chapter of the United Daughters of the Confederacy. As a young Confederate soldier, Lott volunteered for service under Capt. Hamilton Mayson. However, he later served in the 12th Mississippi Infantry, a regiment assigned to service in the East. His obituary stated that he fought in many battles in Virginia in A.P. Hill's corps until he was wounded on August 17, 1864, near Petersburg, Virginia. Lott's experience is rare as he is one of the few residents of Marion County known to serve in the Army of Northern Virginia. This photograph was taken on Saturday, April 27, 1912. (Courtesy of Marion County Historical Society.)

Four

Industry, Logging, and Railroads

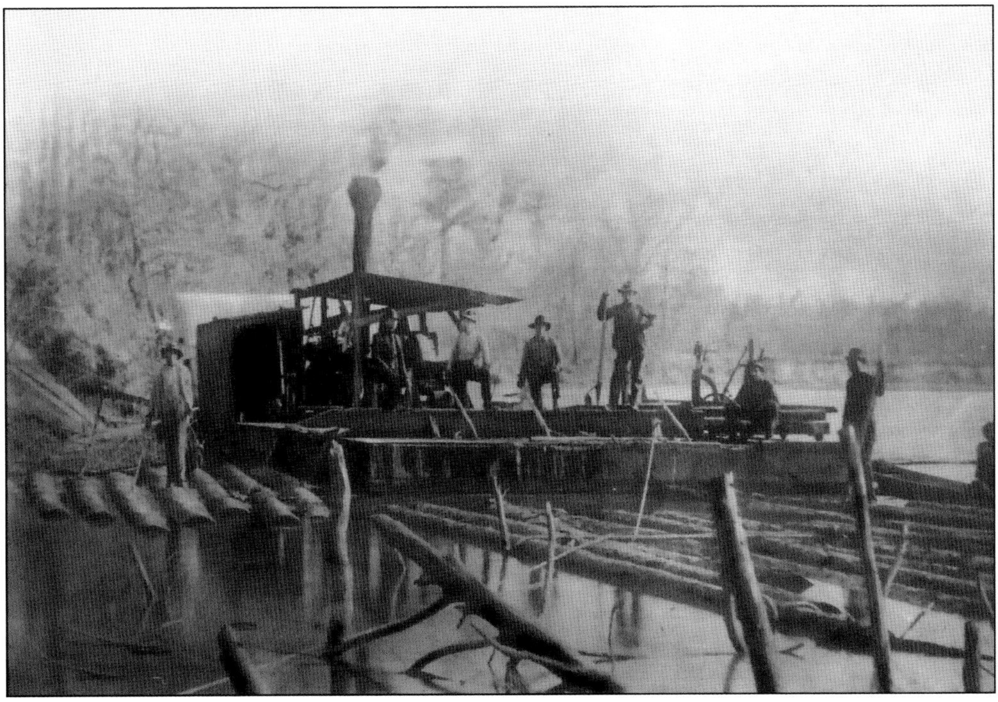

The logging crew of Chas. S. Jordan's floating sawmill on Pearl River momentarily pauses from work for the photographer. From left to right are Mr. Toney, Chas. S. Jordan Sr., Neal Coker, Robert Jordan, Tom Coker, Bob Coker, Mr. Galloway, and Mr. Wolfe. The photograph was taken around 1910. (Courtesy of Cass Barnes.)

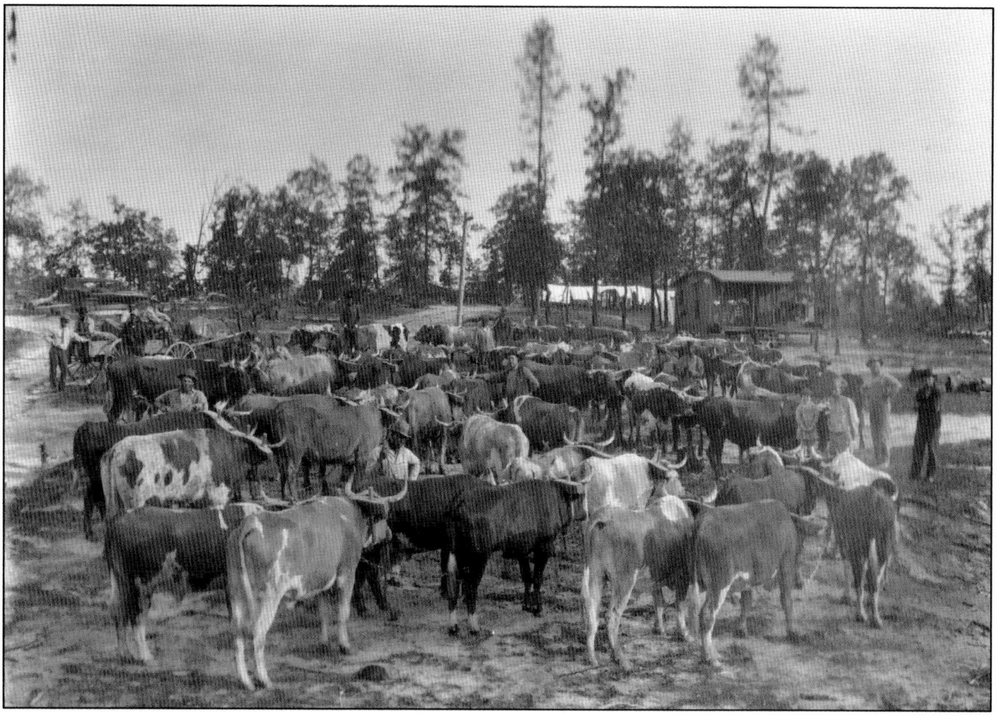

As the wash dries on the line in the background, teams of oxen and their handlers are photographed in this logging camp scene. (Courtesy of Marion County Historical Society.)

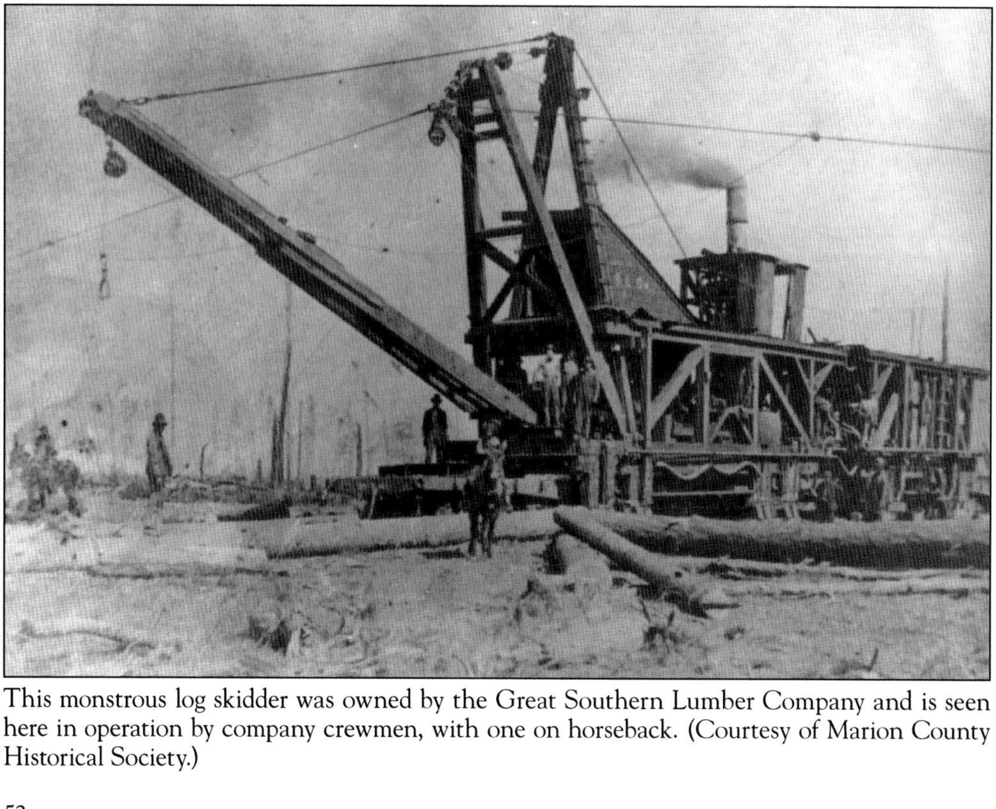

This monstrous log skidder was owned by the Great Southern Lumber Company and is seen here in operation by company crewmen, with one on horseback. (Courtesy of Marion County Historical Society.)

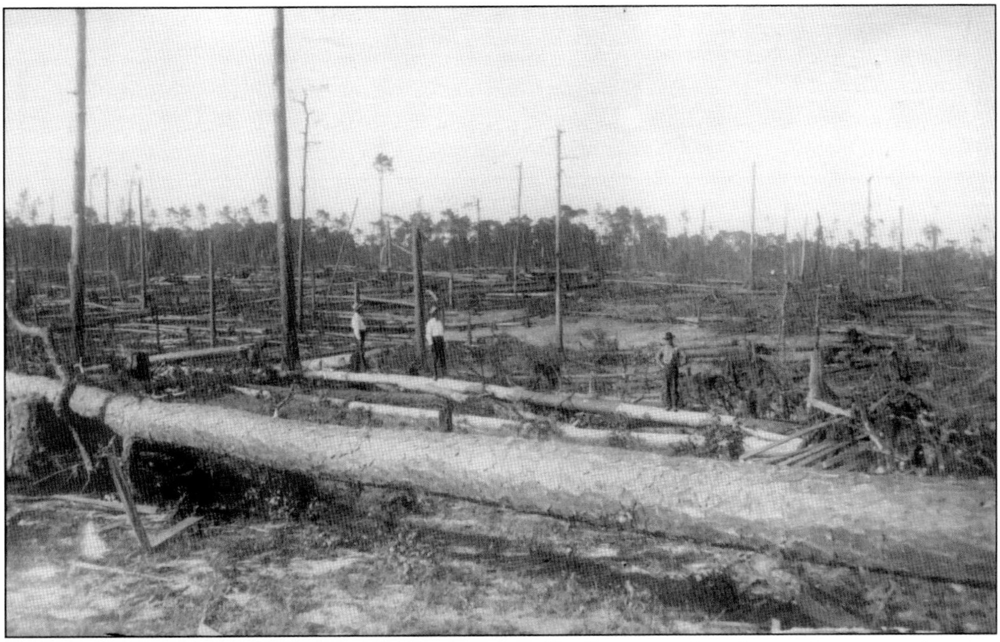

This 1902 photograph, taken near Cheraw, graphically illustrates the effects of intensive logging operations on the Marion County landscape. In more ways than one, the timber boom forever changed the face of South Mississippi. (Courtesy of Marion County Public Library.)

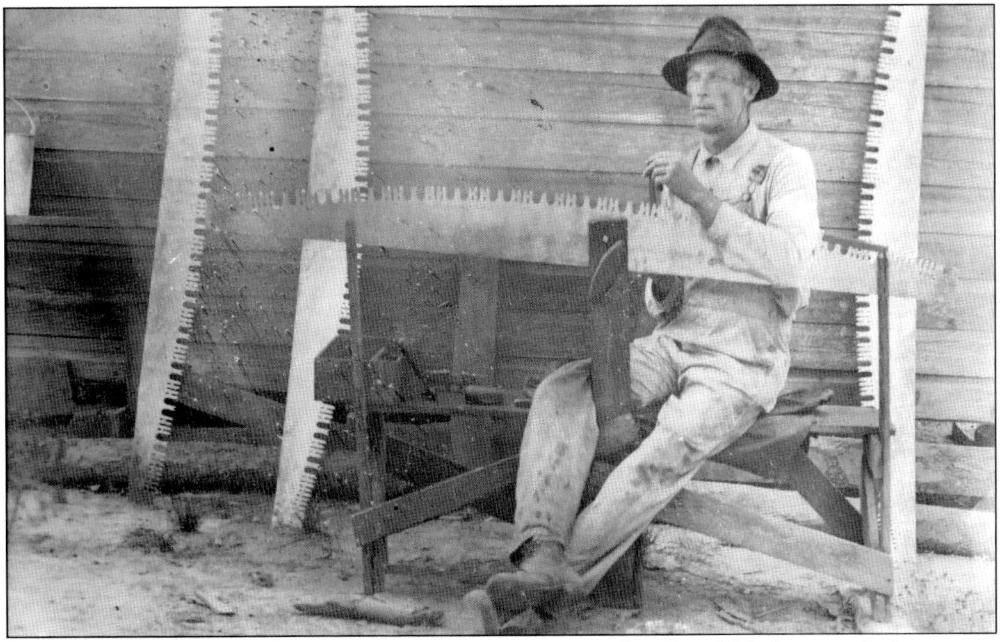

Arthur Tyner of the Spring Cottage community was captured in this 1910 photograph sharpening his saw blades. During his youth, his family attended school and church at the Payne's Chapel Methodist Church in Spring Cottage, where he and his siblings sang in the choir. He was named after his great-great-grandfather Arthur Pearce Tyner, a veteran of the Revolutionary War and prominent farmer who settled in Marion County prior to 1820 in the Cedar Grove section of the county. (Louis F. Morgan collection.)

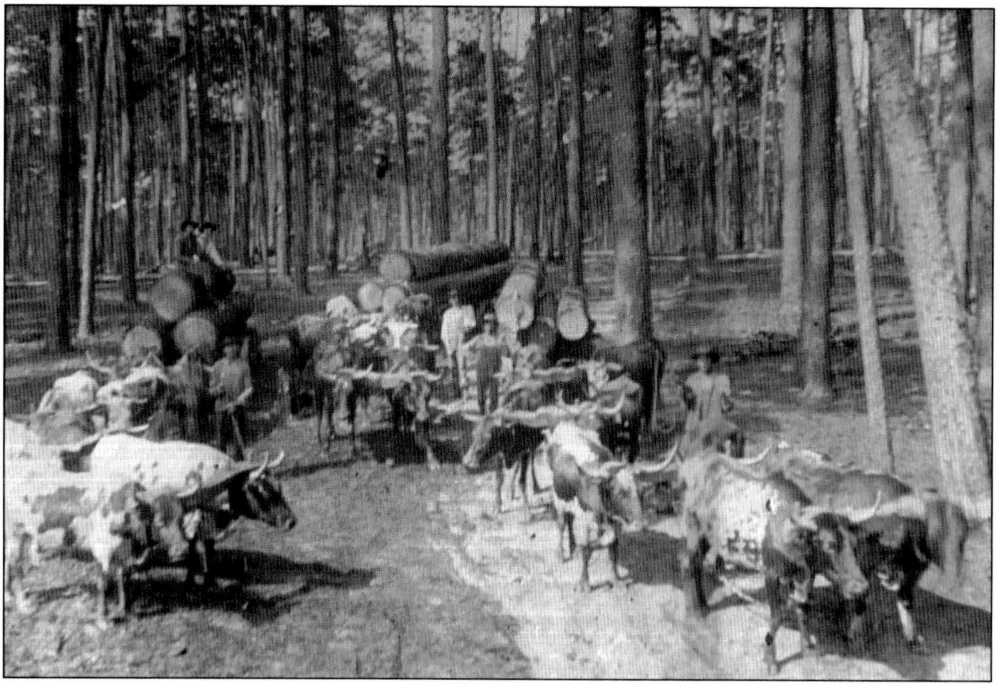

This scene of massive pine logs being hauled on wagons pulled by teams of oxen was commonplace in the county for decades. While some of these hardy loggers prefer to ride, others prefer to walk. (Courtesy of Marion County Historical Society.)

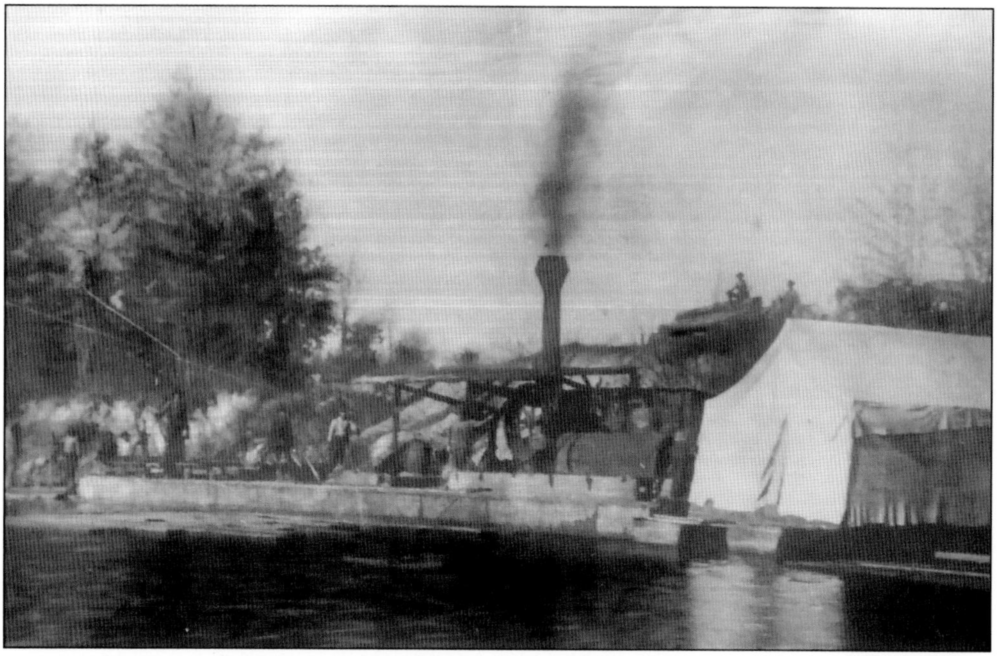

In this c. 1910 view of the Chas. Jordan floating sawmill, the crew is seen at work in the vicinity of Hunt's Hill on Pearl River. The sawmill was built locally, constructed at Old Log Landing above Foxworth, while the boiler was fabricated by Cliff Williams of Corinth, Mississippi. This photograph dates to 1910. (Courtesy of Cass Barnes.)

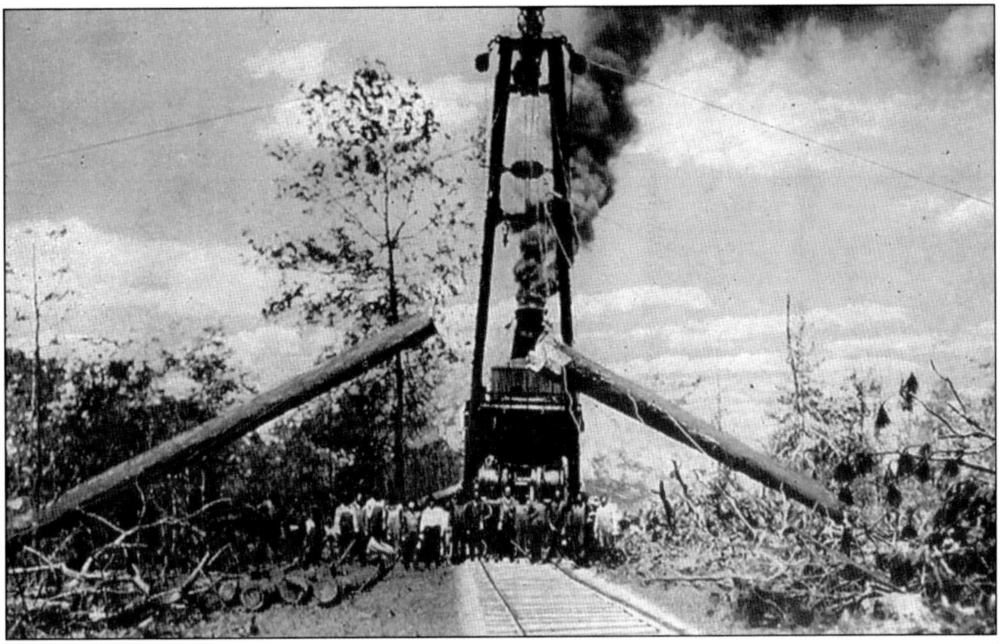

This logging operation is most likely that of the Great Southern Lumber Company. (Courtesy of Mississippi Department of Archives and History.)

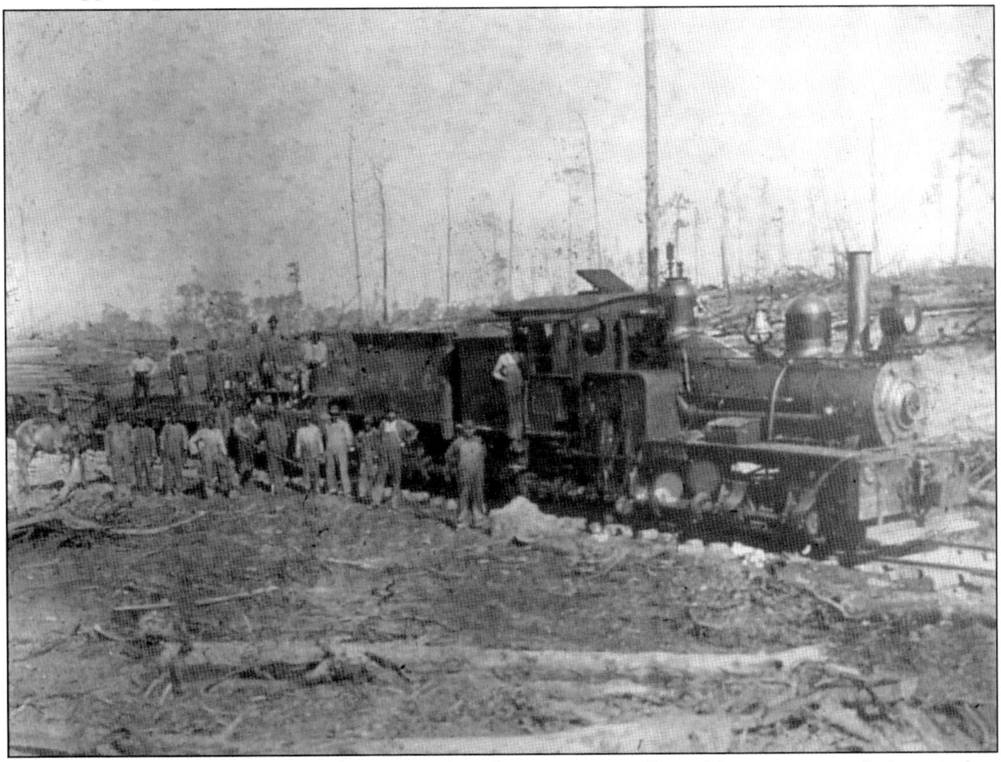

Chartered in 1902, Great Southern Lumber Company purchased large tracts of pine timber and was once the largest sawmill operation in the world. Here, logging crewman pose next to a company locomotive used to haul logs to mill. (Courtesy of Marion County Historical Society.)

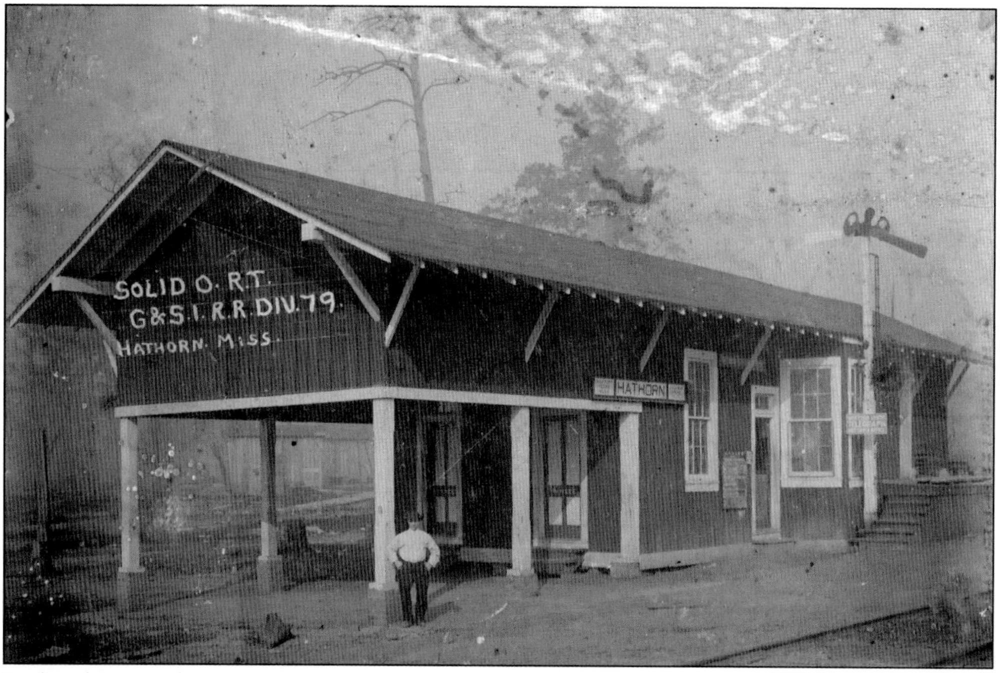

Railroad agent John Rogers is seen here at the Gulf & Ship Island depot at Hathorn, a community that once thrived from the timber industry. Note the segregated entrances marked "white" and "colored." (Courtesy of Marion County Historical Society.)

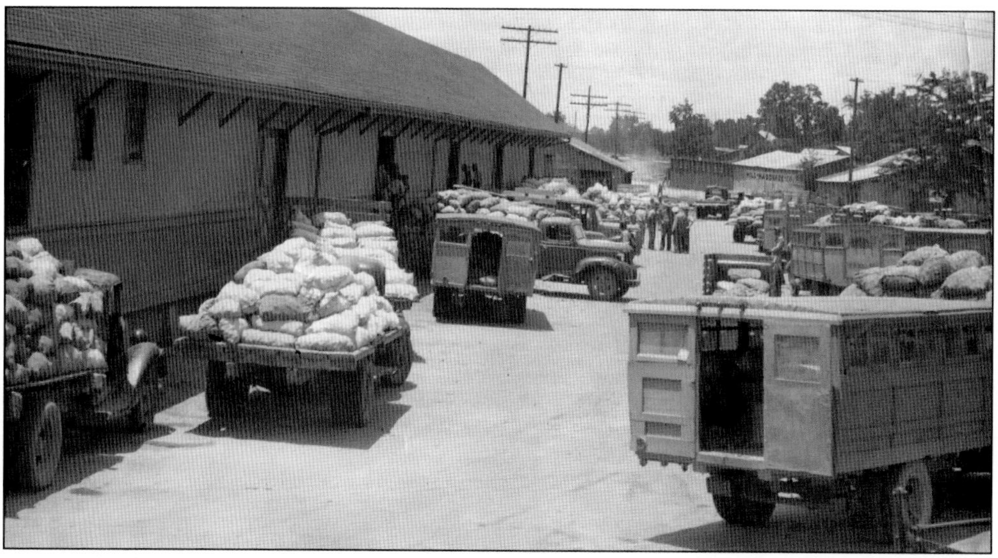

Waiting for the potato grader, truckloads of regionally produced Irish potatoes crowd the Gulf & Ship Island freight depot on Pittman Street. In fact, in 1938, Marion County led all of Mississippi's counties in potato production. Note the privately owned school bus being utilized to haul the spuds to market. (Courtesy of Fran Ginn.)

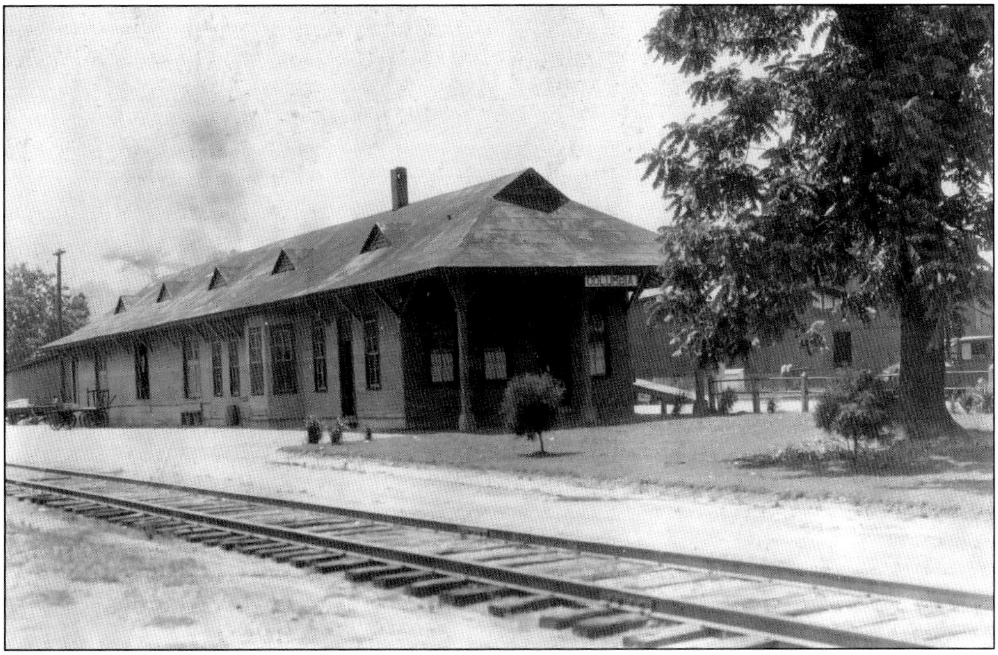

The New Orleans & Great Northern railroad came to Columbia in 1908 as a result of the expanding operations of the Great Southern Lumber Company during the timber boom. The old NO&GN depot once stood southwest of the courthouse near the Pearl River. (Courtesy of Marion County Development Partnership.)

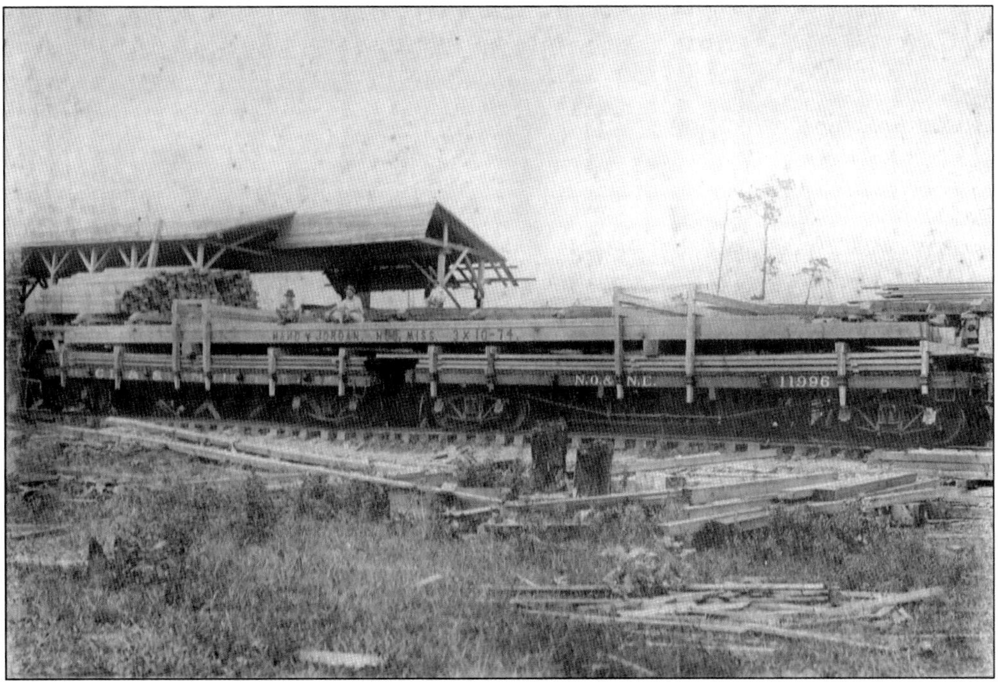

In a photograph likely taken south of Columbia, two employees take a break on a railroad flatcar. Stacks of freshly milled lumber can be seen at left while "Hand & Jordan, Hub, Miss." can be seen embossed on the side of the railroad car. (Courtesy of Marion County Historical Society.)

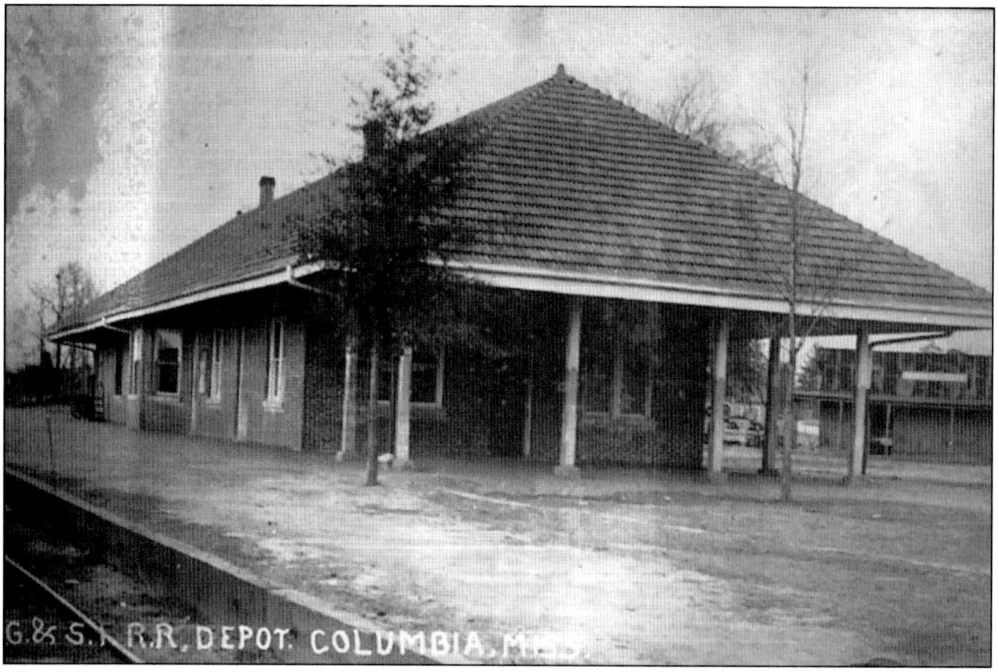

The Gulf & Ship Island passenger depot was built on Second Street in 1907 and was operated by the company until 1925. During World War II, the building was utilized to house soldiers on weekend leave from Camp Shelby. This image is from an early postcard. (Courtesy of Bates Bullock.)

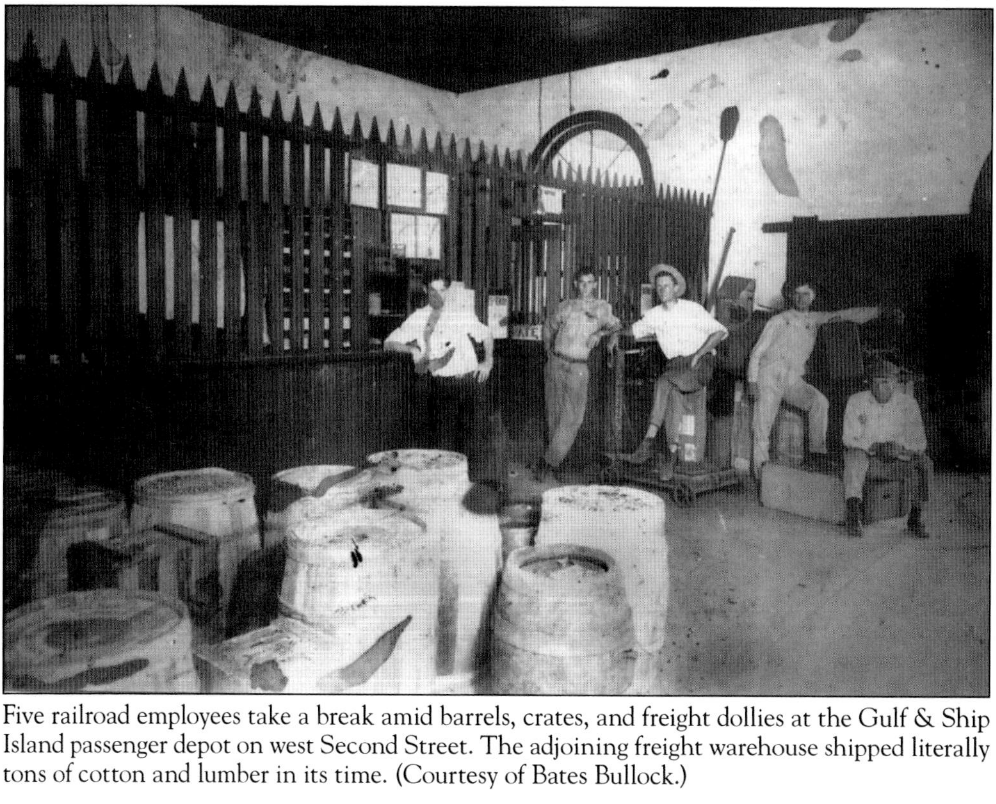

Five railroad employees take a break amid barrels, crates, and freight dollies at the Gulf & Ship Island passenger depot on west Second Street. The adjoining freight warehouse shipped literally tons of cotton and lumber in its time. (Courtesy of Bates Bullock.)

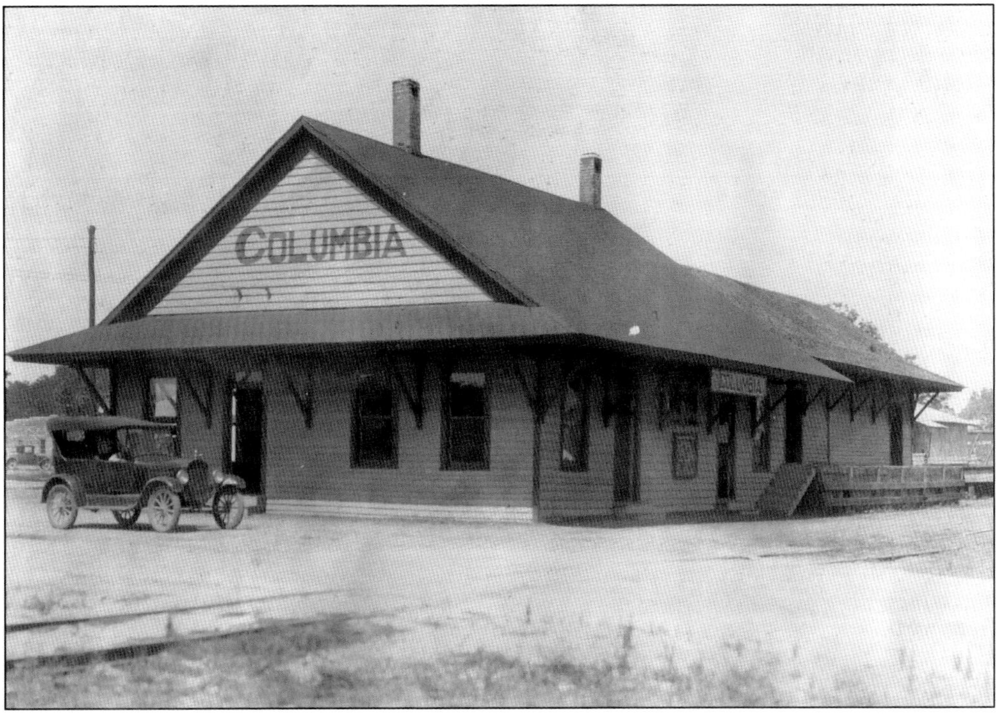

Drawn by the booming timber industry, the Fernwood, Columbia & Gulf Railroad came into Columbia in 1920. The company depot stood on the south side of the courthouse. The railroad's daily schedule can be seen on the exterior wall in this photograph. (Courtesy of Marion County Development Partnership.)

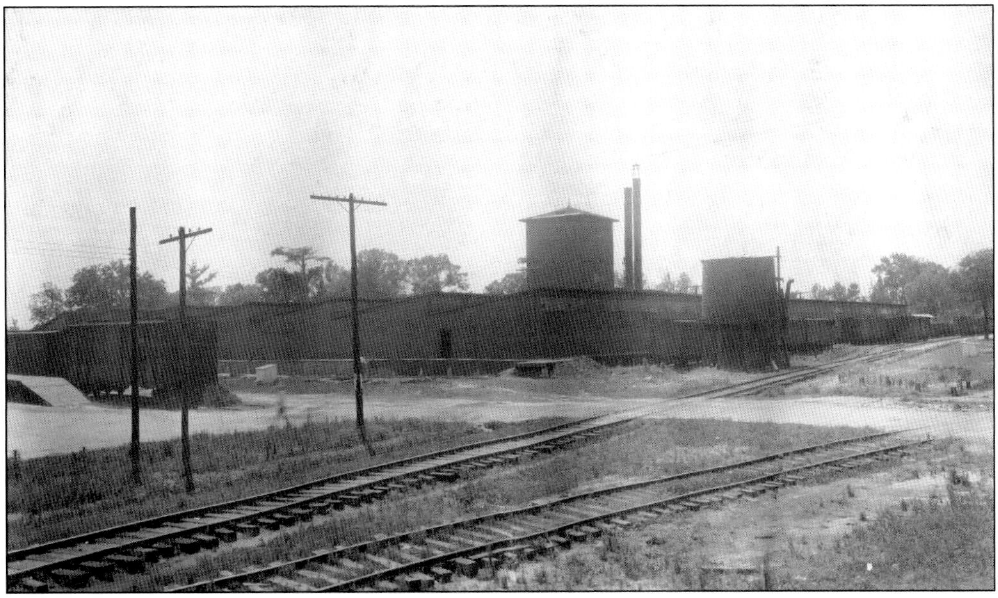

The sprawling facilities of the cotton compress testifies to the dominance of "king cotton" to the Marion County economy. The compress was located near Pearl River on the west side of Columbia. By 1860, Mississippi produced more than one-fourth of America's cotton. (Courtesy of Marion County Development Partnership.)

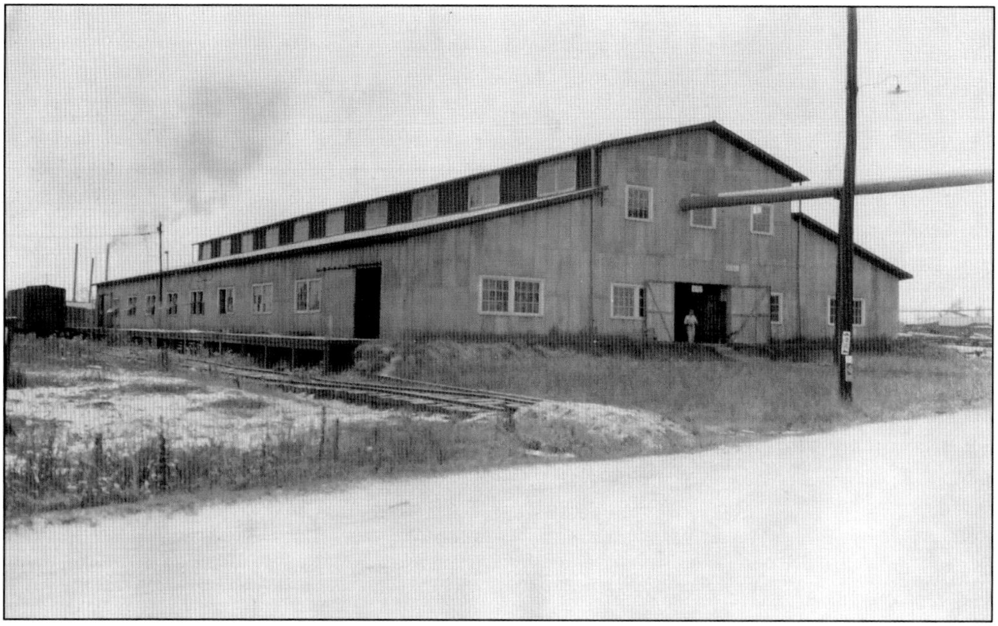

White's Box Company on South High School Avenue manufactured wire-bound boxes. The company came to Columbia as a result of Hugh White's groundbreaking "Balance Agriculture with Industry" program. (Courtesy of Marion County Development Partnership.)

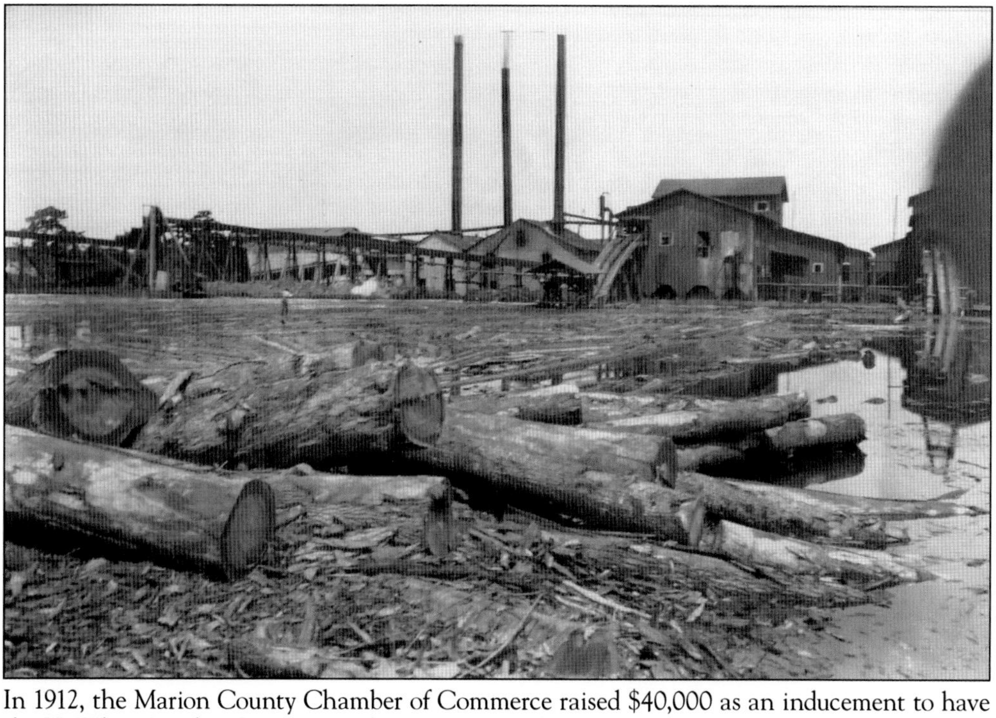

In 1912, the Marion County Chamber of Commerce raised $40,000 as an inducement to have the J.J. White Lumber Company to locate a new mill at Columbia. At peak production, the mill manufactured 250,000 feet of pine lumber per day. In 1931, the mill whistle blew for the last time, an event long remembered with grief by Columbia citizens. (Courtesy of Marion County Development Partnership.)

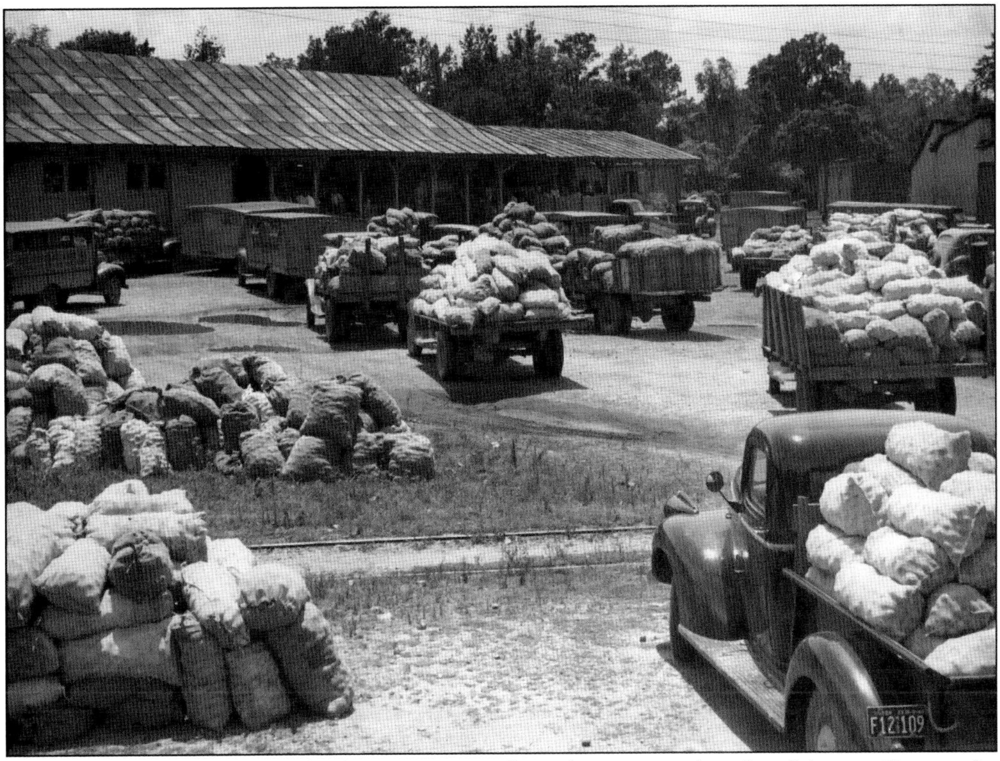

Irish potatoes were one of the first commercial truck crops produced in Marion County. In this 1944 photograph, truckloads of potatoes crowd the Gulf, Mobile & Ohio depot near the courthouse. (Courtesy of Fran Ginn.)

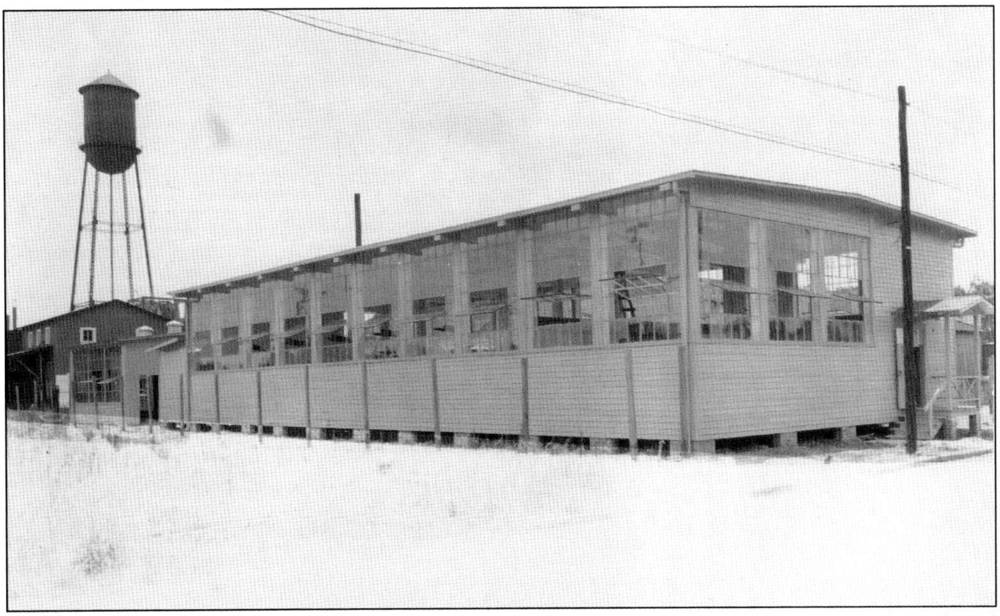

The Columbine Knitting Mill was located across from Reliance Manufacturing and employed some 100 employees and, at peak production, churned out 2,500 pairs of socks per week during the Depression years. (Courtesy of Marion County Development Partnership.)

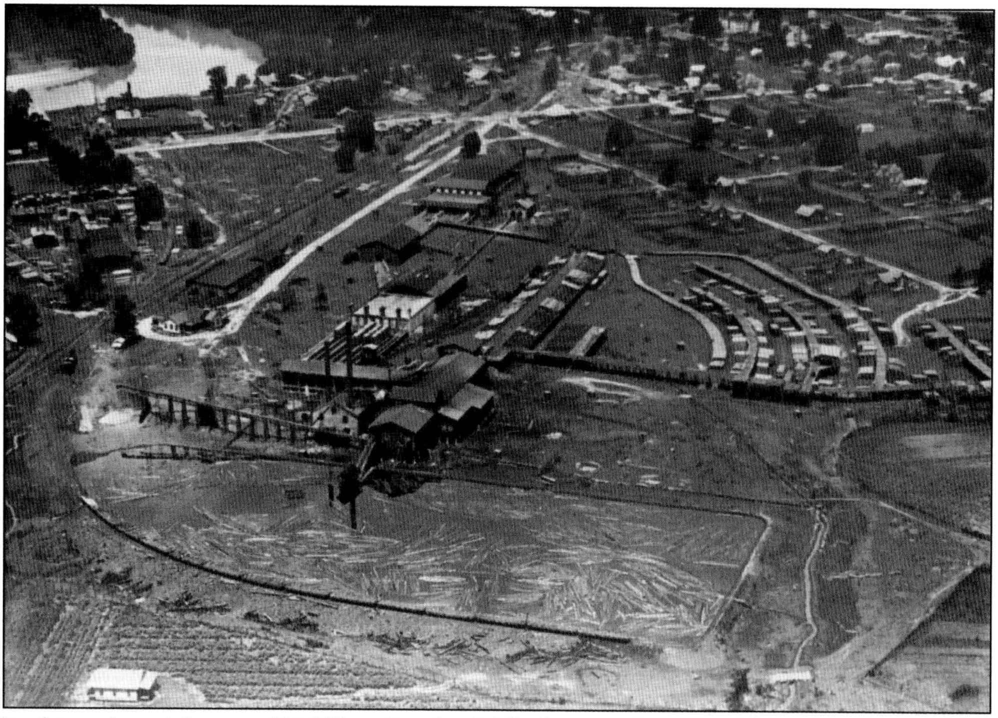

In this early aerial view of J.J. White Lumber Mill, the sprawling sawmill complex can be seen, including the large millpond. A curve in the Pearl River is visible at the top of the frame. (Courtesy of Marion County Development Partnership.)

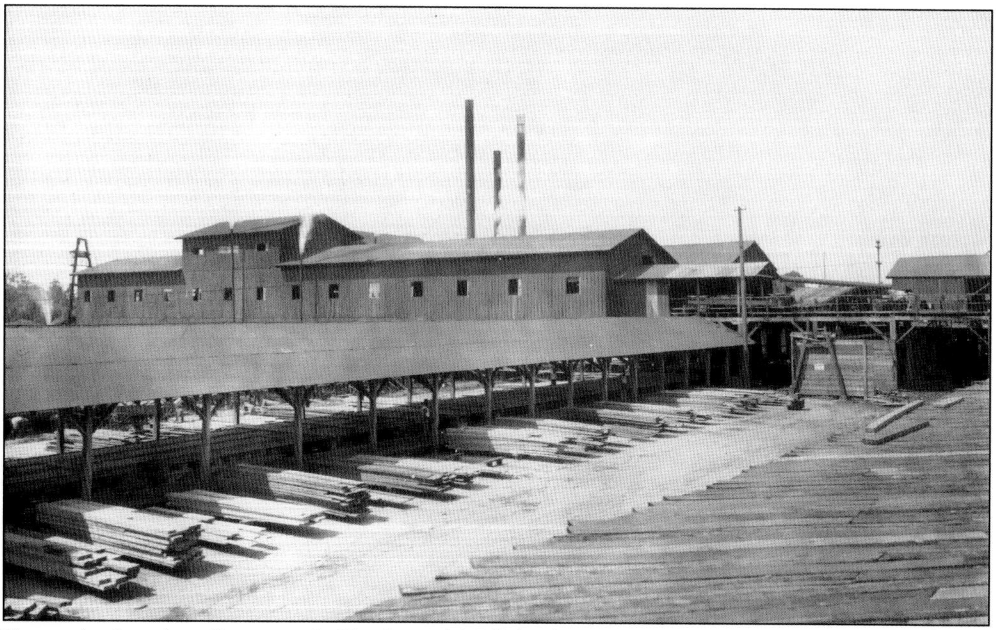

Kentucky Lumber Company's Hardwood Mill had a capacity of 50,000 feet per day. It is thought this mill was located near South High School Avenue. (Courtesy of Marion County Development Partnership.)

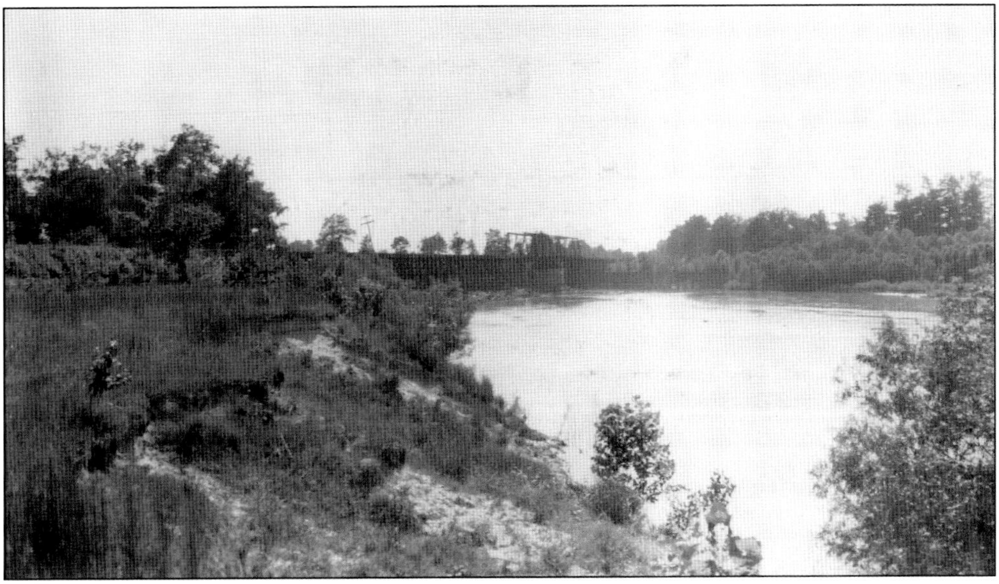

Built in 1897, the famous New Orleans & Great Northern Railroad turn bridge on Pearl River is seen in this c. 1930 image. The pile driver necessary for the construction took three months to arrive from New Orleans before work could begin. (Courtesy of Marion County Development Partnership.)

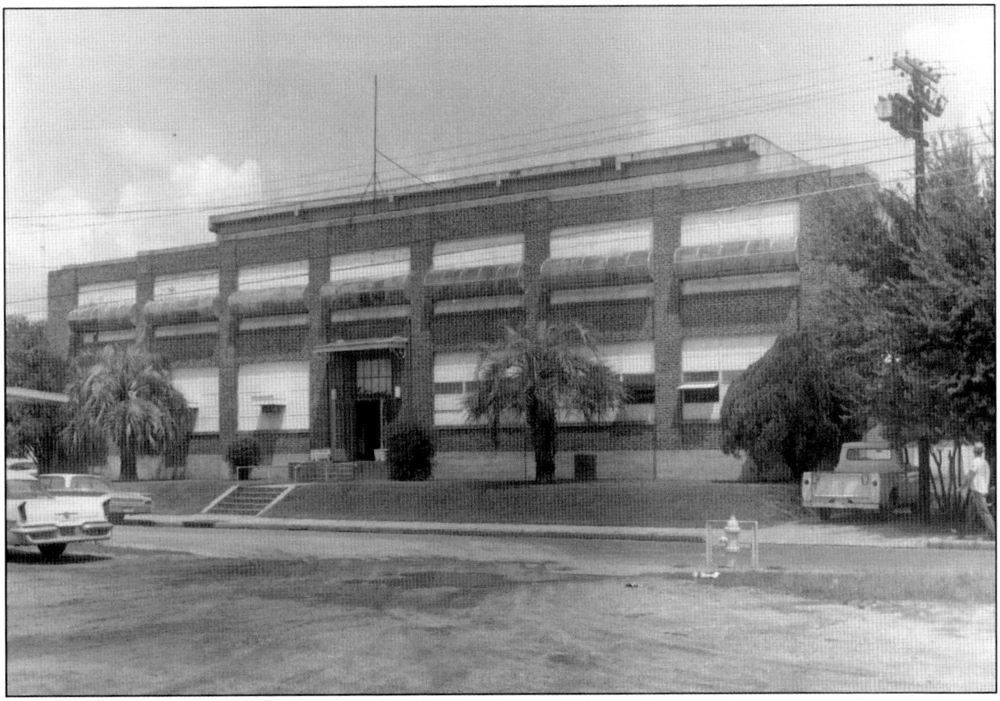

Reliance Manufacturing Company Building began production in 1933 on west Church Street. At the outset, the factory produced clothing but by World War II was manufacturing tents and parachutes and won the "E" award for production from the Army and Navy. When the factory began operations, it had 70,000 square feet of floor space and employed around 1,000 employees. Interestingly, *National Geographic* reporters visiting Columbia in 1937 mistook the Reliance building for a high school. (Courtesy of Marion County Development Partnership.)

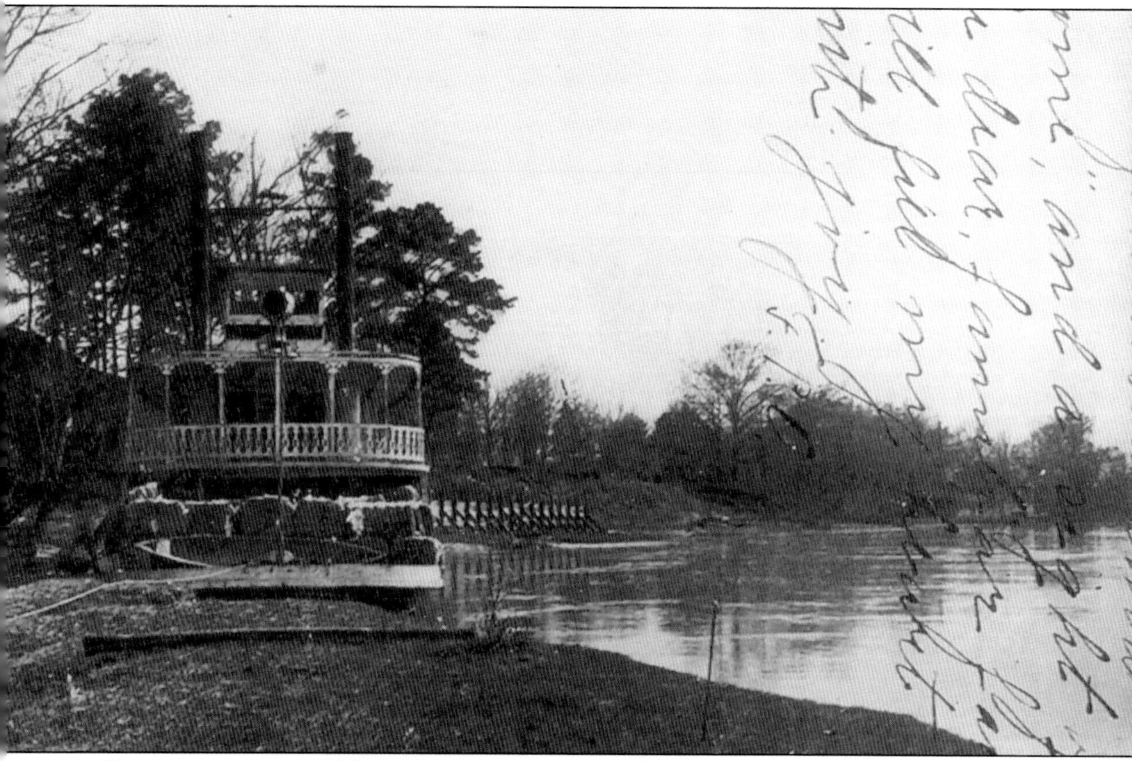

The *Fountain City and Black Warrior* is pictured on the Pearl River at Columbia in this pre-1910 image. This rare postcard image shows the grand Pearl River at the end of the romantic steamboat era. Note the cotton bales stacked on the lower deck. (Courtesy of Mississippi Department of Archives and History.)

Five

All around Columbia

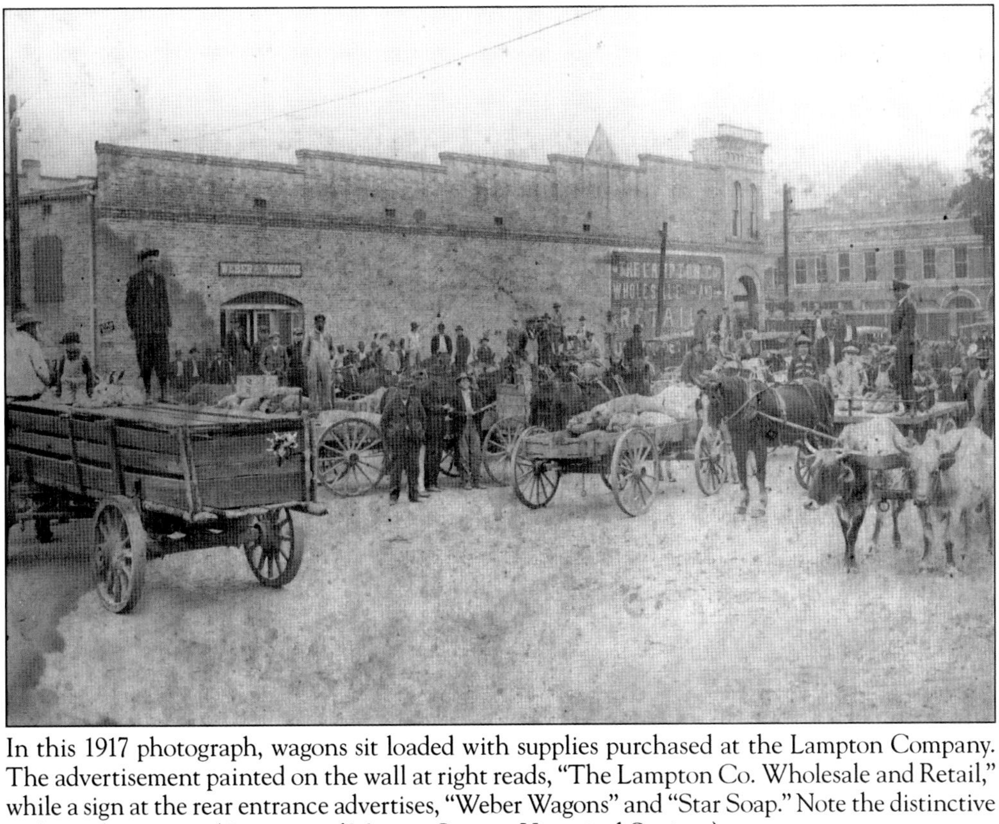

In this 1917 photograph, wagons sit loaded with supplies purchased at the Lampton Company. The advertisement painted on the wall at right reads, "The Lampton Co. Wholesale and Retail," while a sign at the rear entrance advertises, "Weber Wagons" and "Star Soap." Note the distinctive arch on the corner. (Courtesy of Marion County Historical Society.)

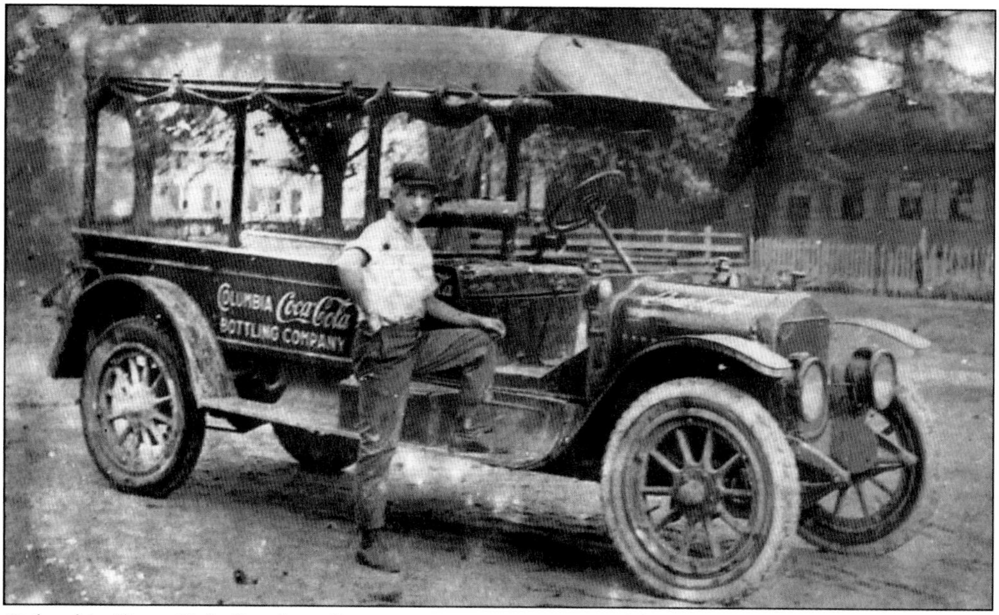

Columbia Coca-Cola Bottling Company came to town and began operations around 1910 on South Main Street near Short Cola Avenue. Alfred Evans was the early manager of the Columbia division, which, by the 1920s, was competing against another local bottling company, NuGrape Bottling Works. In 1917, Columbia Bottling enacted the cash deposit system of returning empty bottles in order to save the customer from inflated prices. (Courtesy of Bates Bullock.)

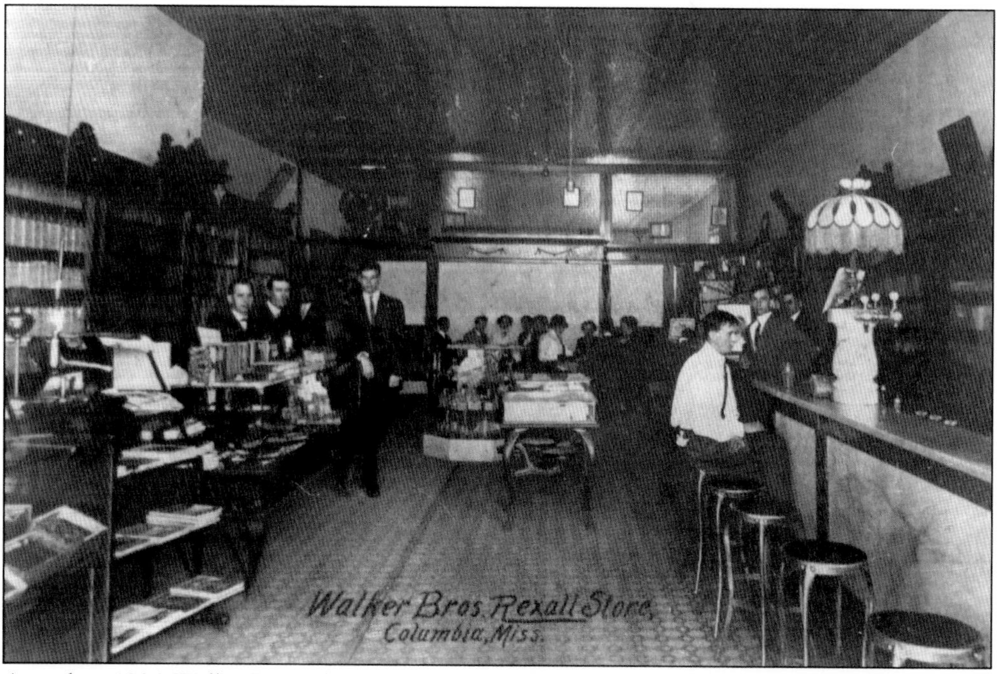

As early as 1906, Walker Bros. advertised, "The Swellest Ice Cream Parlor in Southern Mississippi," perhaps evident by the patrons gathered in the store. Note the bar and early soda fountain located on the right side of the room and the sitting area in the rear. Scenes such as this were common for the period. (Courtesy of Marion County Historical Society.)

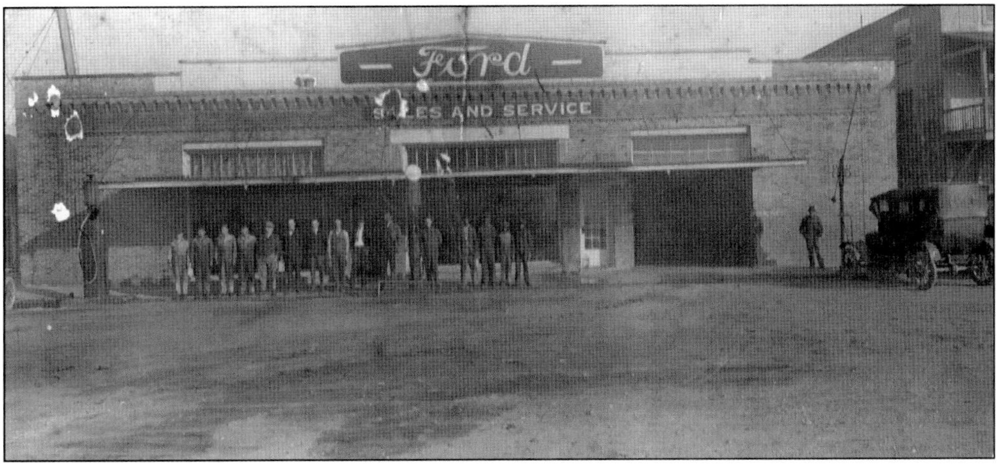

Offering both sales and service, Universal Motor Company was established around 1918 on west Second Street. They advertised the following: "Authorized dealers for Ford, Lincoln and Fordson, genuine parts, prompt repair service, battery work, air water and advice free." The first Ford car sold in the county was sold by Hill Hardware Company in 1917, forever changing the mode of travel in the county. (Courtesy of Marion County Historical Society.)

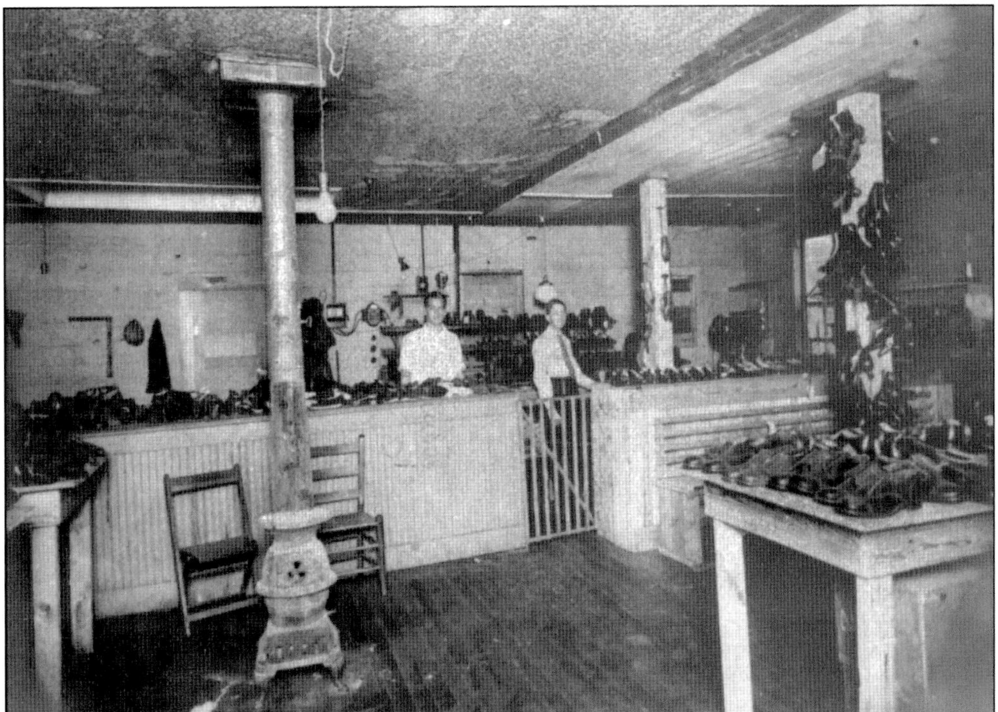

Shoes of every make can be been seen on tables of the Welch Shoe Shop. At a time when it was more cost effective to repair footwear rather than buy new, the two employees kept busy. Note the rudimentary wood-burning heater and the single bulb for light. (Courtesy of Marion County Historical Society.)

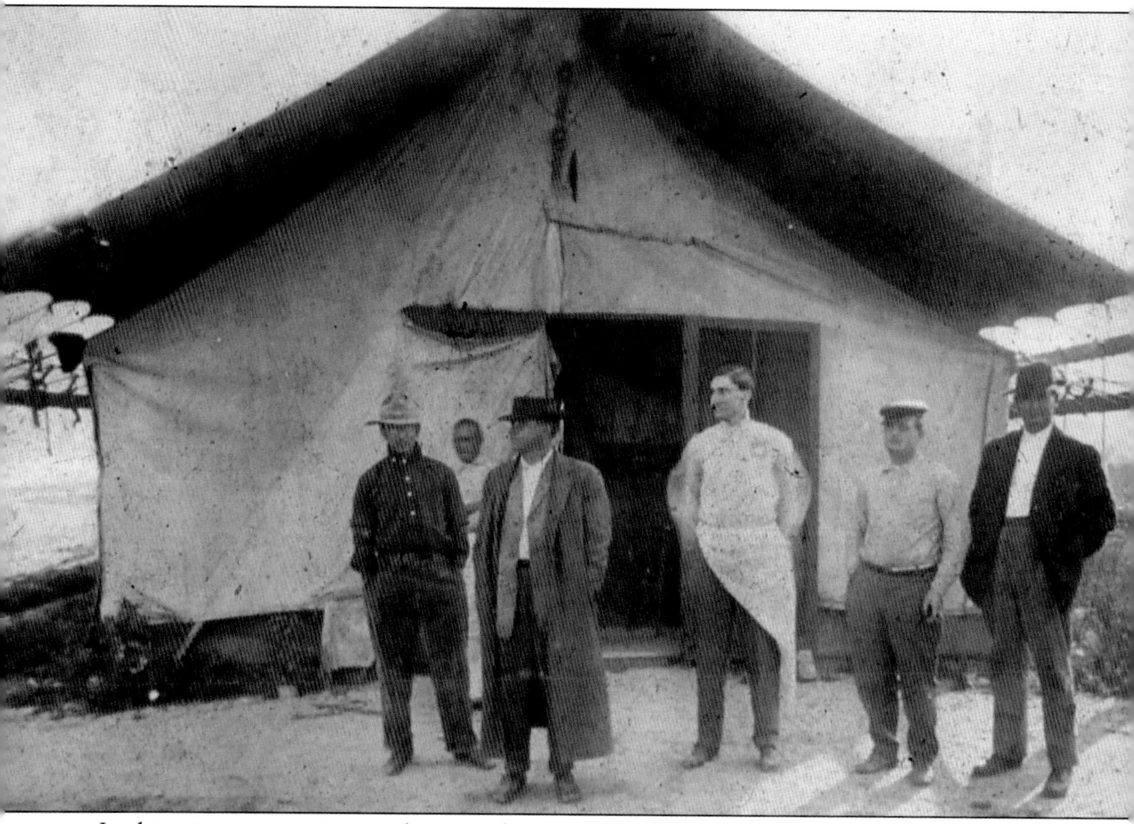

In this winter scene, six men loiter at the entrance of Tom Robertson's tent café that was once located near Courthouse Square. (Courtesy of Marion County Historical Society.)

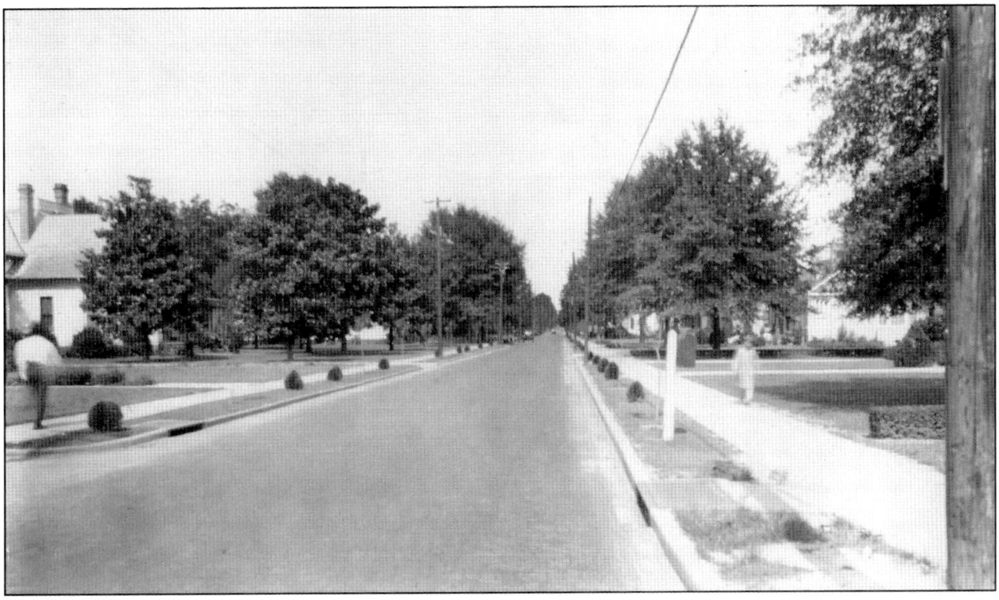

Residences line Broad Street in this 1930s photograph, looking east from High School Avenue. In the 19th century, this thoroughfare was known as "Purvis Road" and ran past Keys Hill, a legendary hill known for its role in numerous hangings. At least two can be documented to this hill, although it is widely believed that many more occurred. (Courtesy of Marion County Development Partnership.)

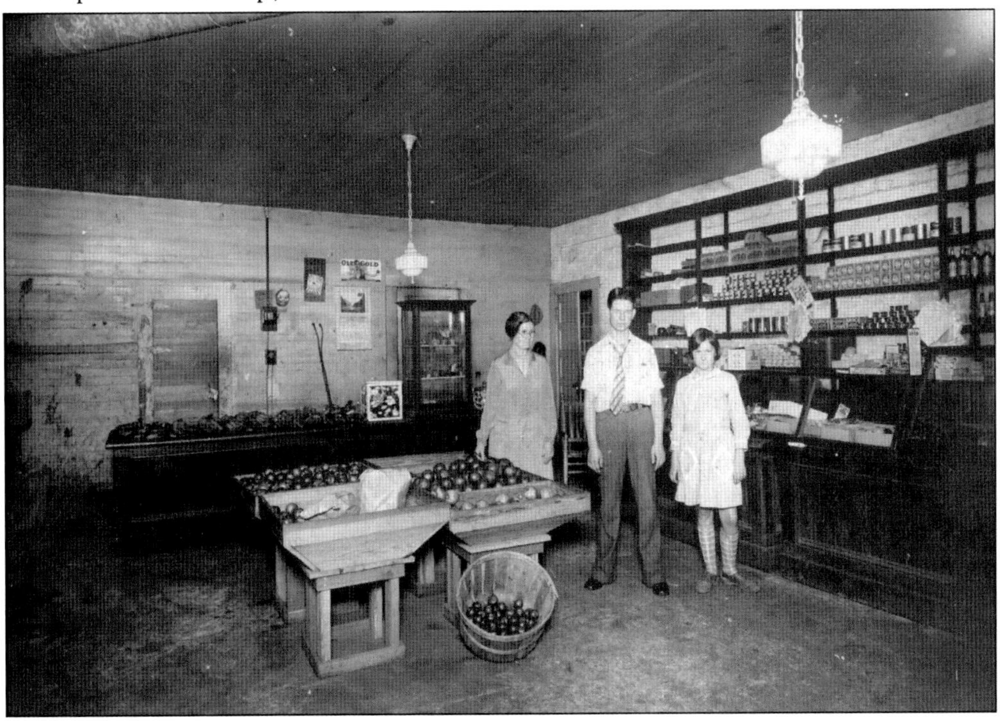

Fresh produce, as well as staples such as baking soda, canned beans, and cornstarch, can be seen in the Fruit Store on Second Street. Pictured are employee Dick Ross and the two ladies identified only as Alice and Lucy. Note the period advertisements on the walls. (Courtesy of Fran Ginn.)

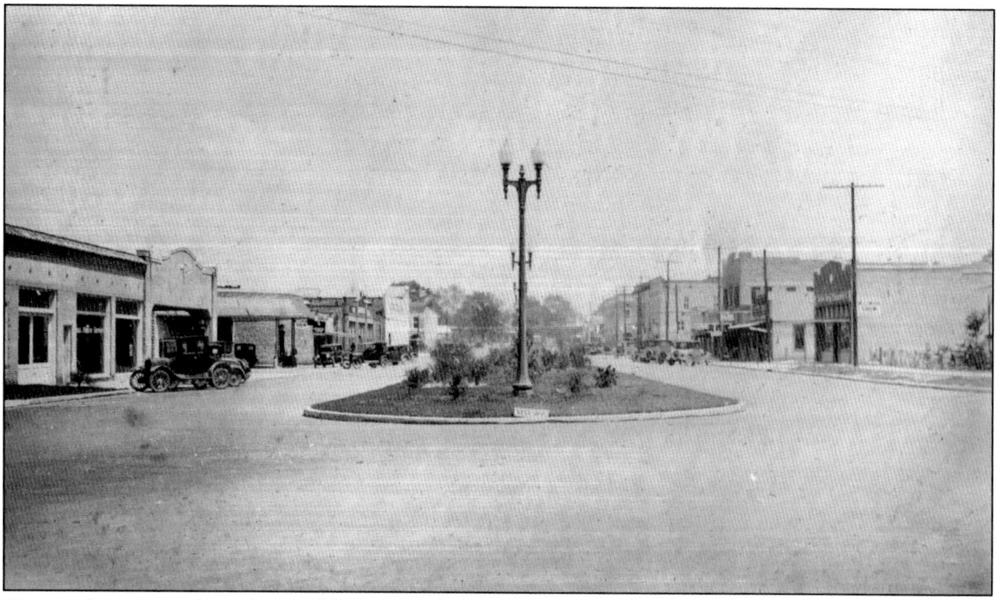

Various businesses line Second Street in this 1920s view from the vantage point of the Gulf & Ship Island passenger depot. The neutral grounds of Second Street look freshly planted, complete with a posted sign-imploring that pedestrians to "keep off." Universal Motor Company can be seen at the left of the frame. (Courtesy of Marion County Development Partnership.)

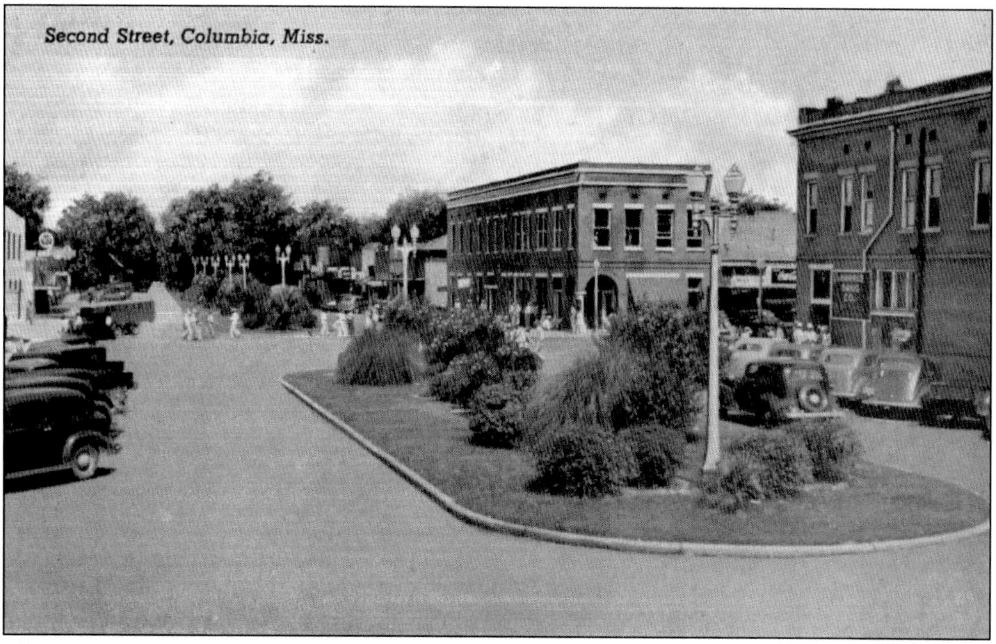

This postcard depicts a typical World War II–era scene in downtown Columbia, looking east toward the Main Street intersection. Large gardens were planted in the center of Second Street, and decorative electric lampposts lined the center of the street. On the far right is Harris Drug Company, and across the street is Citizen's Bank. What appear to be uniformed soldiers can be seen loitering about town. (Courtesy of Randy Davis.)

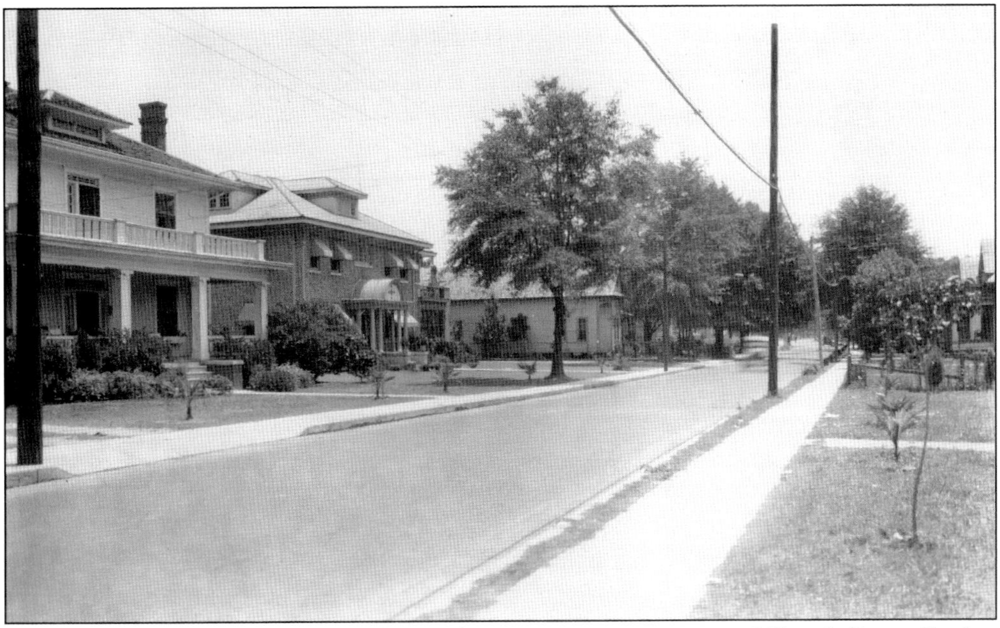

Looking east from near Main Street, houses line a picturesque segment of Church Street. Farther to the right, an approaching car can be seen blurred by motion. Off of frame to the right is the Round Table, a historic eatery that has been a Columbia landmark for decades. (Courtesy of Marion County Development Partnership.)

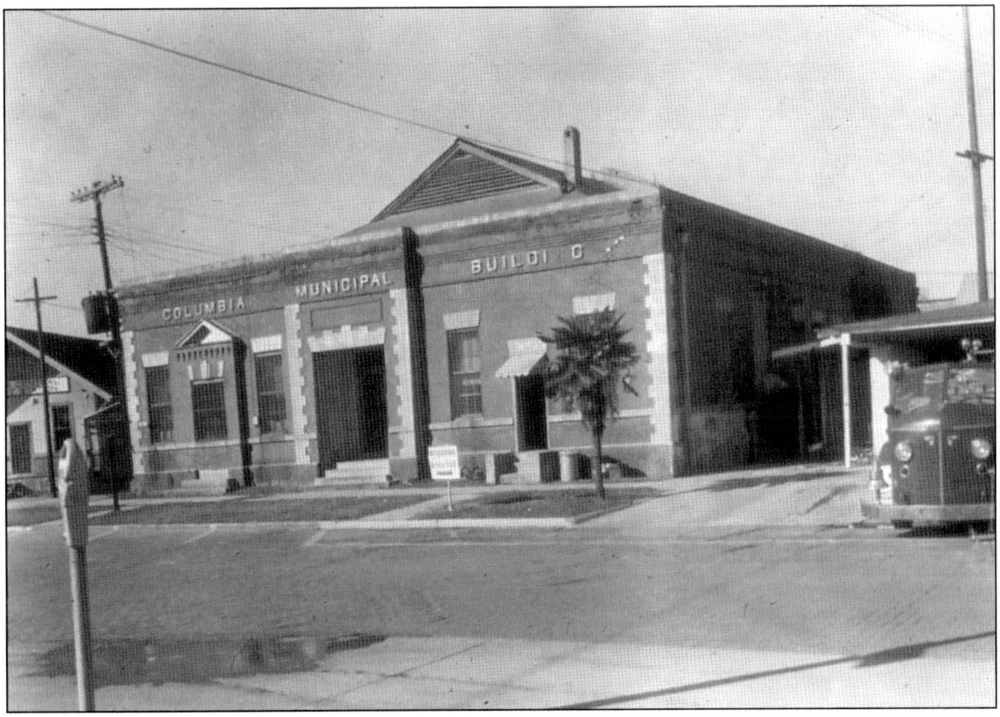

Columbia City Hall was constructed in 1908 on the west end of Second Street and was eventually replaced. At the time, the Columbia City Jail was located just inside the front door to the left. (Courtesy of Marion County Historical Society.)

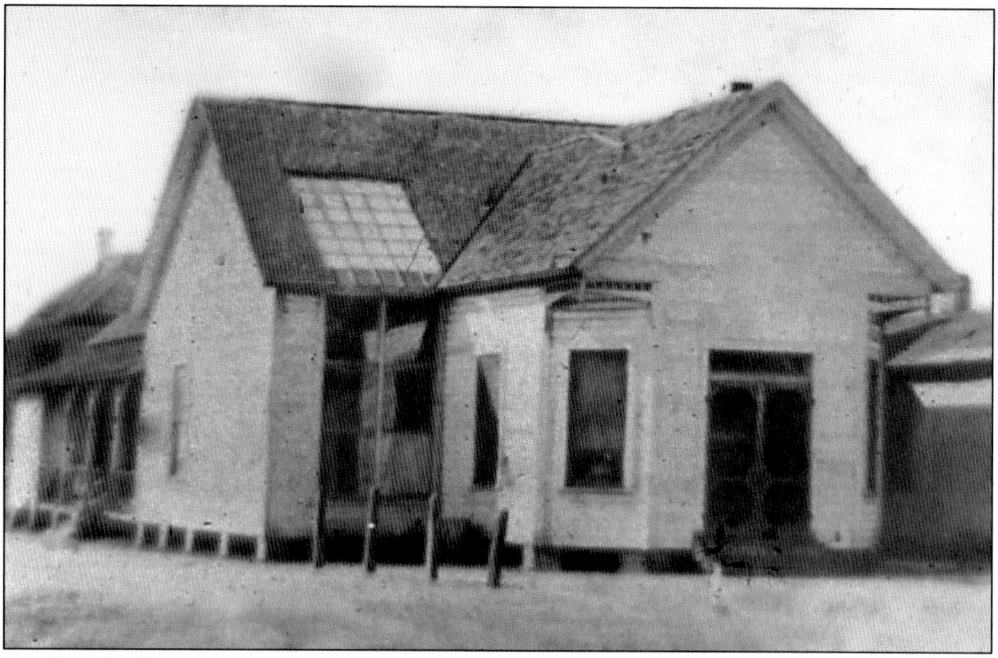

It is thought that Benjamin Franklin Mobley was likely the first professional photographer to call Columbia home. His early photographic studio and dark room stood on Second Street. (Courtesy of Marion County Historical Society.)

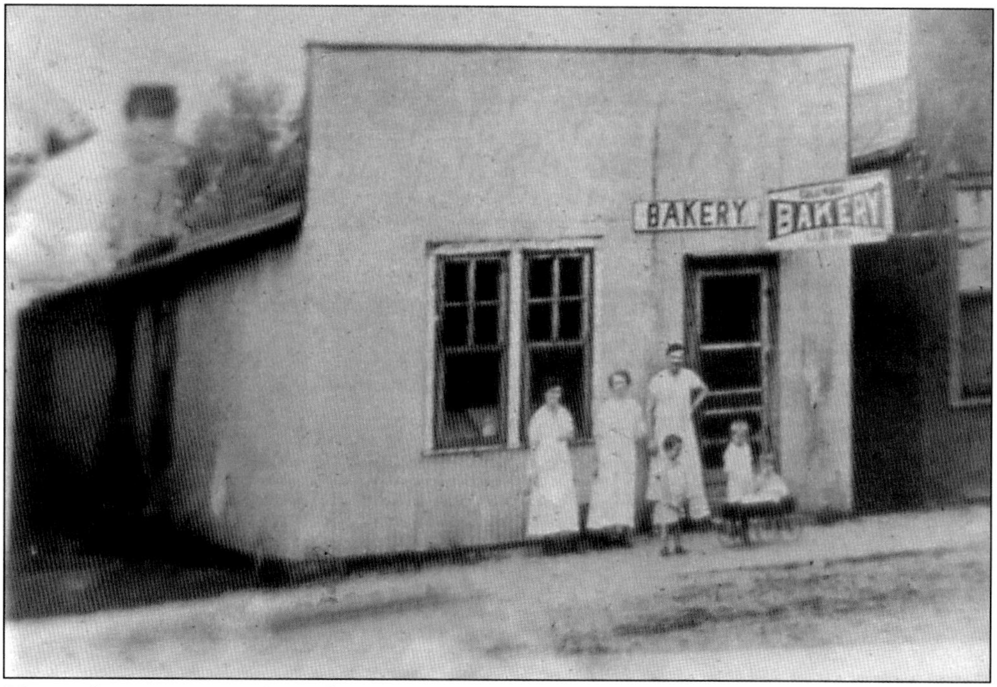

This modest structure on Second Street, complete with an ornate screened door, housed Columbia Bakery, "bakers of better bread, cakes and pastries." As early as 1911, the bakery advertised, "See the wagon for bread every morning. Out of town orders solicited. Shipments made on all trains." (Courtesy of Marion County Historical Society.)

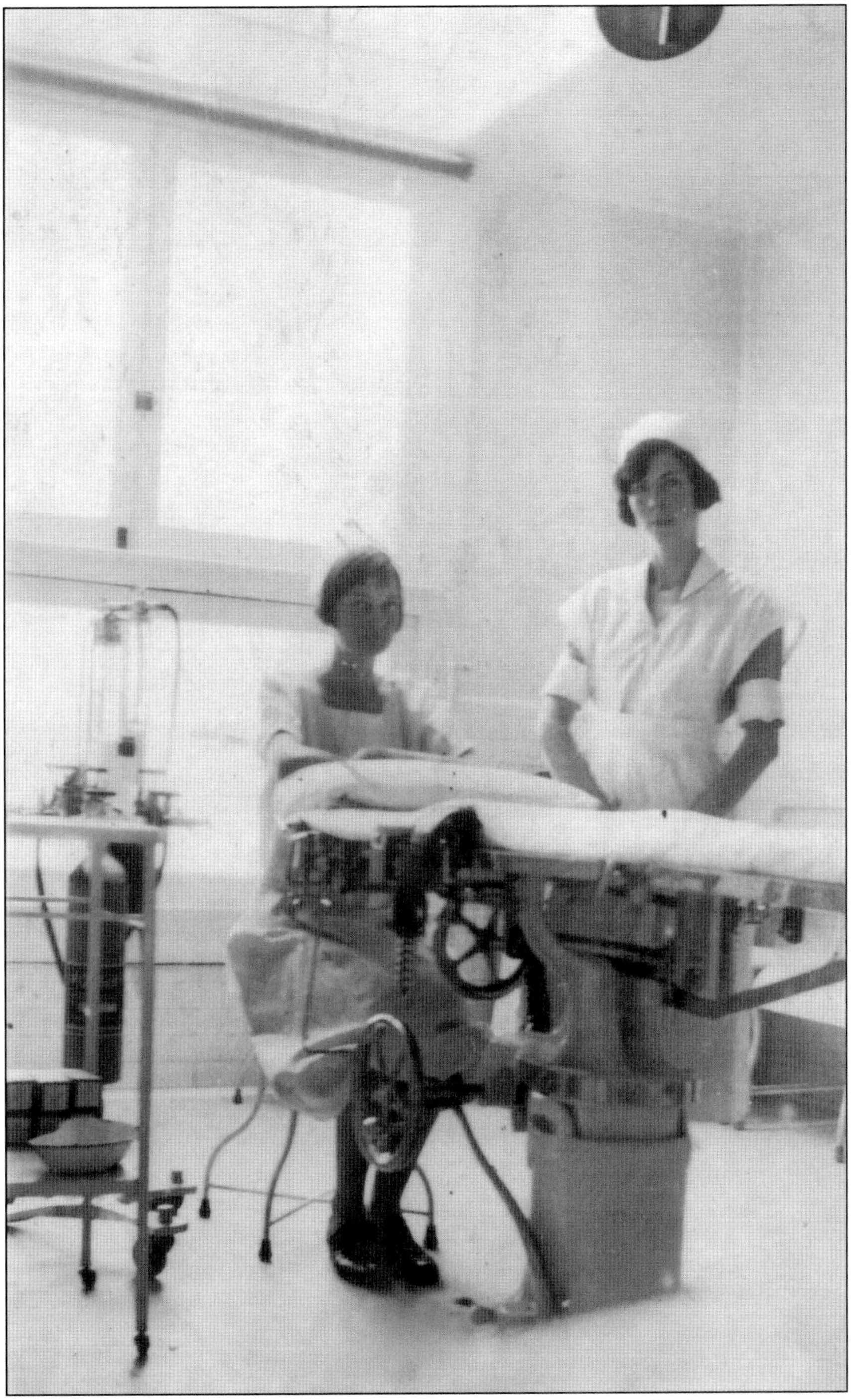

This 1930s photograph shows Alma Pittman Pickett (seated), originally from Kokomo, working in the operating room of Columbia Hospital. This early hospital adhered to high standards for the period and became one of the first hospitals in the South to comply with the standards of the American College of Surgeons, as well as being an accredited nursing training facility. (Louis F. Morgan collection.)

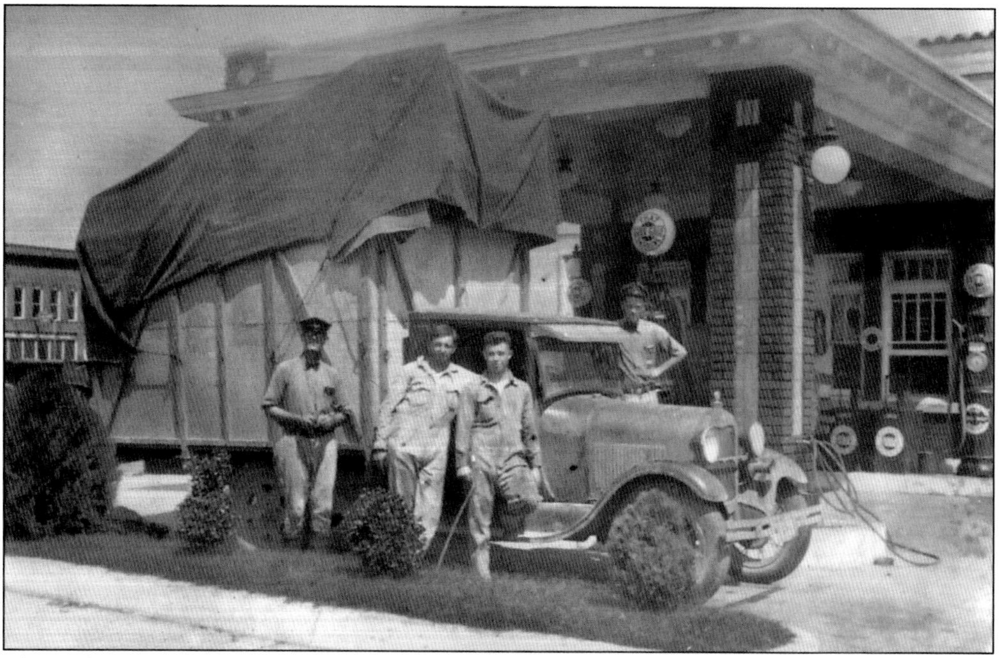

The Gulf Service Station was located near the courthouse on the corner of Broad Street. This 1940s photograph shows two uniformed station attendants posed with two customers with a heavily loaded truck. In the background at left, what is thought to be the Rankin Company Building can be seen. (Courtesy of Bates Bullock.)

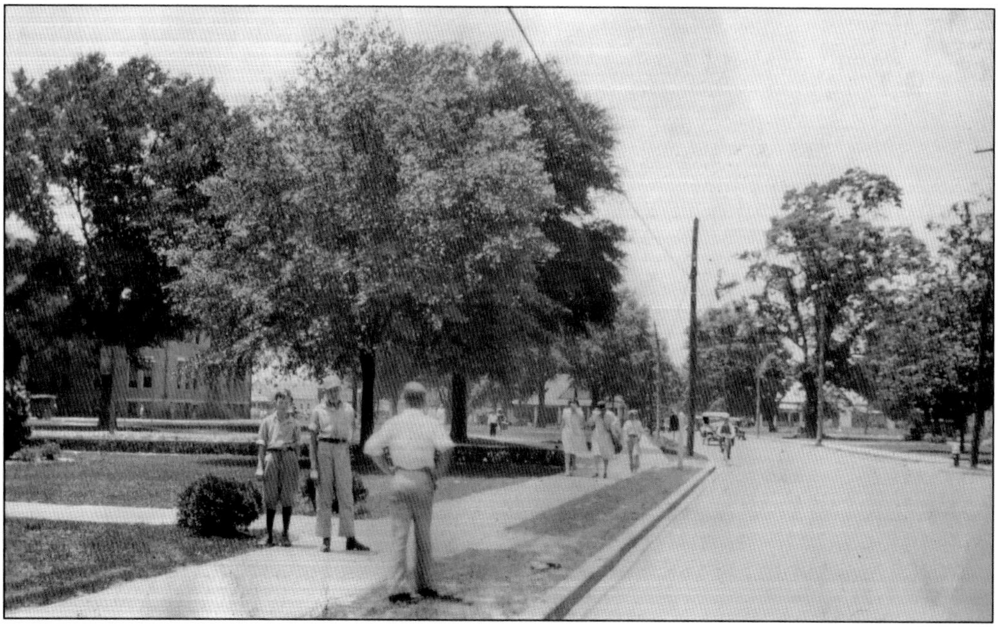

It was a sunny day when this photograph was taken showing Church Street, as one looks east toward Main. Perhaps, the conclusion of a school day, to the far left is the rear of the Columbia High School building as children walk along the sidewalks. Note the basketball goal in the schoolyard and the early mailbox on the curb. This photograph was taken in the 1920s. (Courtesy of Marion County Development Partnership.)

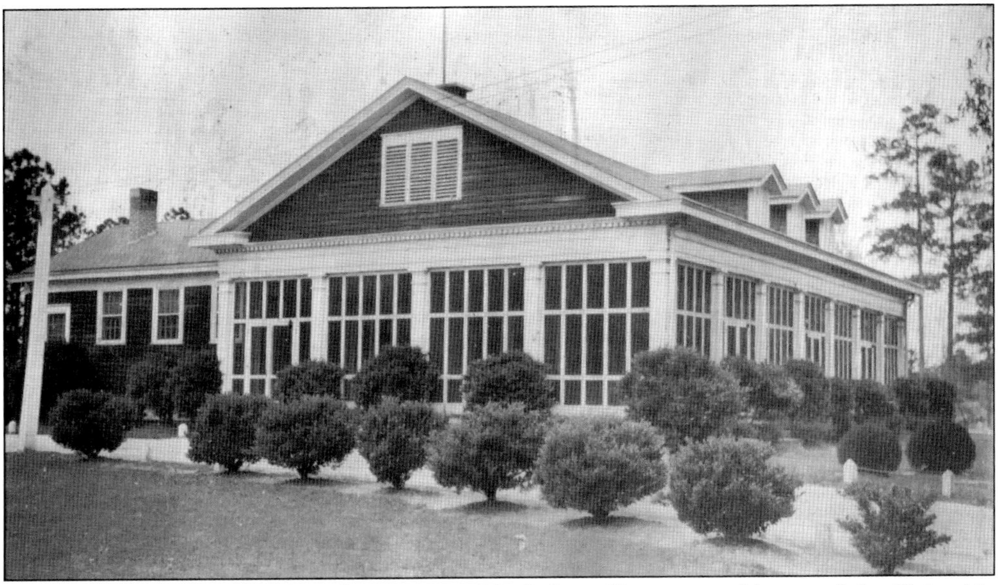

In 1923, Hugh White purchased 41 acres and had the golf course and house of the Columbia Country Club constructed. The actual golf course was originally built with mules and slips, while the greens were often plucked by hand. In its first year of operation, the club had grown to a membership of 84. (Courtesy of Marion County Development Partnership.)

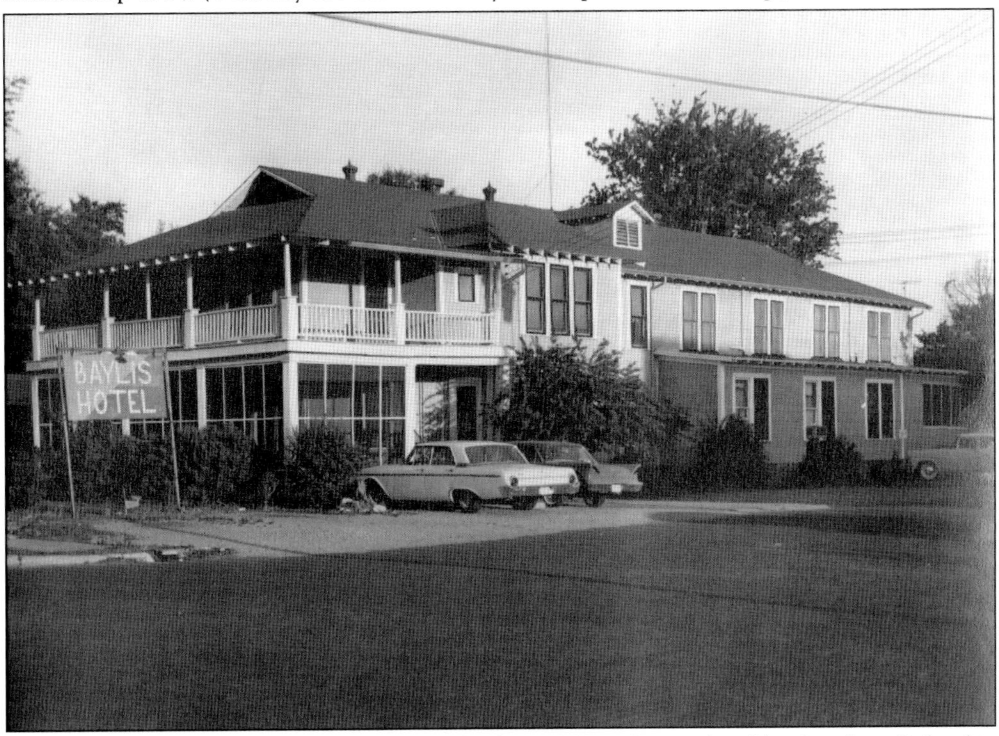

The Baylis Hotel on east Second Street was built in 1920 and was a local landmark in Columbia for decades. It offered 31 bedrooms and a large dining room that was renowned for its food. In the side yard was a sample room available to salesmen passing through to pitch their merchandise. (Courtesy of Marion County Historical Society.)

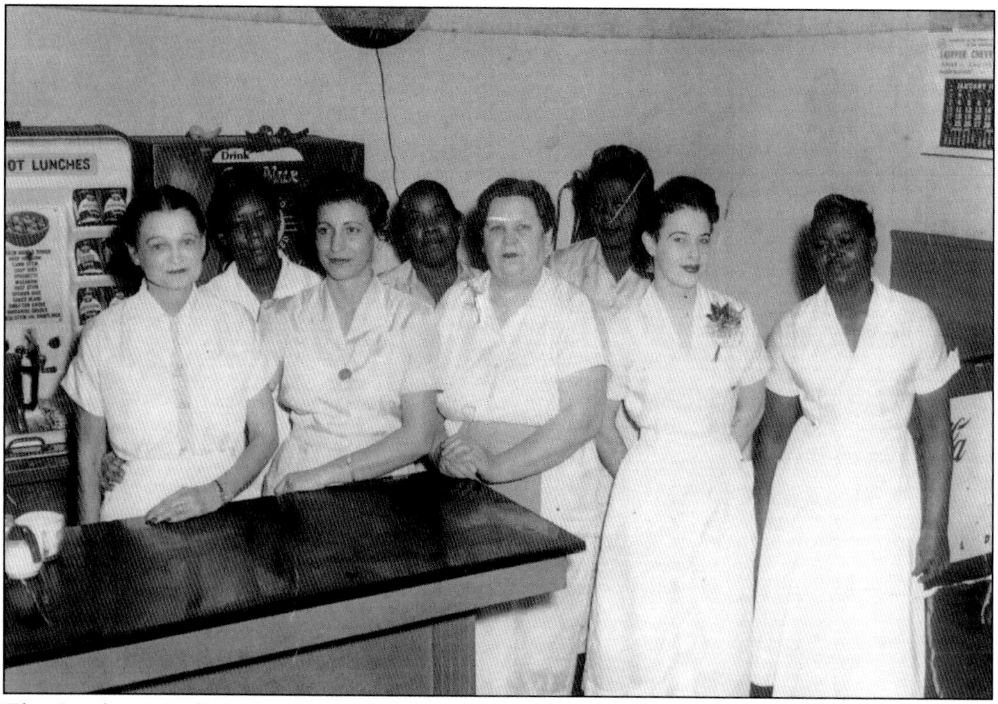

The Southern Grill on Second Street was a well-known diner in Columbia for many years. In this c. 1950 image, the staff poses for a group photograph. Note the Heinz canned soup machine to the left and the Skipper Chevrolet calendar to the right. (Courtesy of Rosa Lee Barnes.)

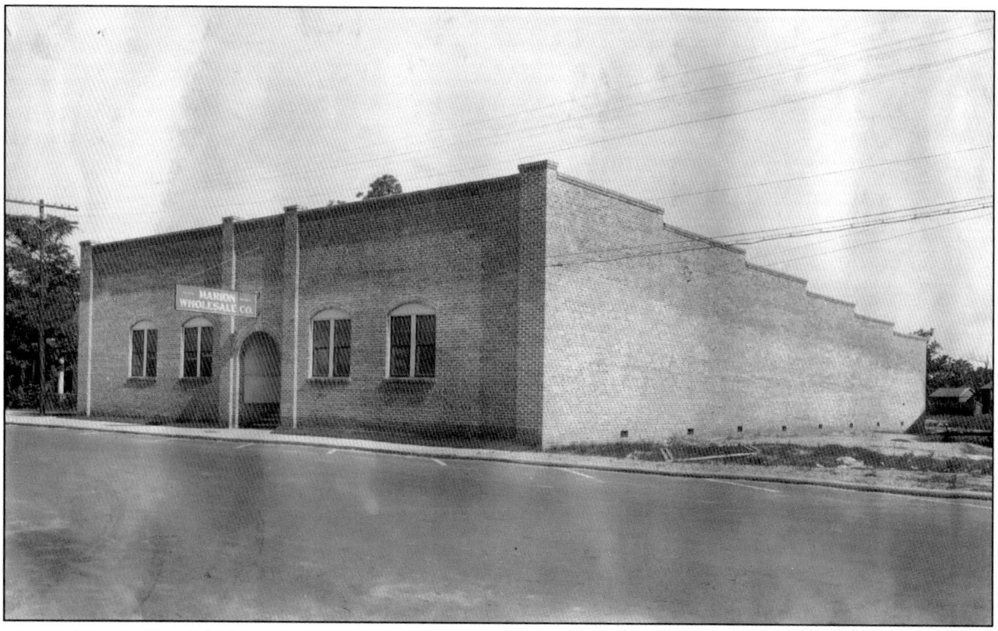

In 1927, Marion Wholesale Company advertised it was a wholesale distributor of White Crest and Globe A1 flour, promising "service and satisfaction." The company's building has stood as a landmark on Broad Street for many decades, most of the time spent as a wholesale grocery company. (Courtesy of Marion County Development Partnership.)

Six

Some Citizens of the Past

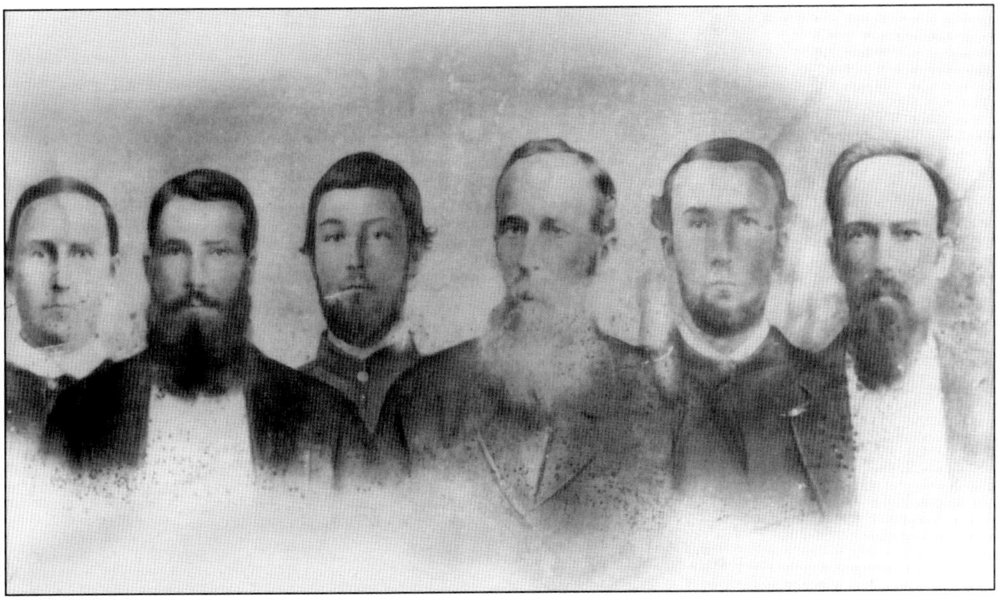

Pictured are six of the seven Pittman brothers who enlisted for the Confederacy on August 10, 1861. The children of John and Susanna Ward Pittman, they are, from left to right, Enoch, Richard, Daniel, Stephen, Charles, and Jesse. Only two of these brothers returned home from the Civil War. (Louis F. Morgan collection.)

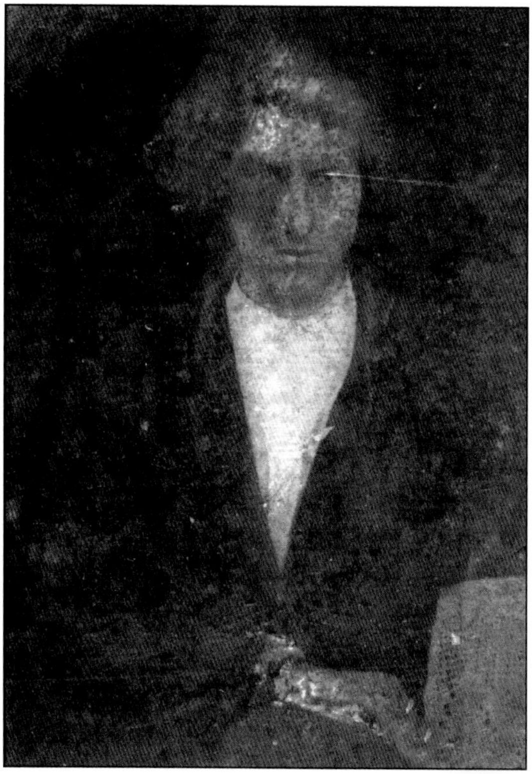

Estranged from his father and working as a cowboy in Texas, William "Little Bill" Morris nevertheless felt it his duty to avenge his father's death and became embroiled in the notorious Cox, Morris, and Pace feud. At least six men and one dog would become casualties before this Reconstruction-era conflict ended. Morris himself was killed in a gunfight on November 22, 1876, near the Bunker Hill community. Upon his gravestone is the simple inscription, "he died for his father." This grainy tintype, likely brought back from Texas, is the only remaining image of Morris. (Courtesy of Damon Watts.)

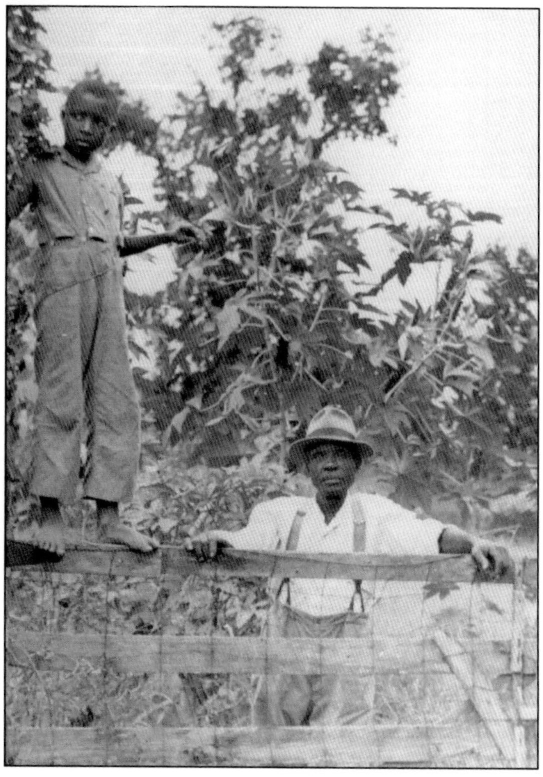

As a young slave, Coleman Davis (right) had vivid recollections of the passing of Union cavalry on the Gainesville Road. Hiding in the forests with other children and livestock, Davis recalled that they subsisted on corn bread and "clabber" skimmed from a trough of raw milk with a spoon. B.B. Bradley, who was well acquainted with Davis, captured this photograph. (Courtesy of Marion County Historical Society.)

Posed in an early portrait, the dashing Hamilton Mayson graduated in the first class from the University of Mississippi. He eventually moved to Columbia, married Mary Pittman, and began practicing law. Always a possessor of strong Southern sentiments, Mayson was a delegate and signatory to Mississippi's Ordinance of Secession. He raised a company of volunteer soldiers in Marion County and was elected its captain. Mayson Avenue in Columbia is named for him. (Courtesy of Martin Hegwood.)

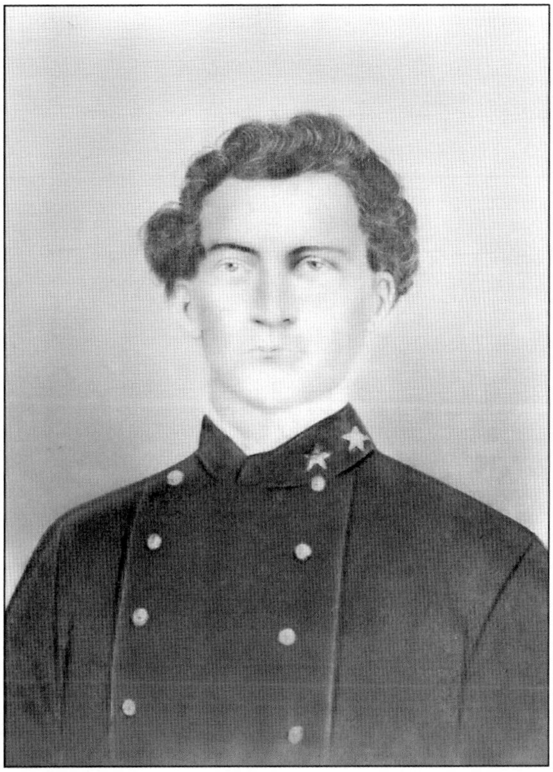

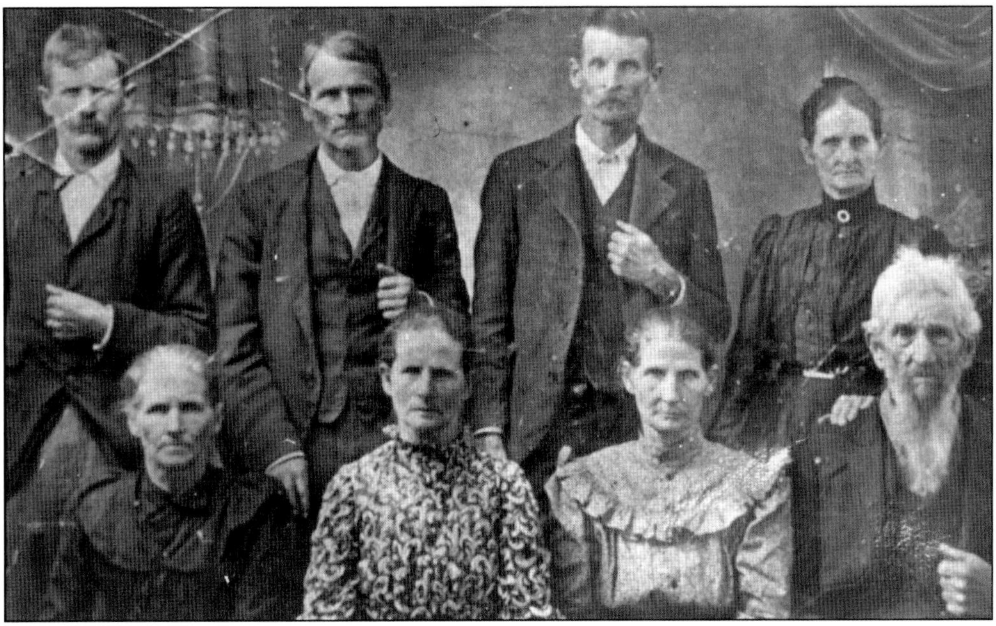

Henry H. Johnson, seated far right, moved to Marion County following the death of his first wife, Eliza Lott Johnson. He is pictured here with the children of his first wife. They are, from left to right, (sitting) Annie Eliza Forbes, Sarah Ann Luter, Amanda Nelson, and father Henry; (standing) Absalom, Robert, and Alex Johnson, and Emily Blackwell Crain. The photograph was made around 1890. (Louis F. Morgan collection.)

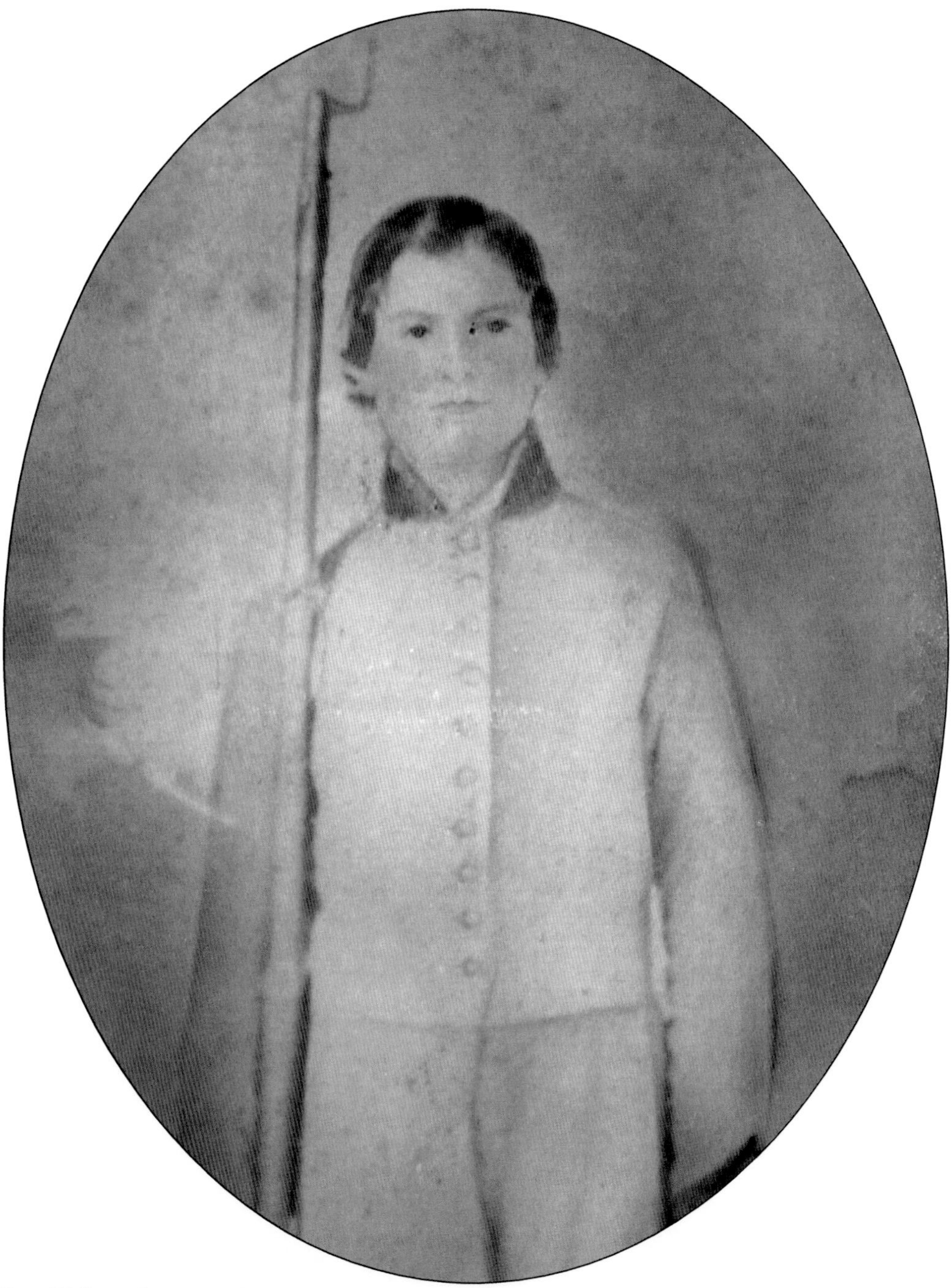

Pvt. William James Ford, posed in his uniform and musket, exhibits the zeal of youth in this photograph from the early Civil War era. In April 1862, his regiment "saw the elephant" and were heavily engaged on the Federal left flank at the Battle of Shiloh. By June of that year, Capt. Henry Pope discharged Ford from service, writing that "the past two months he has been unfit for duty . . . because of clubfoot which he has had from childhood and which is growing worse." Ford worked the rest of his life as a farmer and sometime county surveyor, dying in 1917 at the age of 47. (Courtesy of Annelle Saucier.)

George Washington Forbes was the son of William W. Forbes who arrived in Marion County in 1832. His mother was Rebecca Ivans Forbes, who was a Choctaw and native of Georgia. G.W. Forbes married Annie Eliza Johnson in 1869, and they had 12 children. A farmer, Forbes was raised in the Sandy Hook area and later settled in what became known as the Kokomo area. This photograph was made around 1890. (Louis F. Morgan collection.)

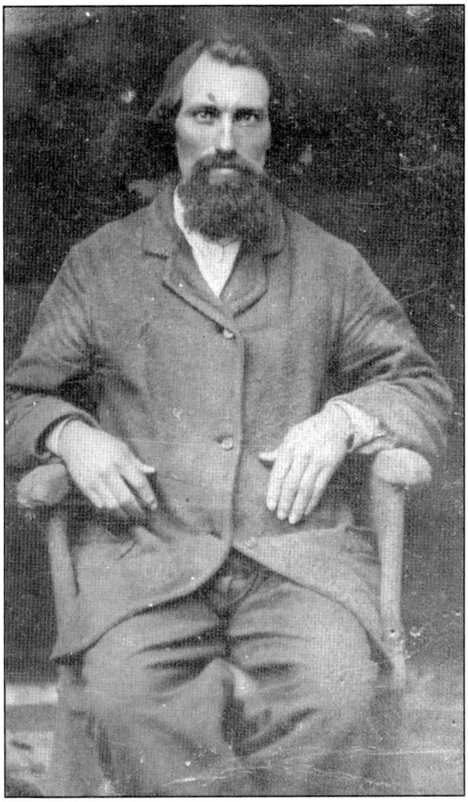

Columbia's Board of Aldermen poses for a formal group portrait. This photograph was made by early Columbia photographer Benjamin Franklin Mobley at his studio in December 1912. (Courtesy of Fran Ginn.)

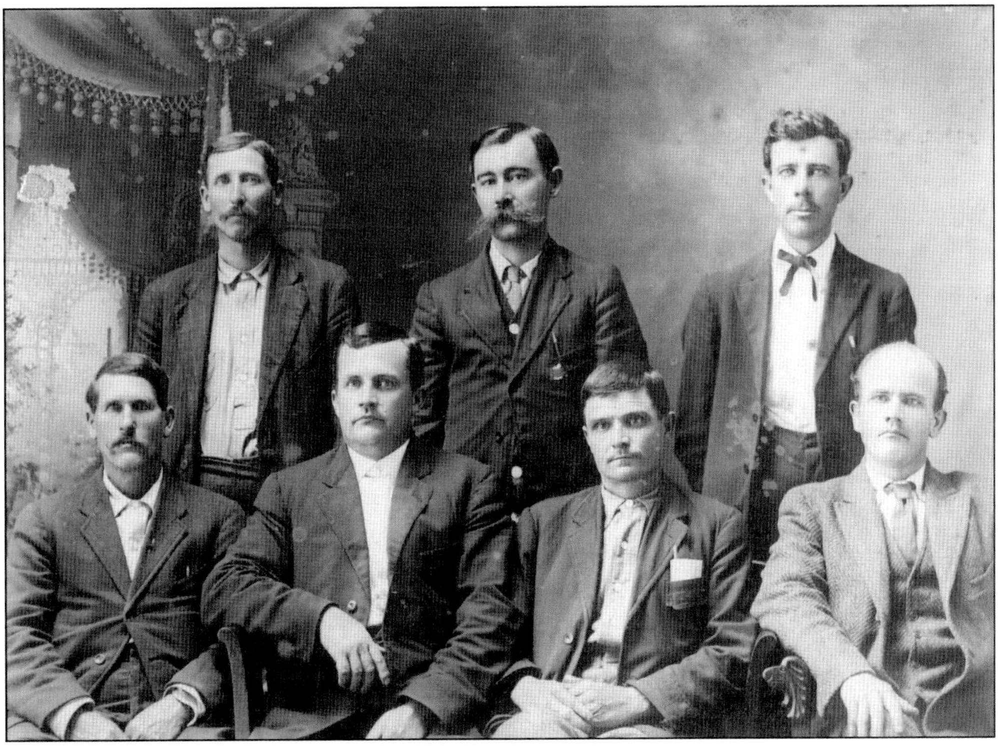

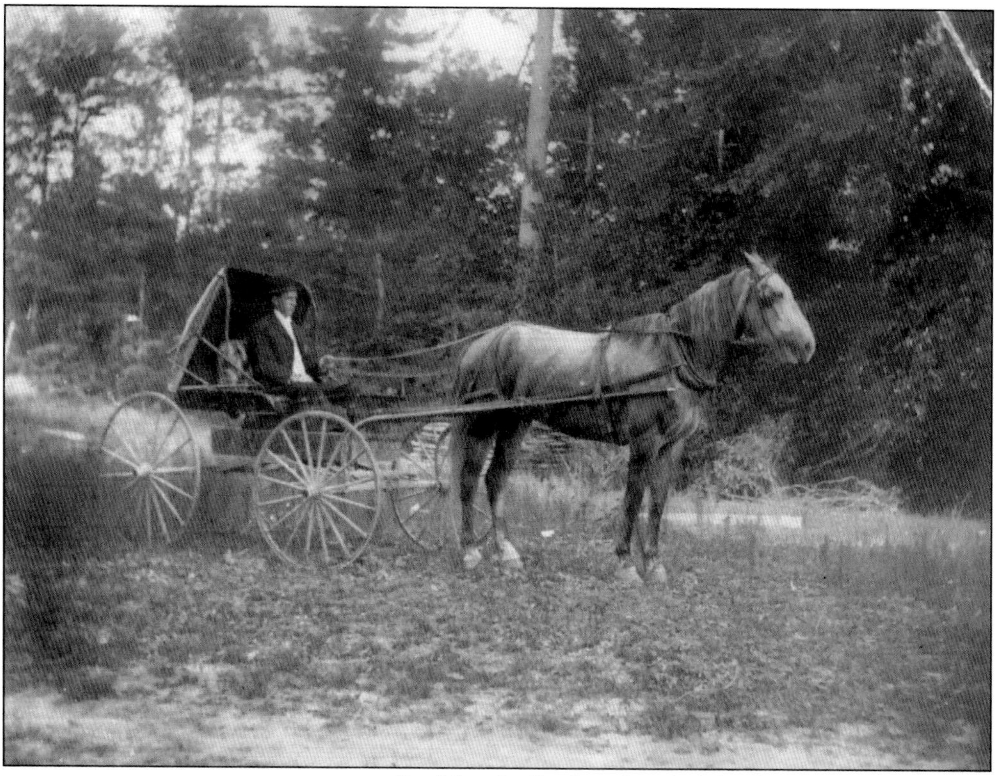

Dr. John G. Gardner founded the first hospital in Marion County and was the president of the Mississippi State Hospital Association at one point in his career. In this 1912 photograph taken in Cheraw, Gardner is seen in the days he was a horse-and-buggy doctor. (Courtesy of Marion County Public Library.)

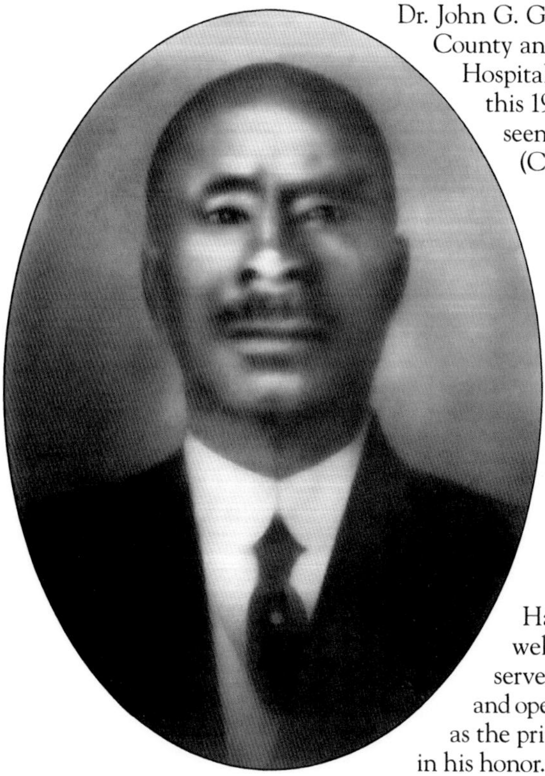

Harry Solomon Expose, born in 1861, was a well-respected leader in his community. He served as the early postmaster of his community and operated a general store. Today, he is remembered as the principle founder of Expose, which was named in his honor. (Courtesy of Patricia Oliver.)

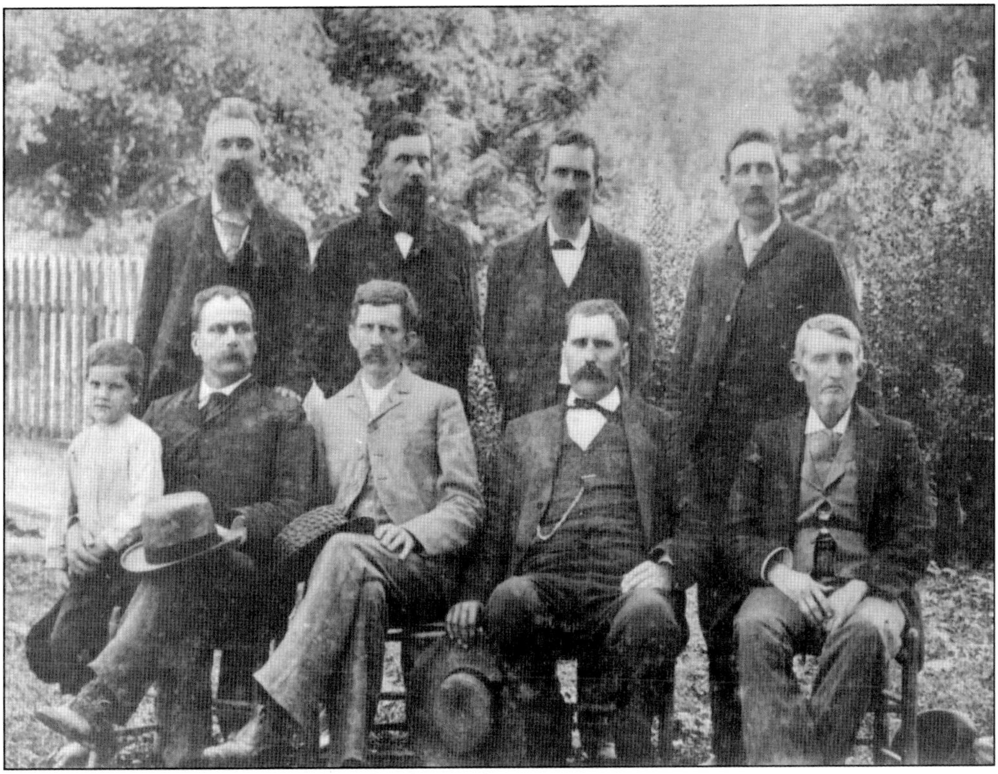

The trustees of Columbia High School pose for a group picture around 1895. They are, from left to right, (first row) Ebb Ford (boy), Thomas Swift Ford, Iddo W. Lampton, Burwell Holloway, and Leon Pittman; (second row) W.B. Stovall, Dr. T.B. Ford, L.E. Bass, and John Watts. (Courtesy of Marion County Historical Society.)

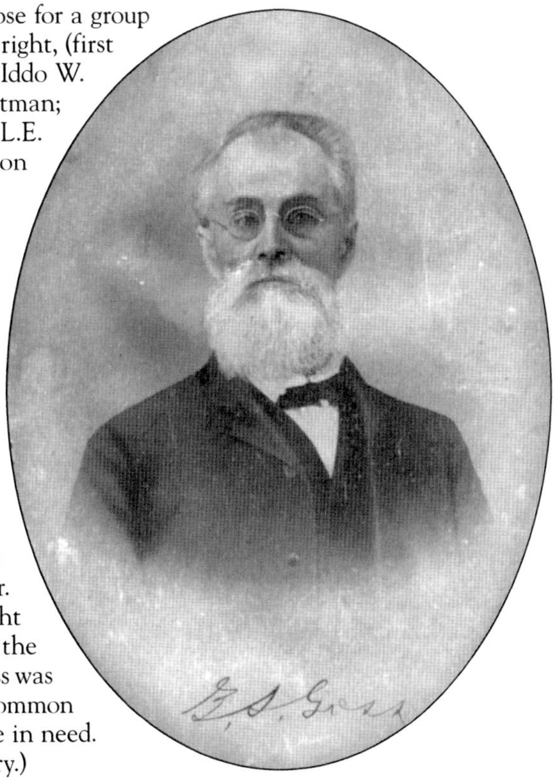

Dr. Zeno Goss practiced medicine for many years along Holiday Creek and was the first postmaster of the community that was named for him, Goss. As a young man, Dr. Goss served in the Confederate army, fought at Shiloh in 1862, and was, at one point in the war, a prisoner of the Federal army. Dr. Goss was remembered as a charitable giver, it being common for him to give away prescriptions to those in need. (Courtesy of Marion County Public Library.)

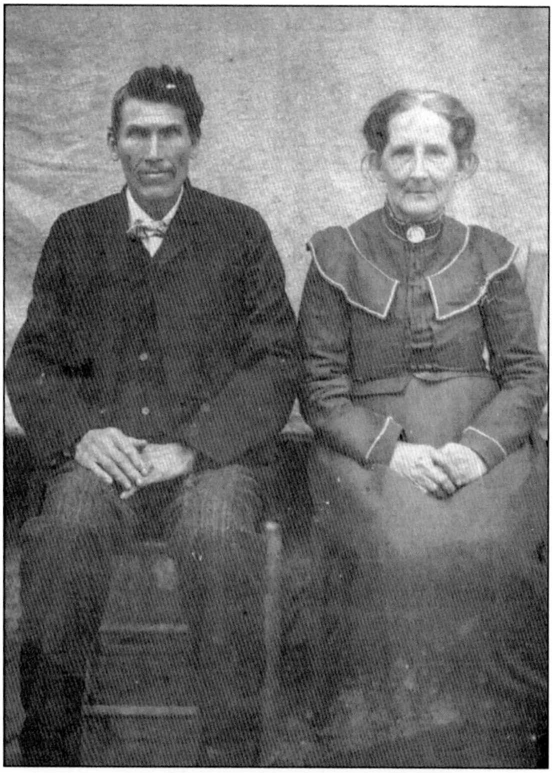

Here are Christopher Nelson Beard and Jane Tracey Beard. Among the early settlers of Marion County was the Beard family. Nelson Beard served as the first postmaster for the village of Claude (now Morgantown) and operated an early store there. The Beard family was large and prominent in agriculture and education in the western section of Marion County. This photograph was made around 1915. (Louis F. Morgan collection.)

Seen here in the automobile that replaced his buggy, Dr. John Walter Montgomery of Foxworth delivered hundreds of babies in his career. Like most doctors of the period, Montgomery was often paid for his services with farm produce and chickens. (Courtesy of Marion County Public Library.)

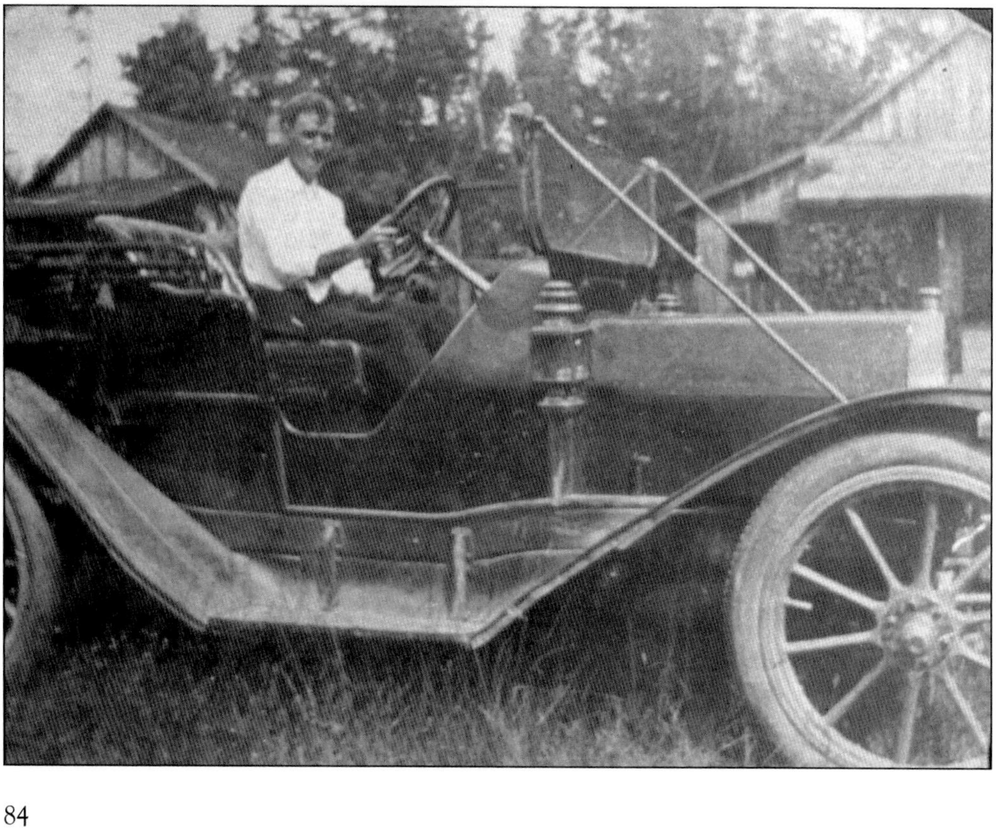

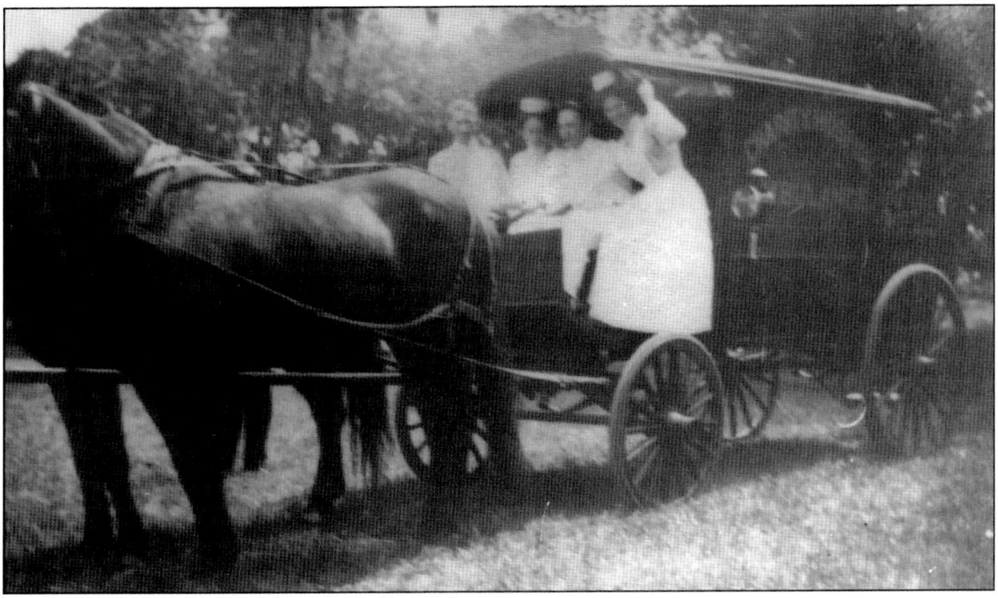

Dr. John Gardner, a young intern at the time this image was made, poses in 1912 with student nurses on the ambulance owned by the Charity Hospital of New Orleans. (Courtesy of Marion County Public Library.)

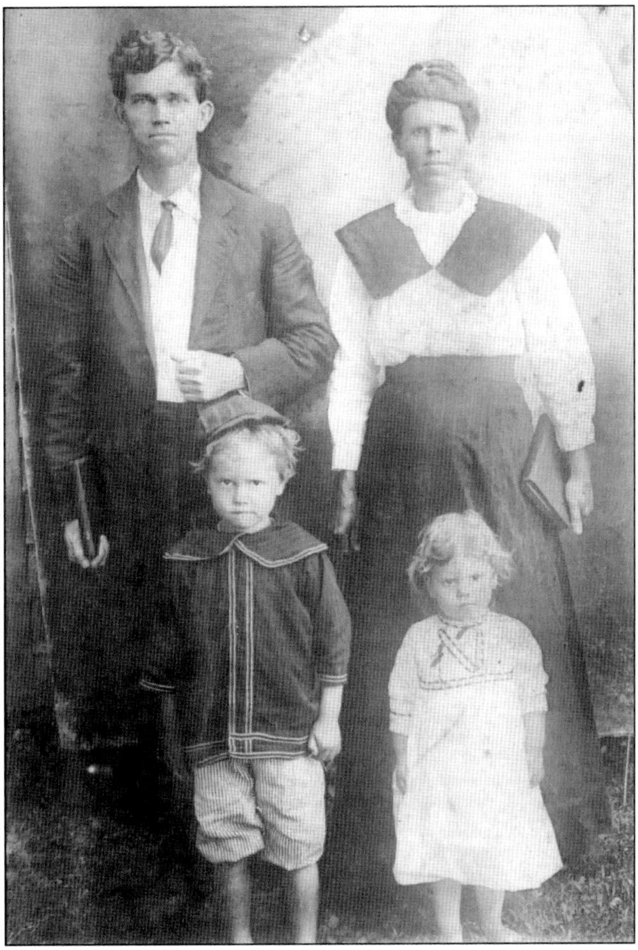

Rev. Warren Evans and his wife, Nancy Beard Evans, returned to Morgantown in 1915 from Florida, where Warren had become a Church of God minister. Evans established the first Pentecostal congregation in Marion County and the first Church of God congregation in South Mississippi under a brush arbor at Morgantown. When trying to establish the church, he was beaten by a mob of White Caps and left for dead but miraculously recovered. Pictured in 1916 with Warren and Nancy are two of their children, J.D. and Melissa. (Louis F. Morgan collection.)

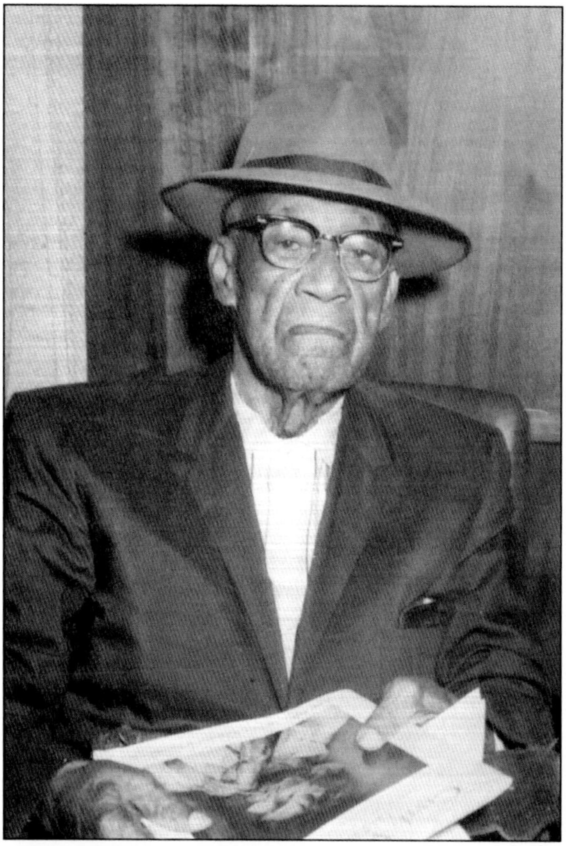

A county resident, Prof. P.S. Bowles taught for 40 years at Alcorn, eventually retiring as president of the institution. In 1928, Bowles Hall, named in his honor, was completed on the campus. (Courtesy of Marion County Historical Society.)

Among neat rows of reference books and a desk with scattered medical instruments, Dr. C.C. Thompson sits in his office, located on the second floor of the Harris Drug Company Building. (Courtesy of Marion County Public Library.)

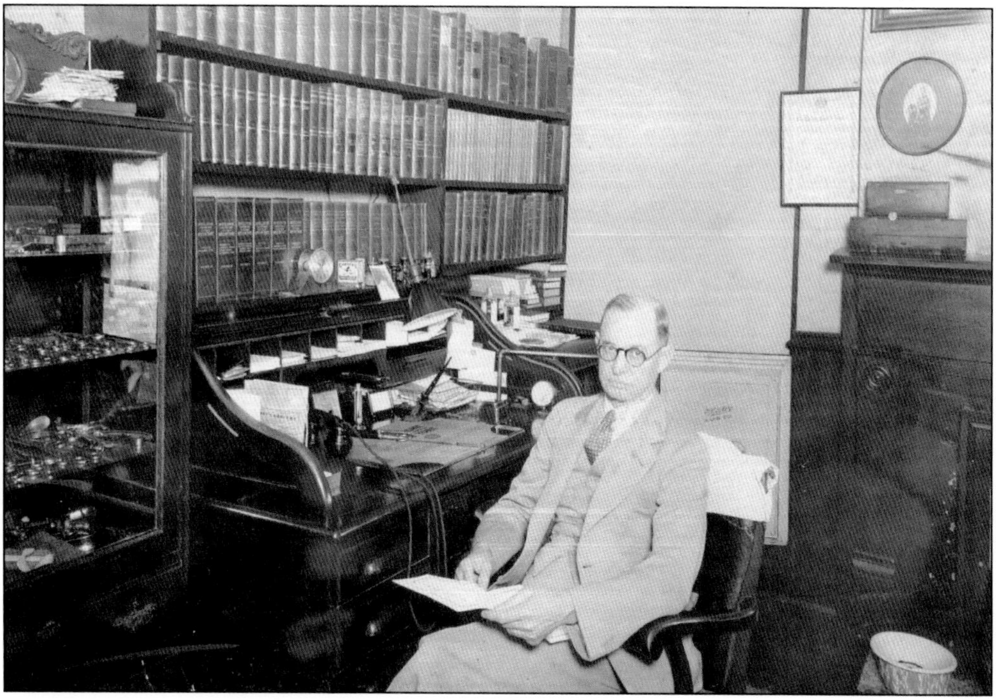

Dr. Theodore B. Ford, perhaps the best known of Columbia's early physicians, poses for a formal portrait with his grandson Bob Ford Thompson. Even in his younger days, Dr. Ford was ever the civic-minded citizen. In 1877, he rode with Sheriff Leon Pittman to capture Nero James, "the leader of a notorious band of thieves." James was held in the Marion County jail for a week, that is until a crowd broke in and lynched him from a large oak tree in Columbia. As late as 1915, residents still considered "Nero's Oak" a local landmark. (Courtesy of Marion County Public Library.)

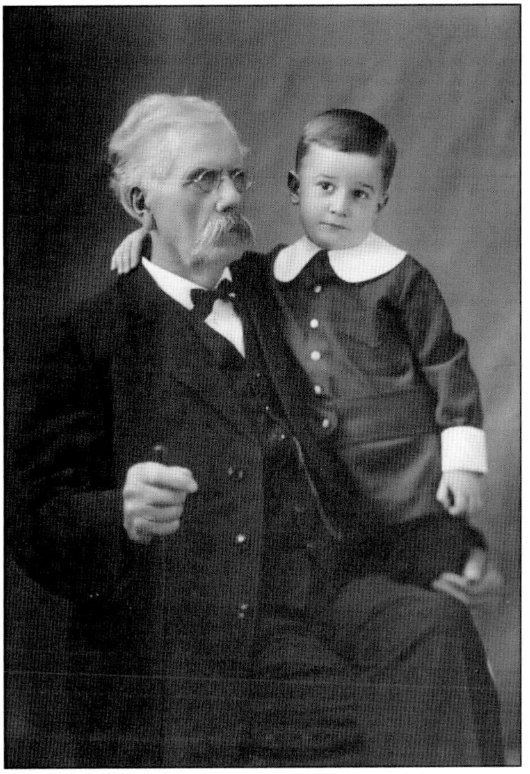

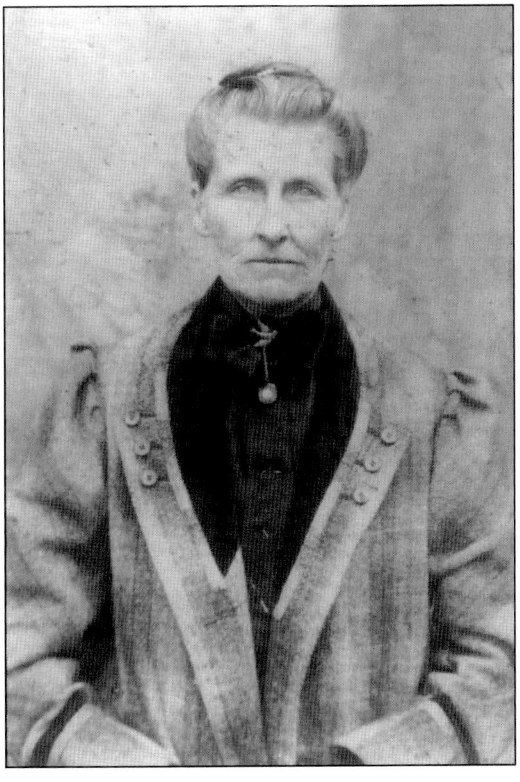

Mary Jane Bullock Tyner was married to James Everett Tyner. Their families were among some of the first settlers of Marion County. She lived in the Kokomo and Spring Cottage communities, where she attended Payne's Chapel Methodist Church and her children sang in the choir. Her children married into the Pittman, Forbes, and Ladner families, and she is the great-grandmother of actress Diane Ladd and the great-great-grandmother of actress Laura Dern. This photograph was made around 1900. (Louis F. Morgan collection.)

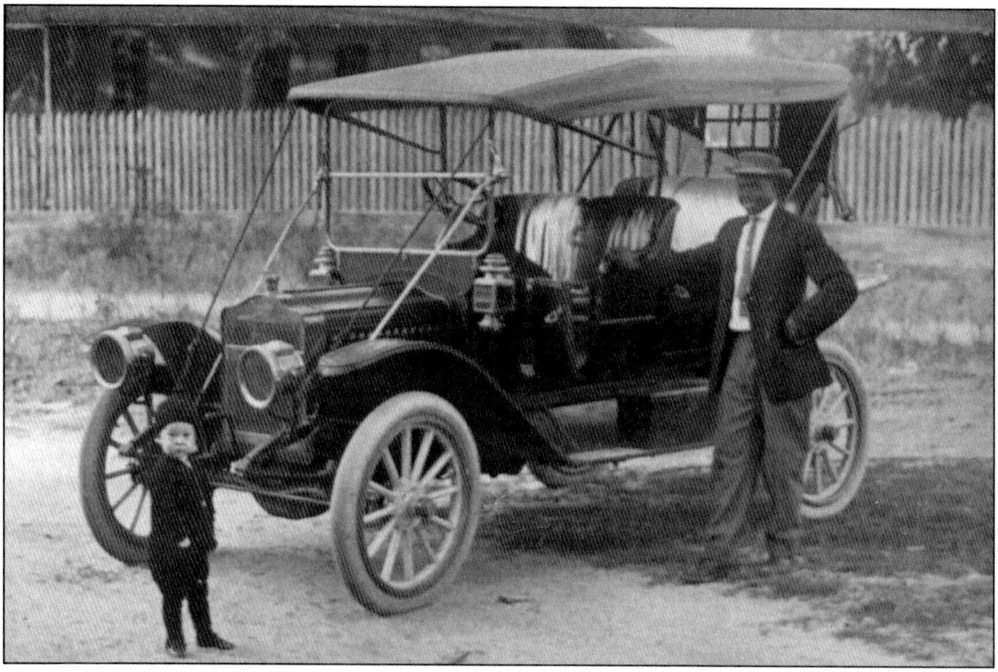

This 1912 Ford Model T touring car was Columbia's third automobile. It was purchased by Dr. C.C. Thompson Sr. Posed with the car is the young son of Dr. Thompson, C.C. Thompson Jr., and John Powell. (Courtesy of Marion County Public Library.)

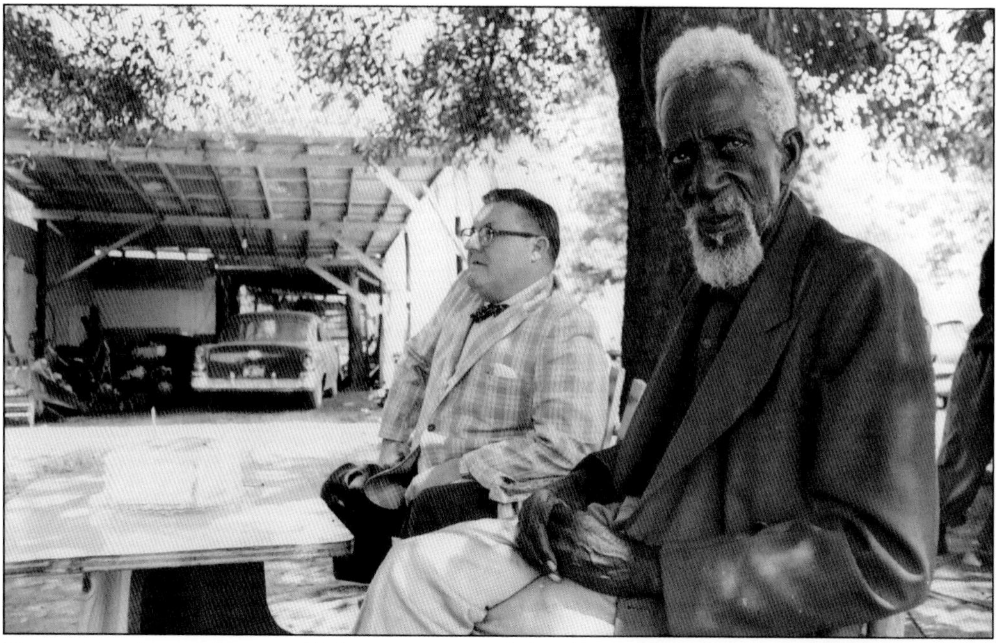

Due to his advanced age and life experiences, Columbia resident Sylvester Magee (right) was courted by the national media during the 1960s, his name appearing in national publications, including *Time* magazine. When he died in October 1971, he was considered by many to have been the last living American slave. B.B. Bradley took this photograph on May 27, 1967, on the occasion of Magee's 126th birthday. (Courtesy of Marion County Historical Society.)

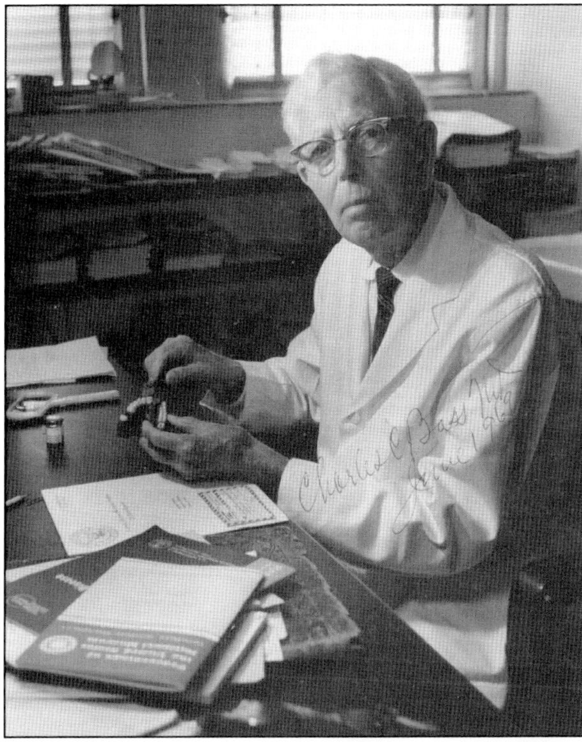

Marion County native Dr. Charles Bass was internationally known for his work in bacteriology and is credited, along with another Tulane pioneer Dr. Foster M. Johns, as the first scientist to cultivate the parasite that causes malaria. Bass was also responsible for the development and establishment of clinical laboratories, now in use throughout the world. He was the first to advocate daily removal of bacteria with the use of a toothbrush and floss, making him the first to describe modern oral hygiene. Today, the American Dental Association considers him the "Father of Preventive Dentistry." (Courtesy of Marion County Public Library.)

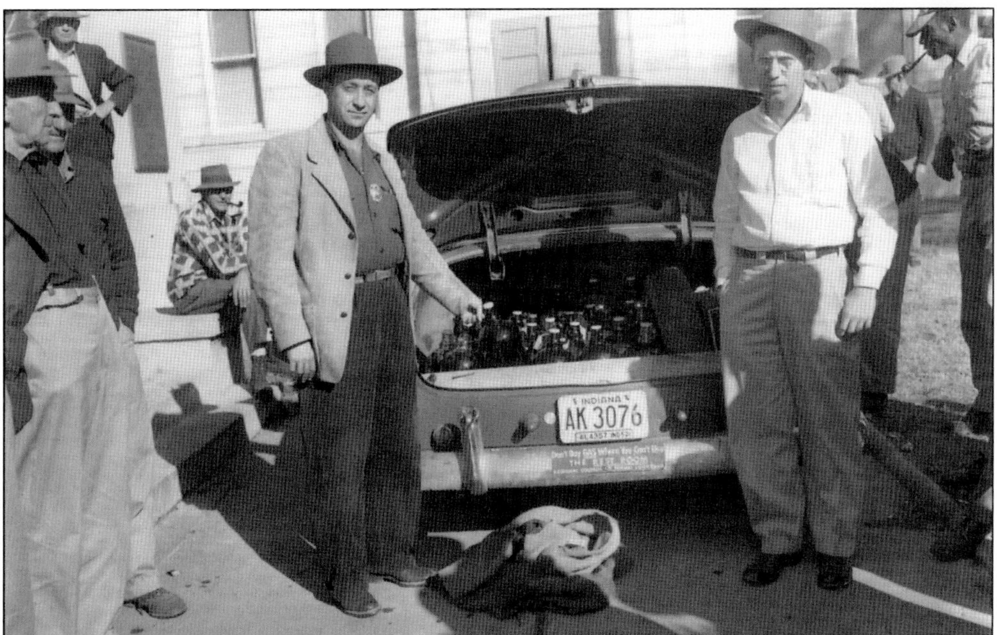

As evident in this photograph taken at the Marion County jail, conflict between law enforcement and bootleggers existed for decades. The bumper sticker on the impounded car reads, "Don't buy gas where you can't use the restroom," a reference to an early-1950s boycott of gas stations that only allowed whites to use restrooms. The officer at left lifting the jug is Marion County deputy Jesse Loftin. (Courtesy of Bates Bullock.)

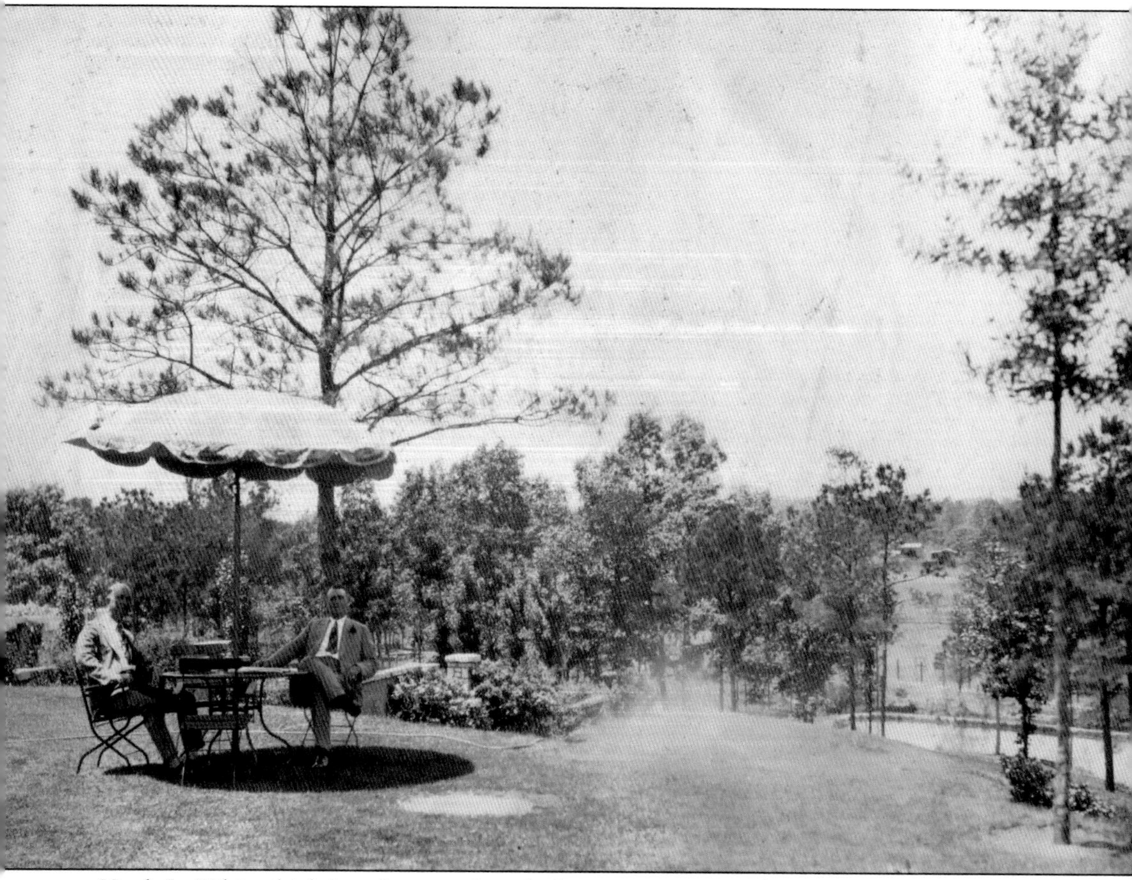

Hugh L. White (right) and an unidentified man converse with one another on the grounds of White's estate. White, a noted Mississippi industrialist and politician, served in numerous capacities, including mayor of Columbia and two-term governor of Mississippi. He is perhaps best known for his groundbreaking "Balance Agriculture with Industry" program introduced in 1936. Remembered as a man of generous character, he purchased band instruments for the Mississippi Industrial Training School children upon overhearing that the institution could not afford the expenditure in 1921. (Courtesy of Marion County Development Partnership.)

Seven

Down on Main Street

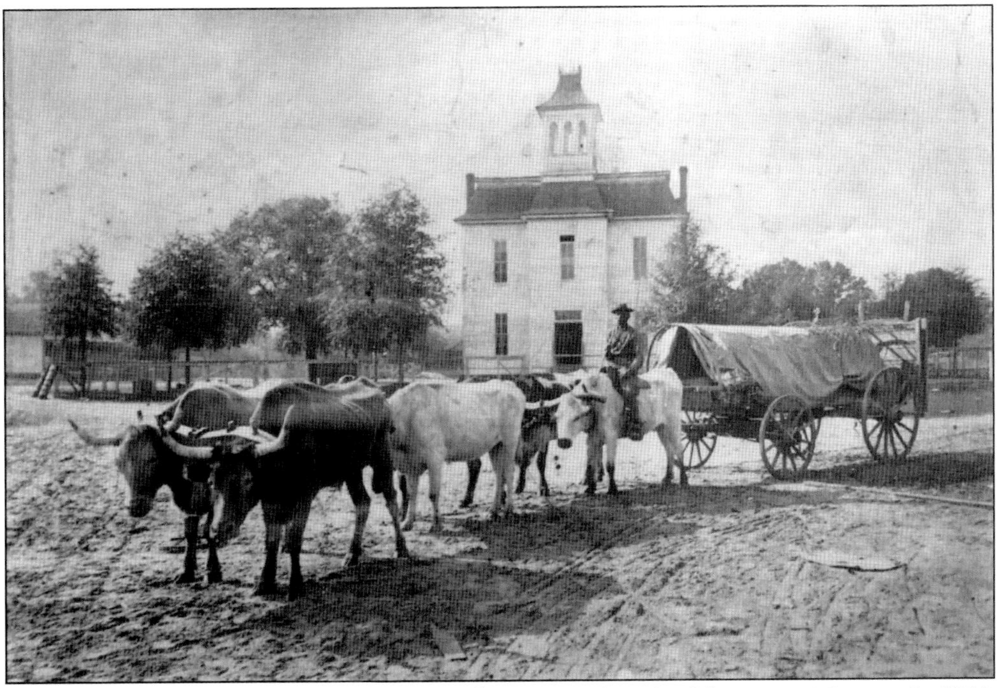

The former Marion County Courthouse was the setting of much of the county's history. In 1864, the building was pillaged by Federal troops and was the setting of the famed Will Purvis hanging 30 years later. Justice during the Jacksonian period was often swift and harsh. In 1826, one unlucky horse thief was fined $100, given 39 lashes, jailed for six months, and locked in the pillory for an hour per day. To make matters worse, before he was released, the letter "T" was branded into the back of the prisoner's right hand. Note the old yard fence around the square to keep free-ranging livestock from grazing too near the county seat of justice. (Courtesy of Bates Bullock.)

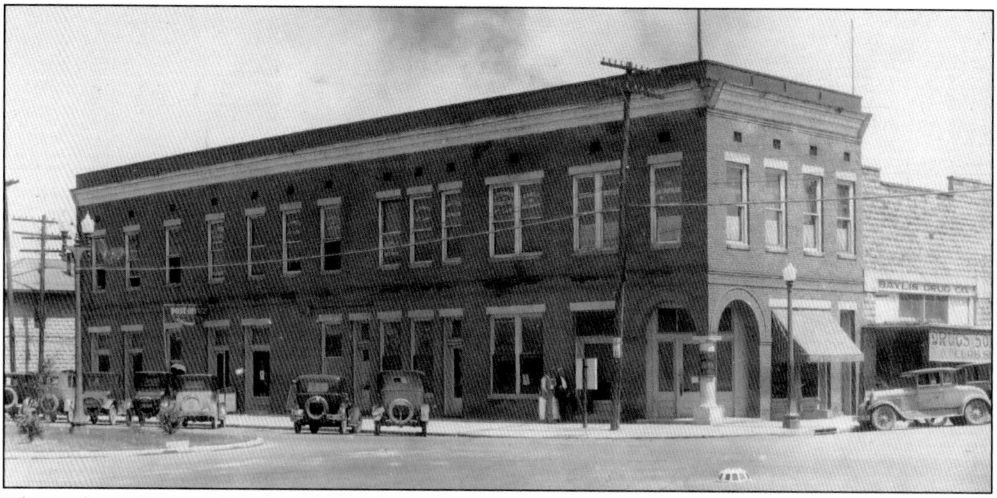

The striking Citizen's Bank building, located on the southeast corner of Main and Second Streets, was built in 1916. While the front of the building housed the bank's operations, the rear served as the Columbia Post Office. Numerous professional offices, including dentist J.H. Chapman, the law firm of Rawls & Hathorn, and Simmons Insurance, occupied the second floor of the building. Baylis Drug Company, advertising "curb service," occupied the adjoining building at the time this photograph was taken. (Courtesy of Marion County Development Partnership.)

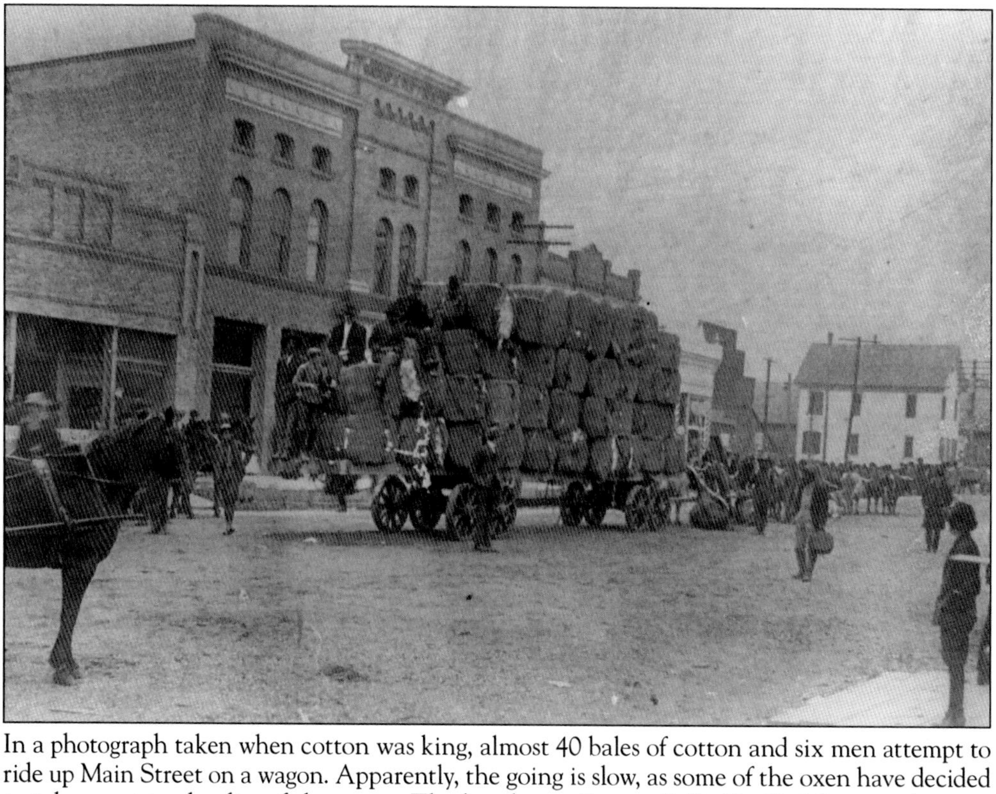

In a photograph taken when cotton was king, almost 40 bales of cotton and six men attempt to ride up Main Street on a wagon. Apparently, the going is slow, as some of the oxen have decided to take a rest in the dirt of the street. The handsome Barnes & Ruffin Building can be seen in the background, which is today occupied by Hill Hardware Company. (Courtesy of Marion County Historical Society.)

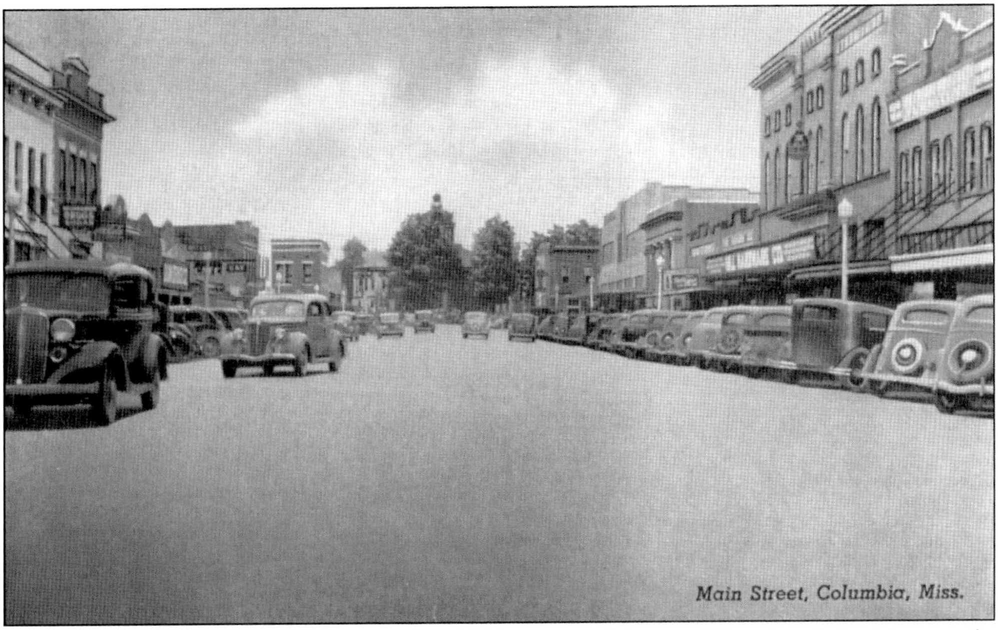

Main Street bustles with activity in this 1940s postcard image. The view is looking south. (Courtesy of Randy Davis.)

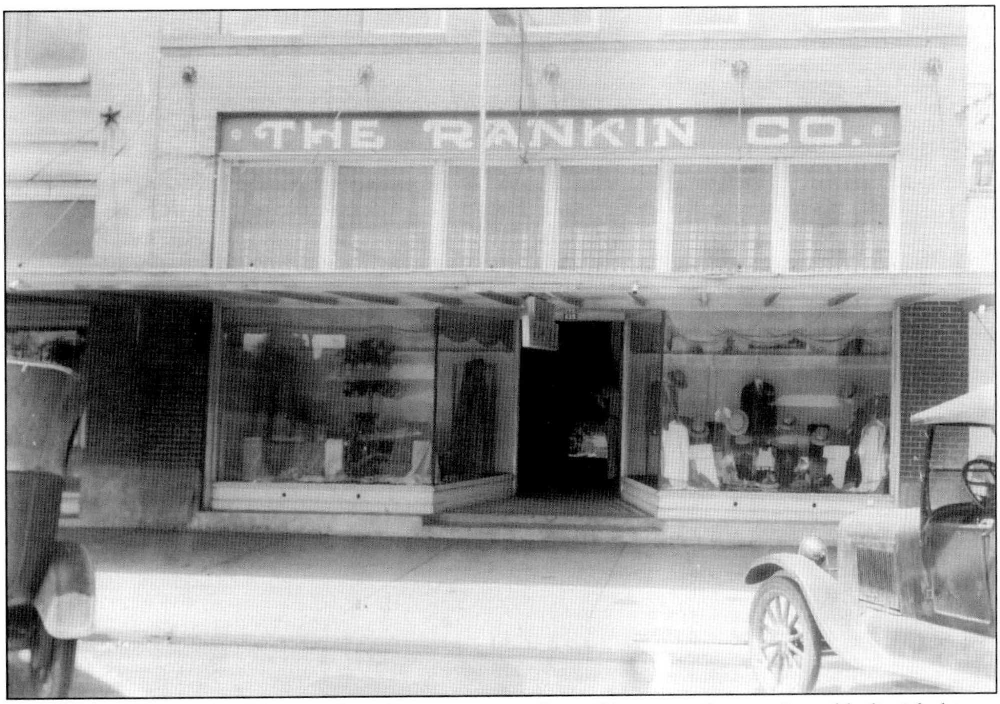

This rare photograph of the Rankin Company storefront illustrates the men's and ladies' fashions of the period. The Rankin Company Building was constructed in 1913 and located on the corner of Main Street and Courthouse Square. (Courtesy of Marion County Historical Society.)

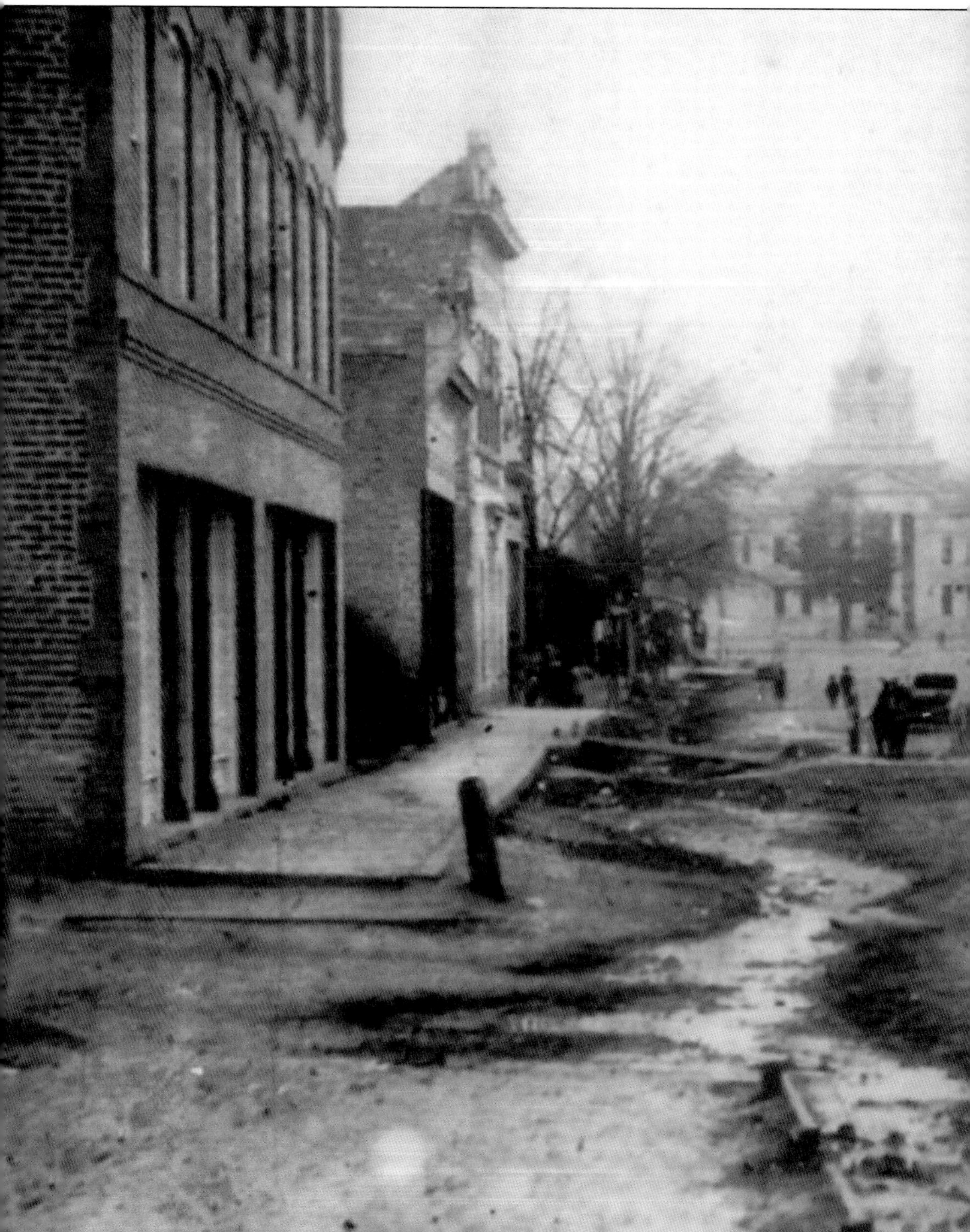

Main Street likely originated as a segment of River Road, constructed during the early settlement period. This historic road once ran from the Choctaw Territory south through Monticello, Columbia, Fordsville, and beyond, paralleling the east bank of the Pearl River. In this famous c.

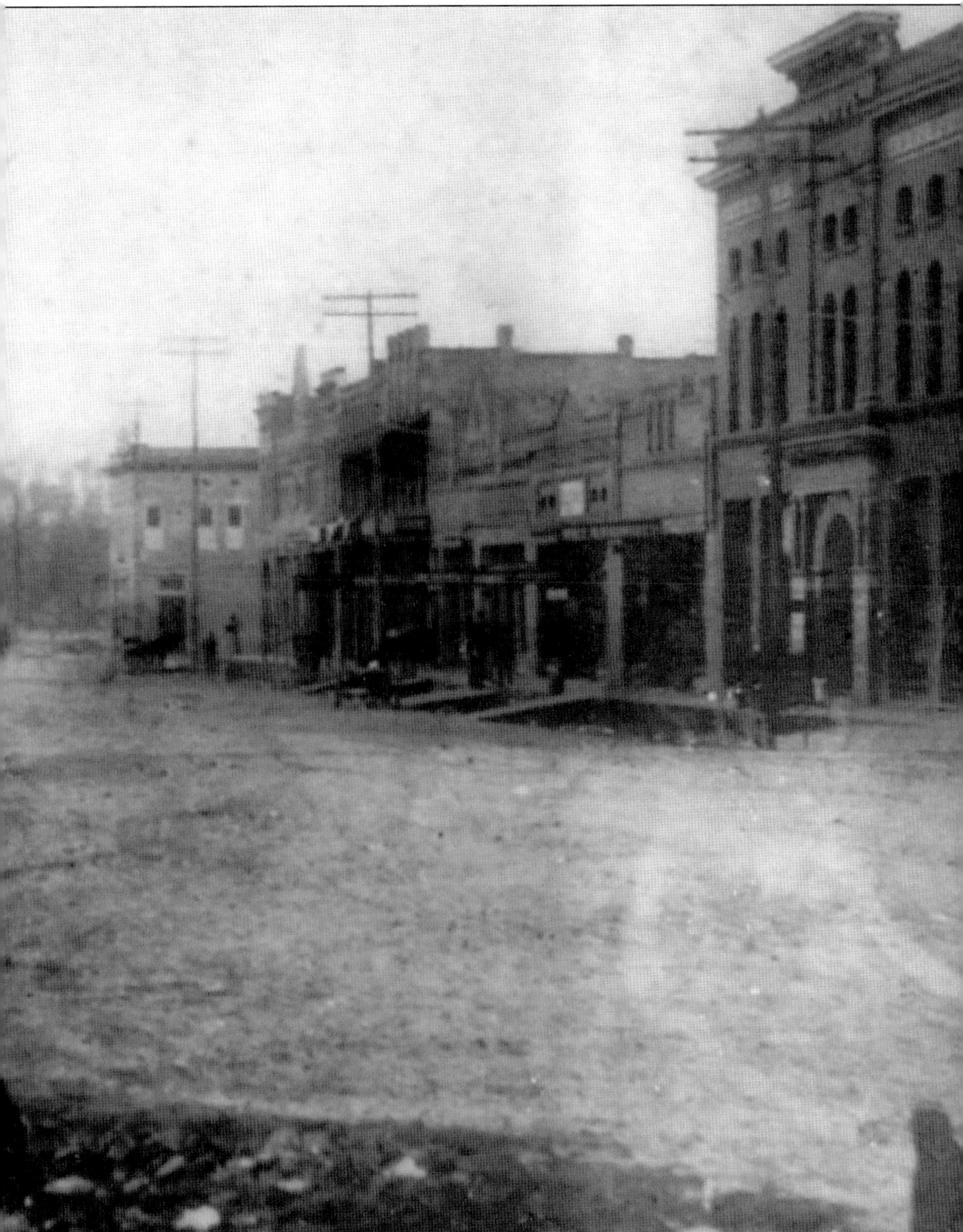

1907 scene, boardwalks and ramps provide access to the storefronts along Main Street. Note the chickens scratching their way about the street. Benjamin Franklin Mobley took this photograph. (Courtesy of Marion County Historical Society.)

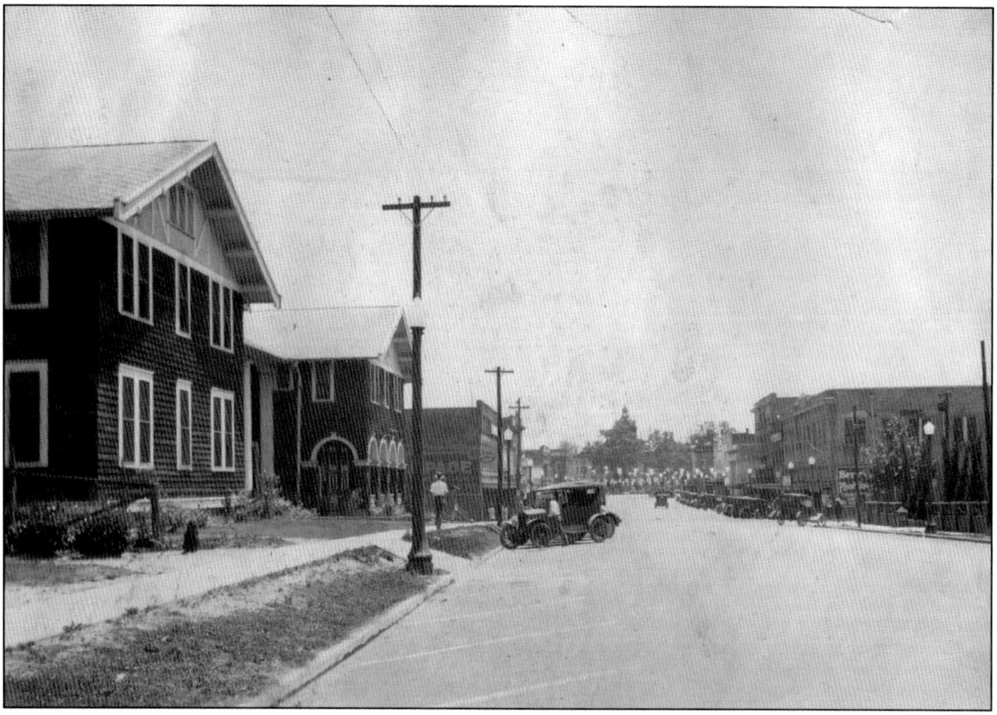

In this 1920s view, the new Hotel Marion can be seen at left, and to the right, the brick fence and trees on the grounds of the Gardner Hospital can be seen. Decorative flags span Main Street, perhaps in anticipation of an upcoming event. Columbia police raided the Dufore Café and Hotel, thought to have been located on nearby Second Street, in August 1921, and the owners were subsequently convicted of running a house of ill fame. (Courtesy of Marion County Development Partnership.)

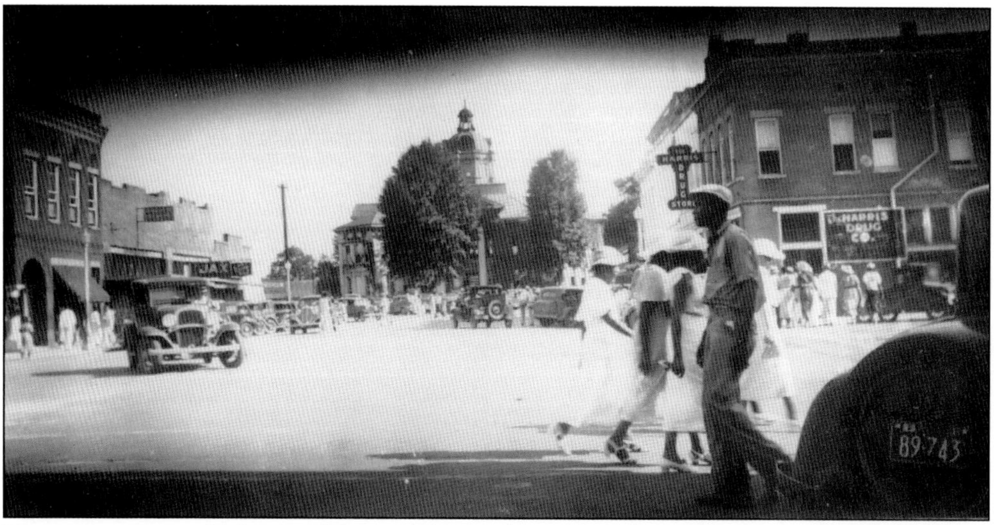

The intersection of Main and Second Streets bustles in this 1930s view. The Harris Drug Company's sign states, "We are always at your service." Note the ivy that covers the courthouse. This photograph was most likely taken by Walter Bullock through the windshield of his car. (Courtesy of Bates Bullock.)

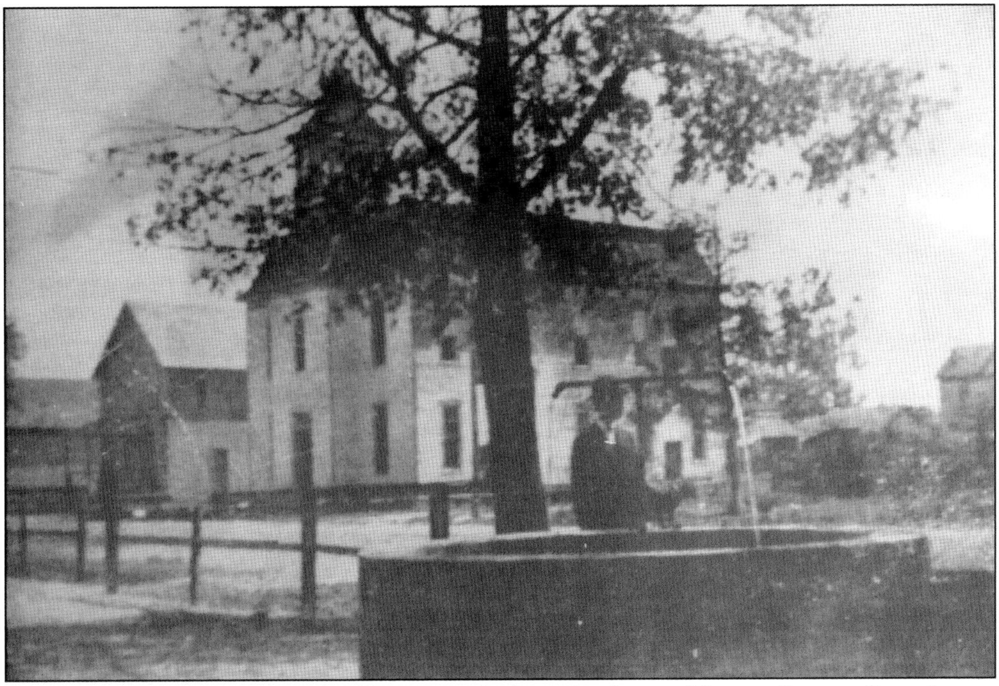

This 19th-century photograph offers a rare look at the former Marion County Courthouse. Although the age of this structure is not presently known, it is documented that some War of 1812 soldiers, who served in George Nixon's 13th Regiment, territorial militia, were sworn in at a place termed the "Marion County Courthouse." Note the artesian well in the foreground and the house cat precariously perched on the edge of the well! This image is from a postcard. (Courtesy of Marion County Development Partnership.)

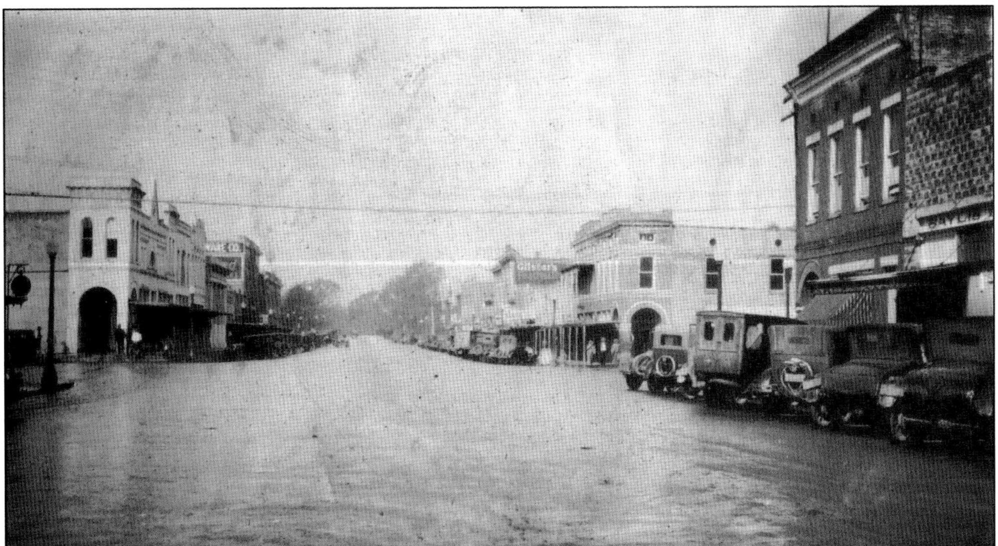

It was a rainy day when this photograph was taken, looking north up Main Street from near Courthouse Square. The landmark clock that once stood on the corner at Harris Drug Company is visible in this photograph. (Courtesy of Marion County Development Partnership.)

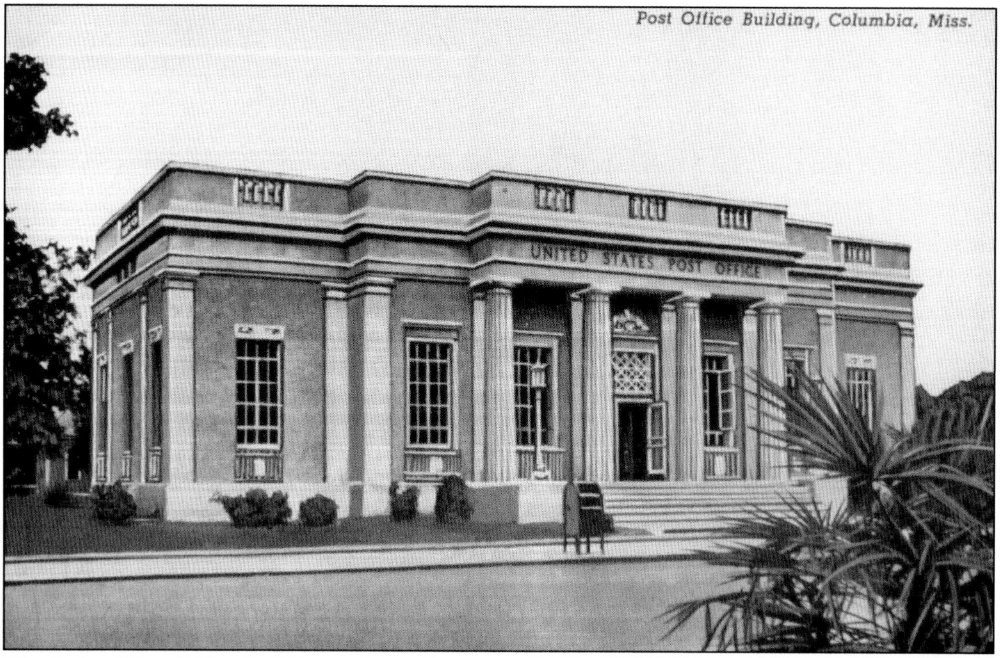

The Federal Post Office Building on Main Street was built in 1933, replacing the post office that had been housed in the rear of the Citizen's Bank building since 1916. (Courtesy of Randy Davis.)

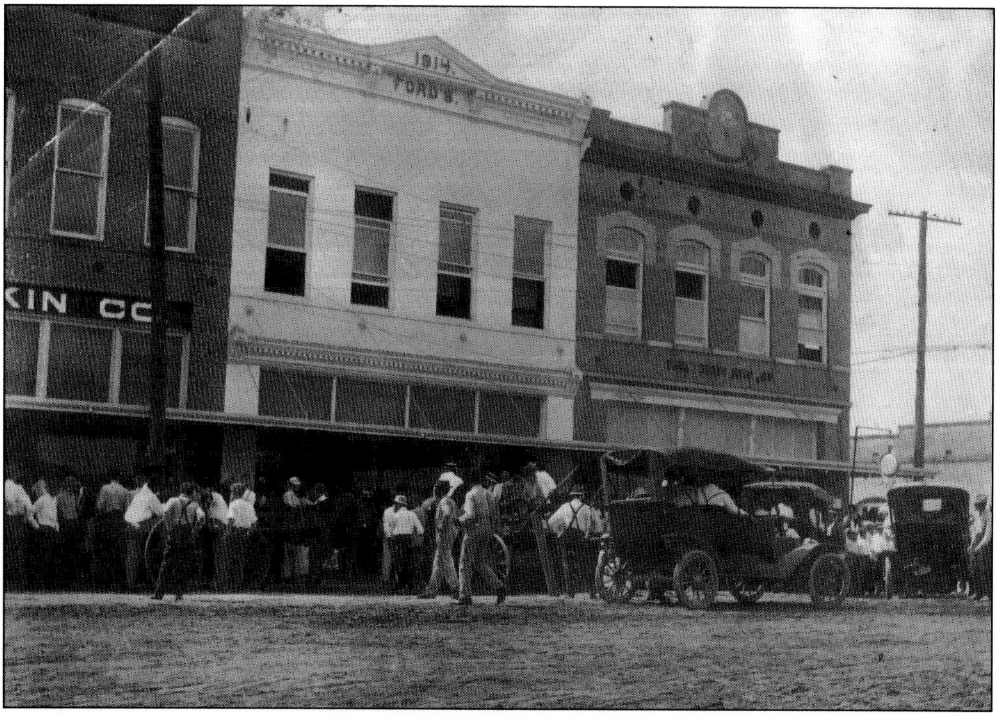

The Berry Drug Company, Ford's, and the Rankin Company can be seen in this early view of the southwest corner of Main Street. This image was most likely captured on a Saturday, the day most shoppers descended upon the business district to do a week's worth of business. (Courtesy of Marion County Historical Society.)

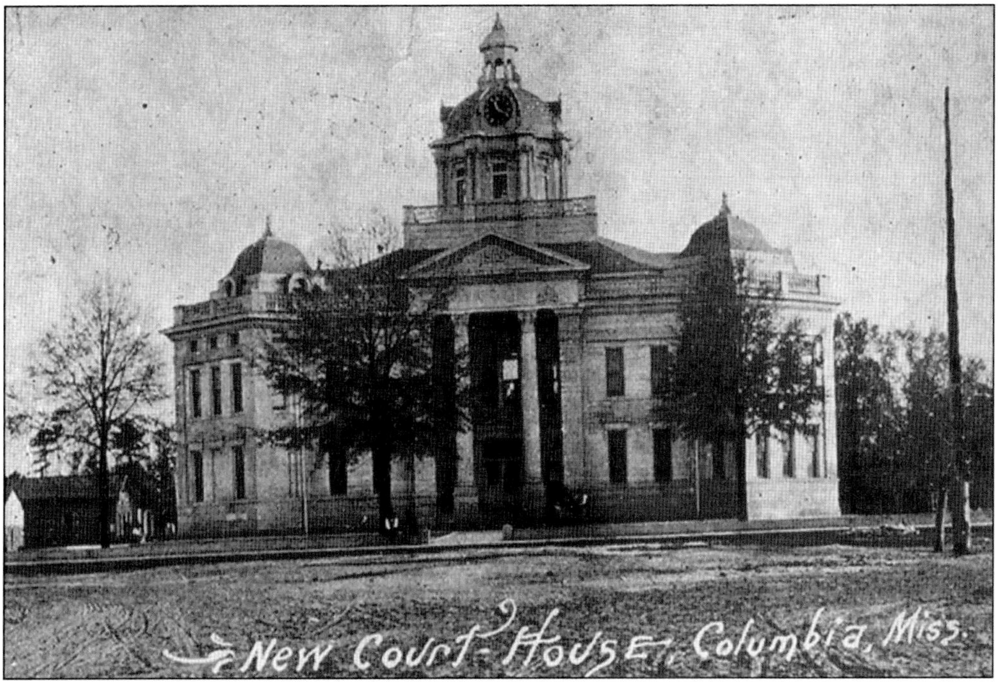

In this c. 1907 image, wagon ruts and dirt streets lead to the new county courthouse, which displays its original architectural details. The structure on the left in rear was the jailhouse, likely the structure that once famously held Will Purvis. This image is from a postcard. (Courtesy of Mississippi Department of Archives and History.)

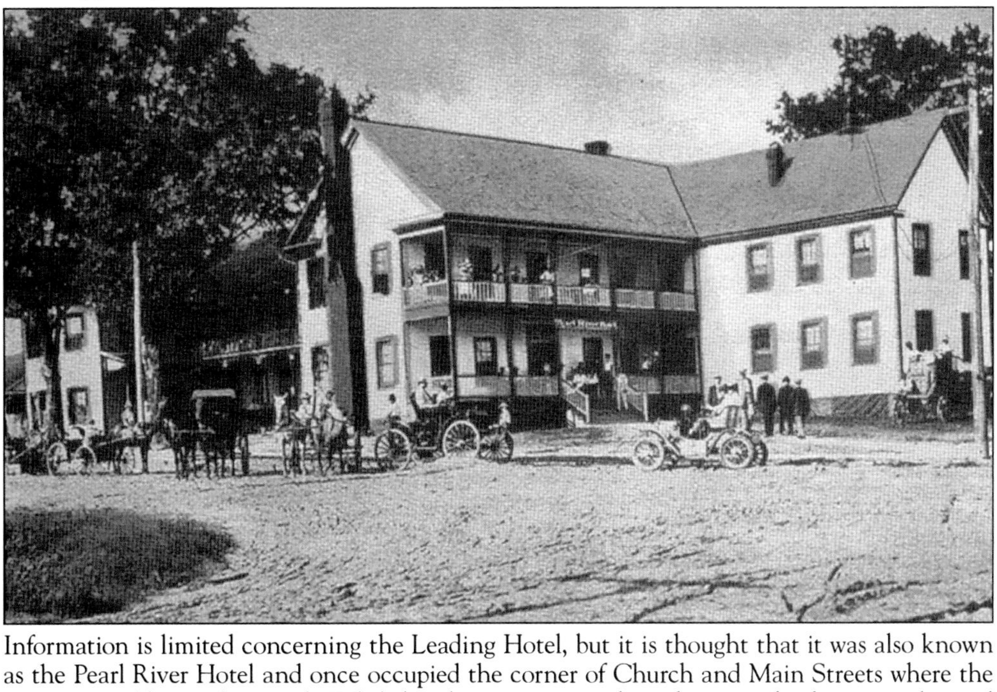

Information is limited concerning the Leading Hotel, but it is thought that it was also known as the Pearl River Hotel and once occupied the corner of Church and Main Streets where the Newsom Building today stands. While hotel rooms were in the right wing, the dining was located in the middle of the building. (Courtesy of Mississippi Department of Archives and History.)

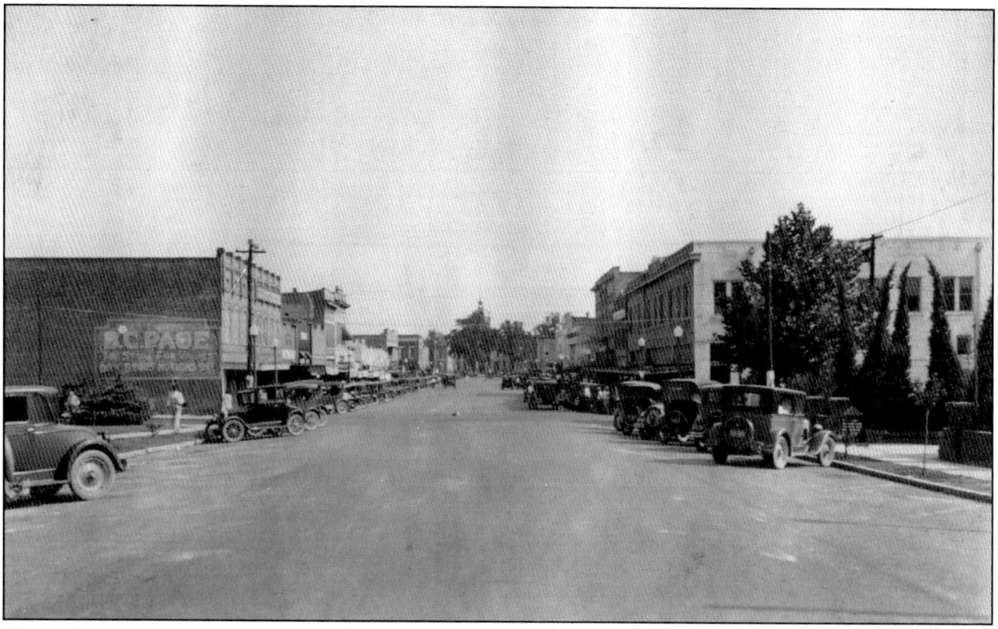

One of the more iconic views of downtown Columbia, it becomes clear that the skyline has remained relatively unchanged in the past century. The following is an advertisement for the B.C. Page Company, which was located farther down the street: "B.C. Page, the store for values, dry goods, notions, shoes." This photograph was made about the time that Columbia's streets were covered with bricks. (Courtesy of Marion County Development Partnership.)

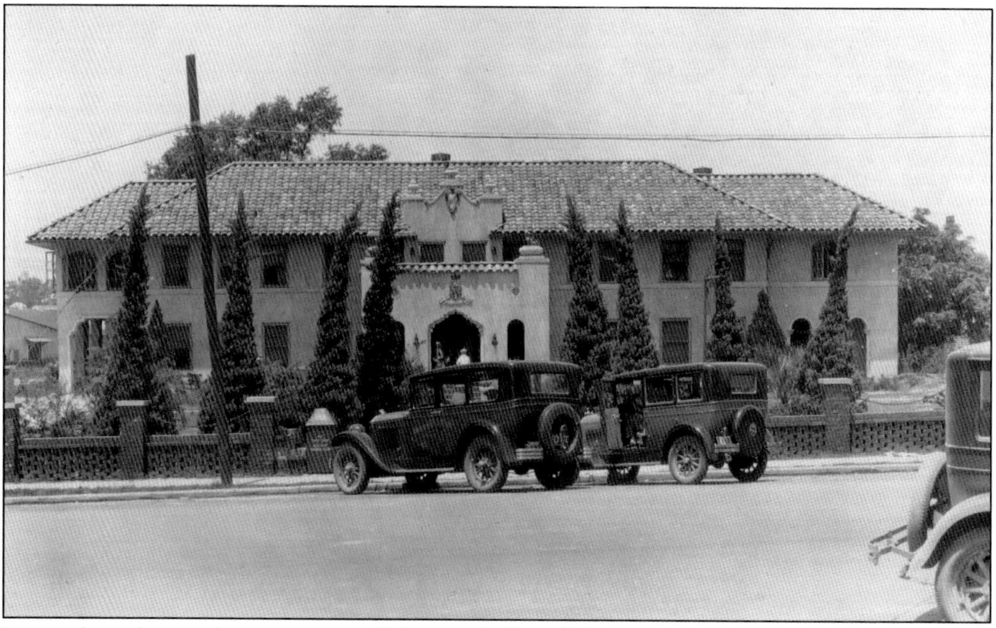

Located on the northwest corner of Main and Church Streets, Columbia Hospital opened its doors to the public in September 1916. Established by Dr. John G. Gardner, the hospital even boasted of being an accredited nursing school. Dr. Gardner later established a drive that led to the construction of a football field at Columbia High School, which was named for him. (Courtesy of Marion County Development Partnership.)

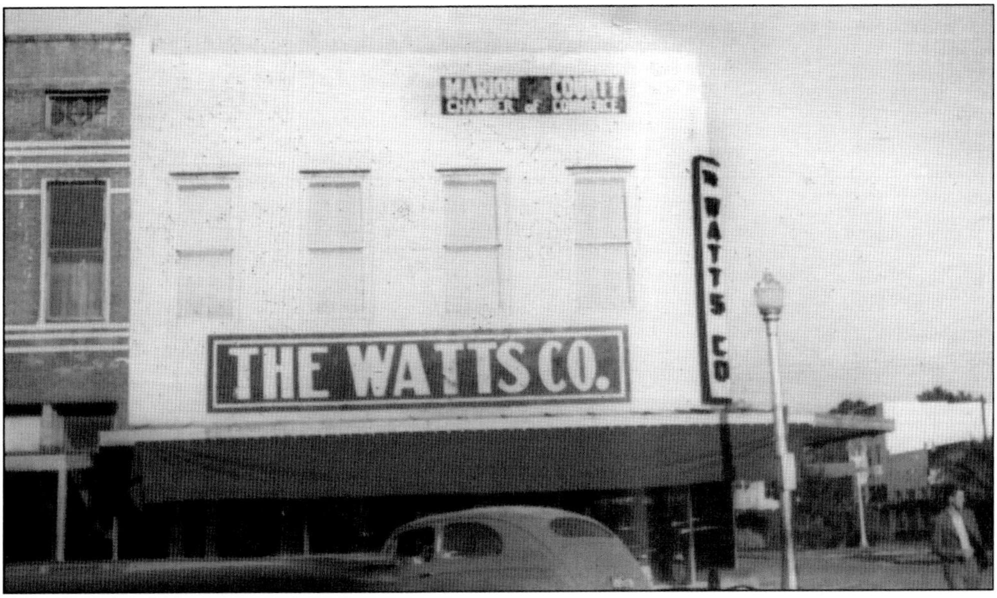

The Watts Company was established by John Watts in 1893 and stood on the northeast corner of Main and Second Streets. It has been frequently told that he added up the shoe bill for his 12 children and decided he should just as well go into the business for himself. This photograph was taken around 1940. (Courtesy of Fran Ginn.)

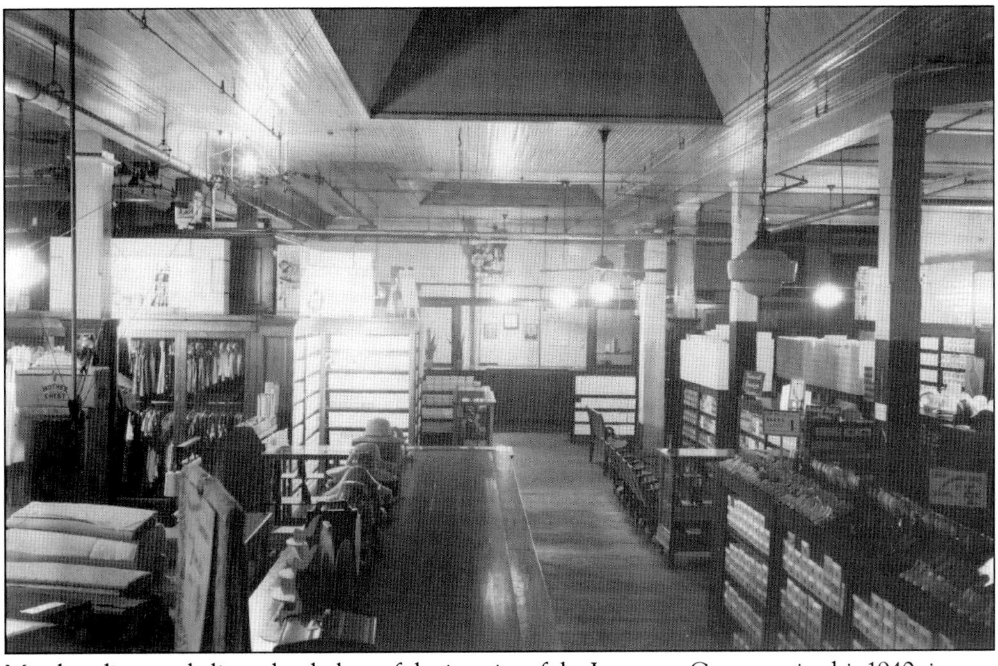

Merchandise neatly lines the shelves of the interior of the Lampton Company in this 1940s image. Lamptons was well known in the area for its innovative use of a network of pneumatic pipes in which transactions were sent from the sales floor to the business office. The Lampton and Rankin Companies once jointly operated their own steamboat, the *Earl*, to transport merchandise from New Orleans. (Courtesy of Marion County Public Library)

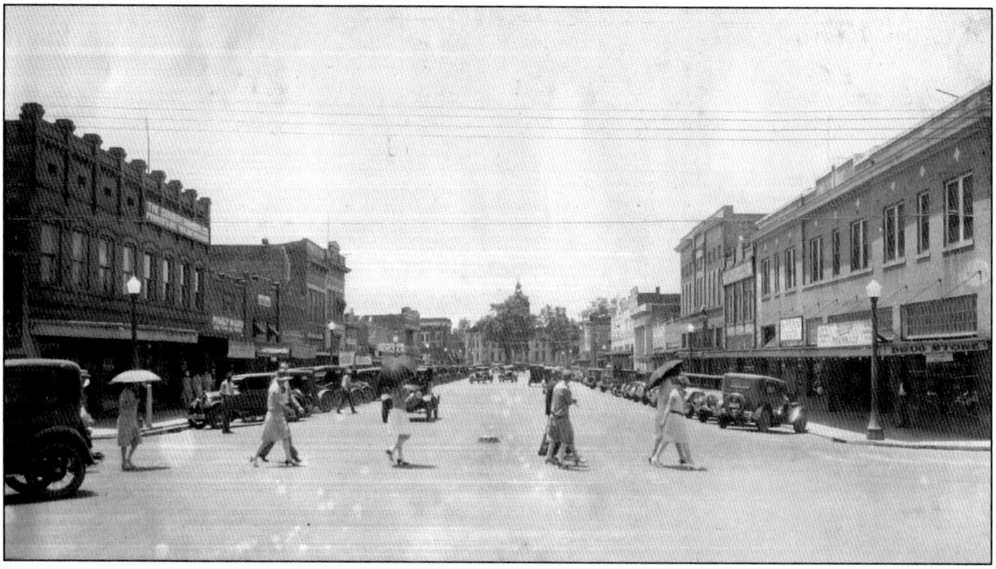

Perhaps the most iconic Main Street photograph, this late 1920s image captures the energy and growing optimism of a thriving Mississippi town on the eve of the Great Depression. As carefree shoppers cross Main Street at the Church Street crossing, Berry's Drugstore can be seen at right, while the Colbert & Brinson Company furniture warehouse can be seen at left. Padgetts Café farther down the street served dinners, short orders, and sandwiches 24 hours a day. (Courtesy of Marion County Development Partnership.)

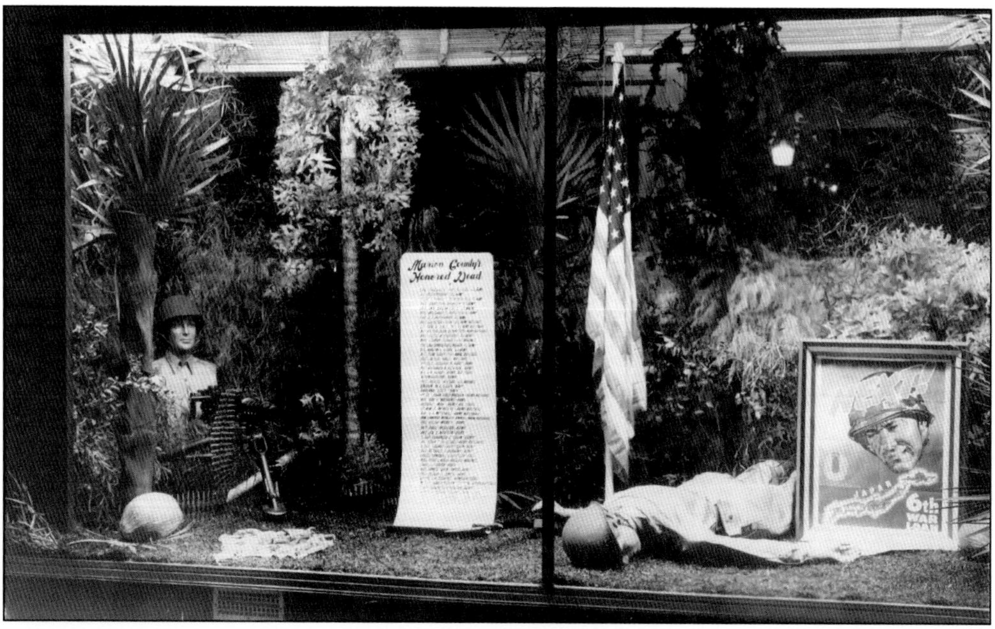

Marion County was heavily involved in World War II. Morgan and Lindsey, Walker Stores, Lampton Company, Rankin Company, and the Marion Theater were just some of the businesses that featured patriotic displays in their windows. This 1944 photograph of the Lampton Company display window sadly lists the names of some 47 local servicemen who had perished in the war up until this point. (Courtesy of Fran Ginn.)

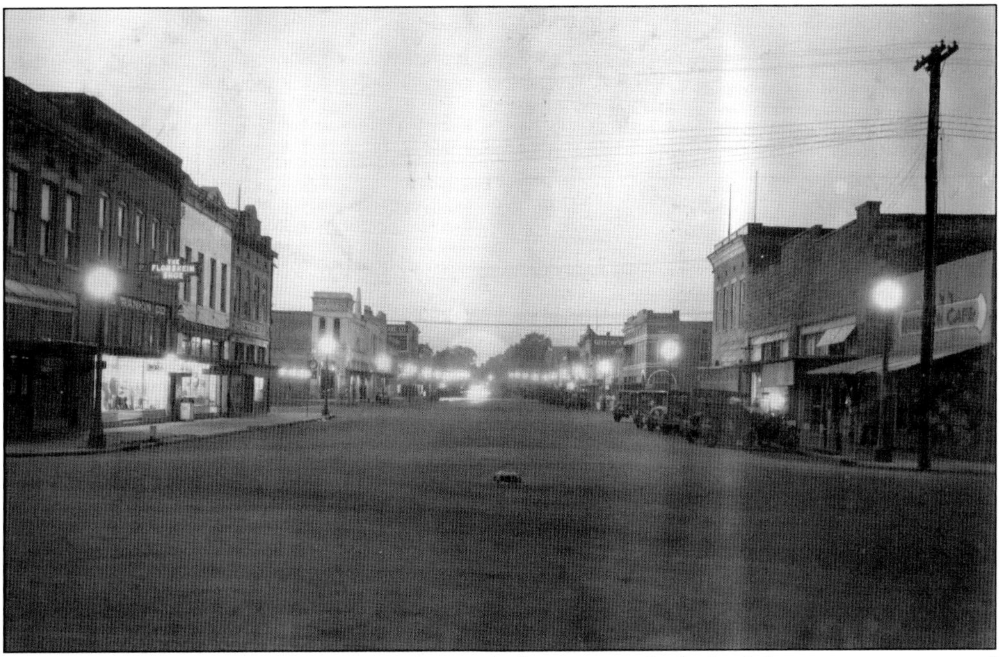

This rare photograph of Main Street, taken at dusk, captures the look of the town as it appeared after dark. A lighted sign on the Rankin Company advertises Florsheim shoes, and the Robertson Café is visible on the east side of the street. The disk-shaped object in the middle of the street contained a flame that was lit each night to mark the middle of the street for motorists. (Courtesy of Marion County Development Partnership.)

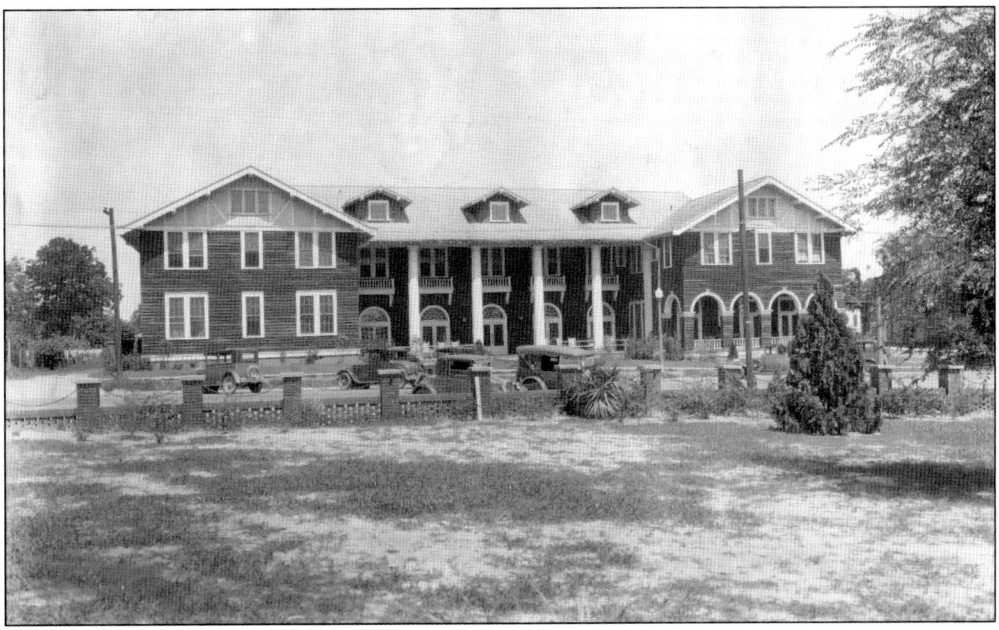

The office of Columbia Western Union could be found inside the grand Marion Hotel. This notable building was constructed in 1923 and was a landmark until its demolition in 1972. This view is from the front door of Columbia Hospital from the west side of Main Street. (Courtesy of Marion County Development Partnership.)

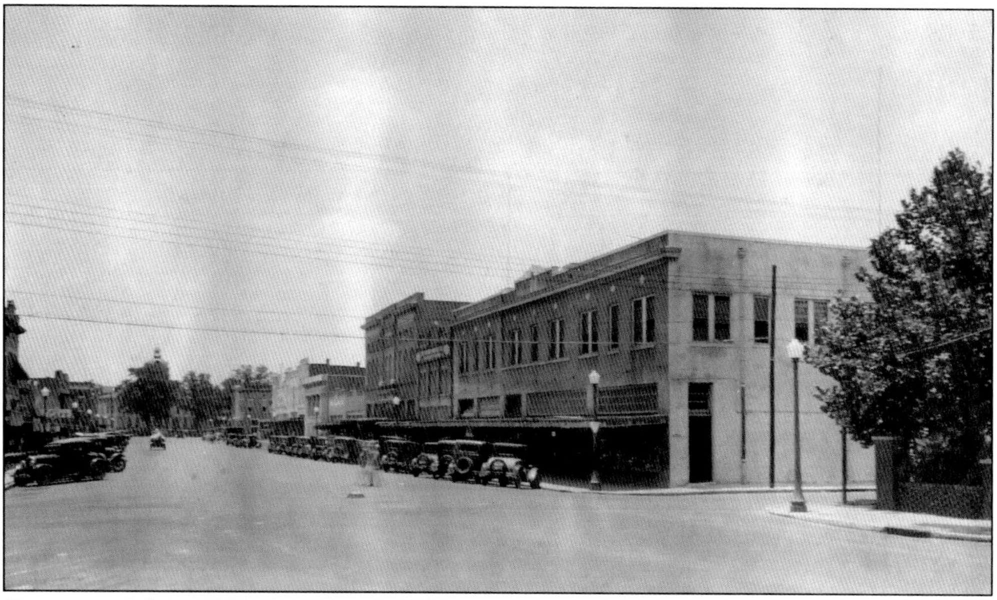

Constructed about 1920, the White Building is seen on the corner of Main and Church Streets. This impressive commercial building housed numerous businesses, including an early motion picture theater, while the second floor was dedicated to professional offices. At the time this photograph was taken, Berry's Pharmacy operated in the White Building, a firm that not only sold prescriptions but was also a well-known dealer in Grafonolas and Victrolas. (Courtesy of Marion County Development Partnership.)

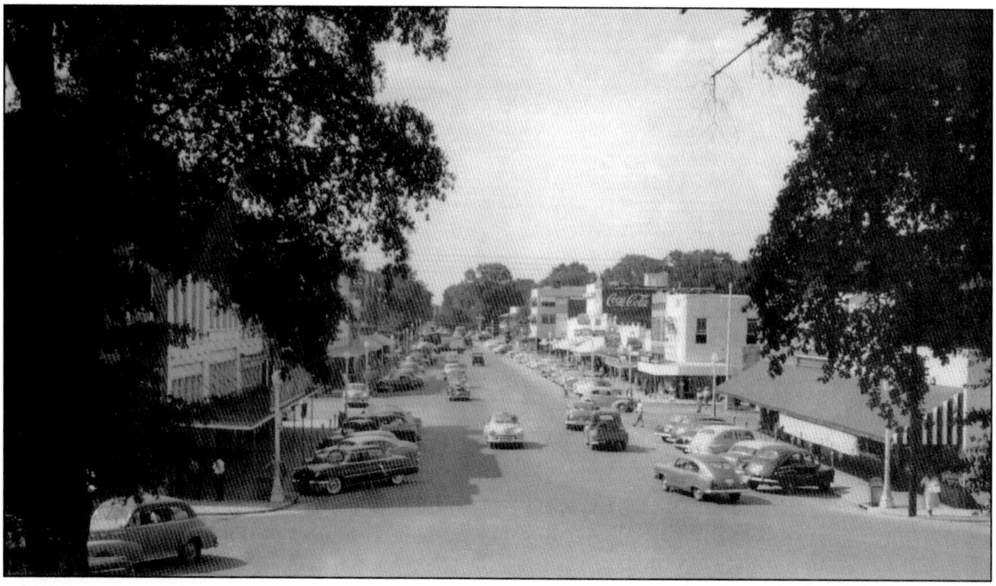

This nostalgic 1950s image captures the downtown business district during its heyday. Municipal parking meters and automobiles line the sidewalks, while awnings cover the storefronts. Note the scaffolding and the painter at work on the Watts Company building. This photograph was taken from the vantage point of the second story of the courthouse. (Courtesy of Marion County Development Partnership.)

Eight

There Is No Place Like Home

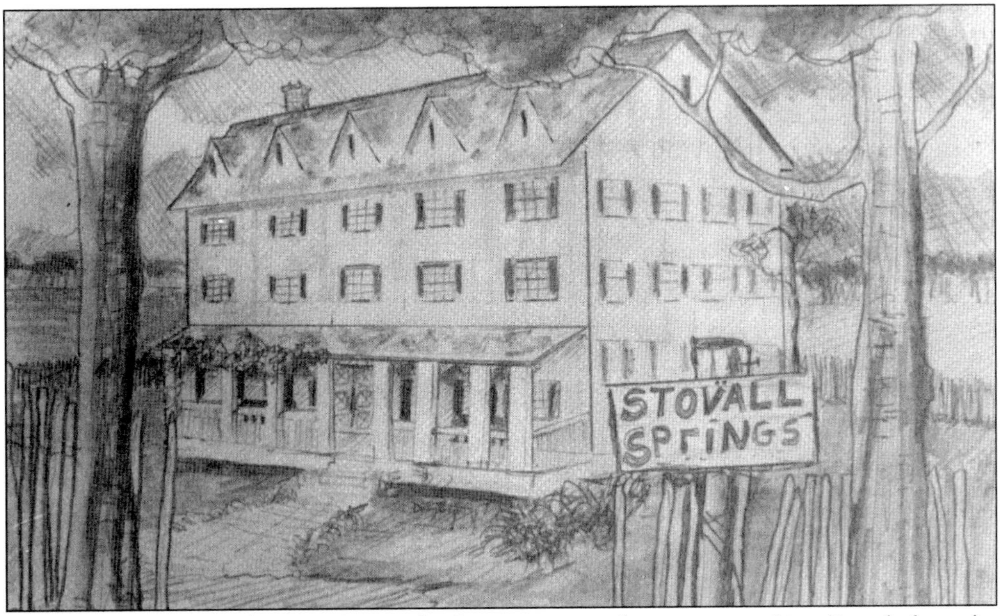

This sketch of Stovall's Springs depicts the famous retreat when it attracted its clientele from the Natchez District and New Orleans. The fifth session of the Mississippi Legislature met here in 1821, temporarily making Columbia the state capital. The legal code of Governor Poindexter was adopted here, and later, Gov. Walter Leake was sworn into office. The reputation of the springs was tarnished after the famous Payson-Stockton duel. In an argument that began at Stovall's Springs, Payson and Stockton squared off in New Orleans, and Stockton was summarily killed. Richard Stockton was a graduate of Princeton and was the attorney general of Mississippi; his father, also named Richard Stockton, was a signer of the Declaration of Independence. (Courtesy of Marion County Historical Society.)

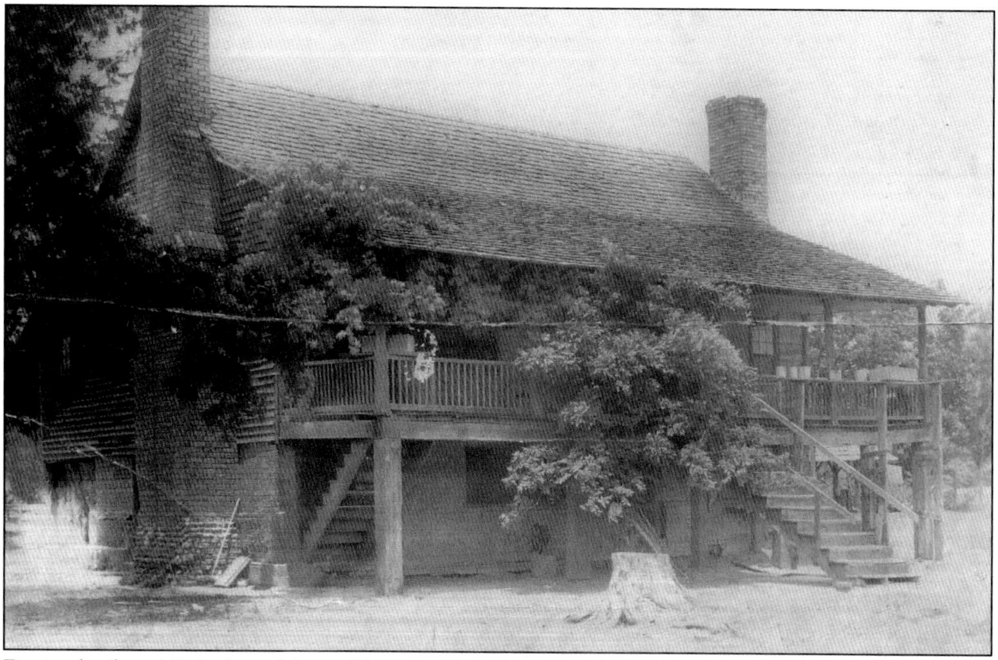

Dating back to 1809, the celebrated home of Rev. John Ford is today the finest example of Frontier architecture found in the South. The house was the setting of two Mississippi Methodist conferences, the Pearl River Convention and it saw service as a fort, territorial post office, and as an inn for travelers. The most famous visitor was Andrew Jackson, who along with troops, was making his way to New Orleans to confront the invading British. (Courtesy of Marion County Historical Society.)

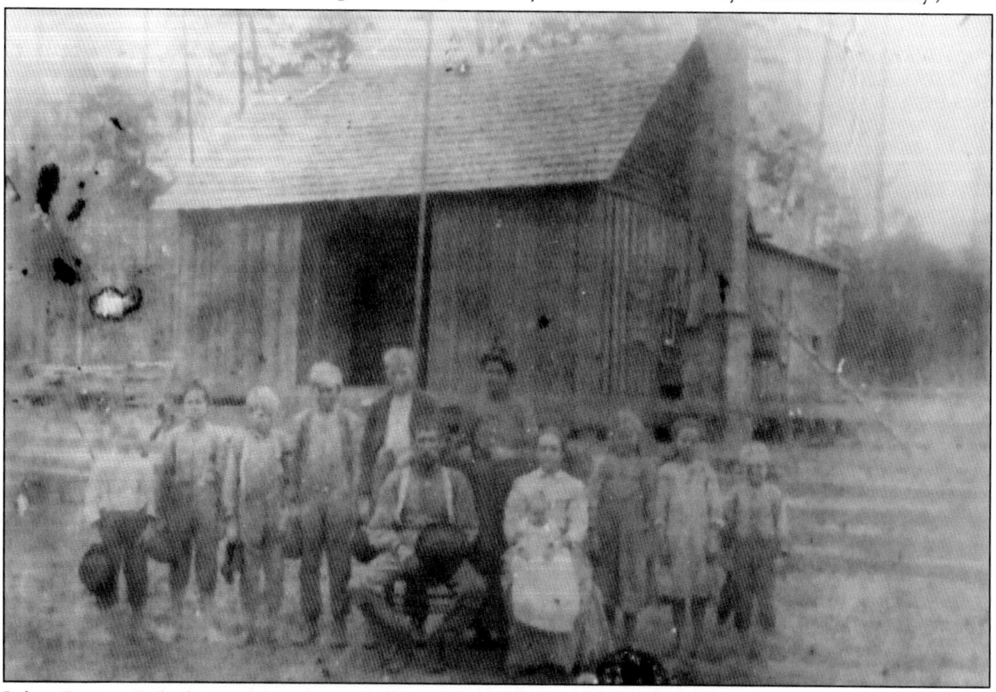

John Green Oglesby and family pose for a photograph at the family home in 1903. The residence was located on Columbia Purvis Road. (Courtesy of Marion County Historical Society.)

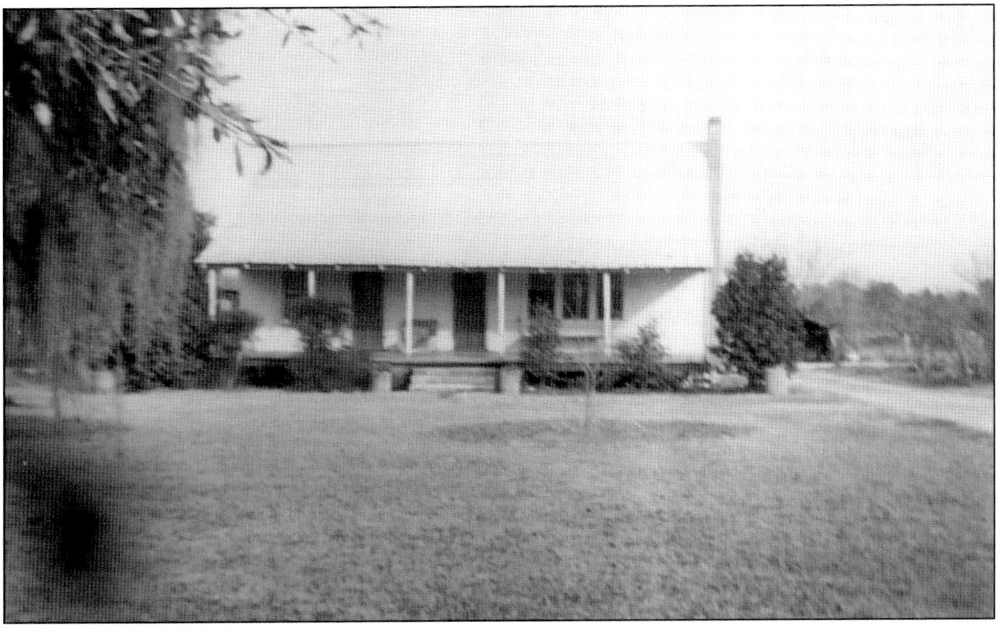

The Evan Powell home was built in 1839, three miles south of Columbia on the Gainesville Road. The original structure consisted of two large rooms, three smaller bedrooms, a full-length front porch, and a separate kitchen some distance away from the house. The historically significant old home is today one of the four oldest standing in the county. (Courtesy of Marion County Historical Society.)

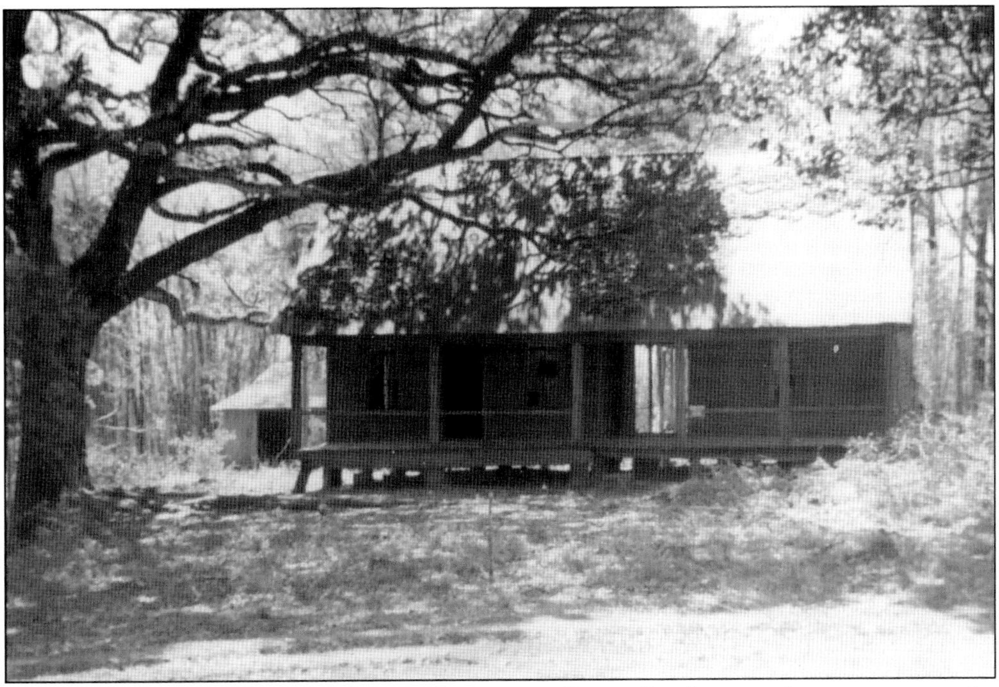

Now demolished, the 1880s Ben Stringer home near Graves Creek was an Improve community landmark for generations. The old home was likely one of the last "Dogtrot-style" houses in Marion County. (Courtesy of Damon Watts.)

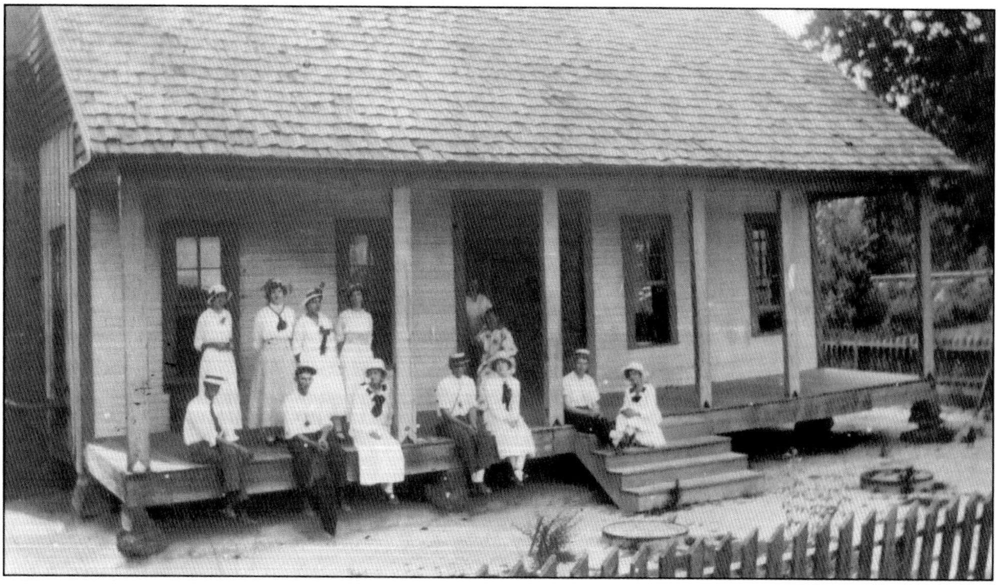

Located in Morgantown, the Baylor-Newsom House is one of the four oldest existing buildings in Marion County. The original room and chimney (shown on the left in the picture) were built around 1815 by Robert Baylor as his residence when he was hired to construct the William T. LeNoir house along Pearl River. The house also served as a depot and post office, operated by Effie Newsom. (Louis F. Morgan collection.)

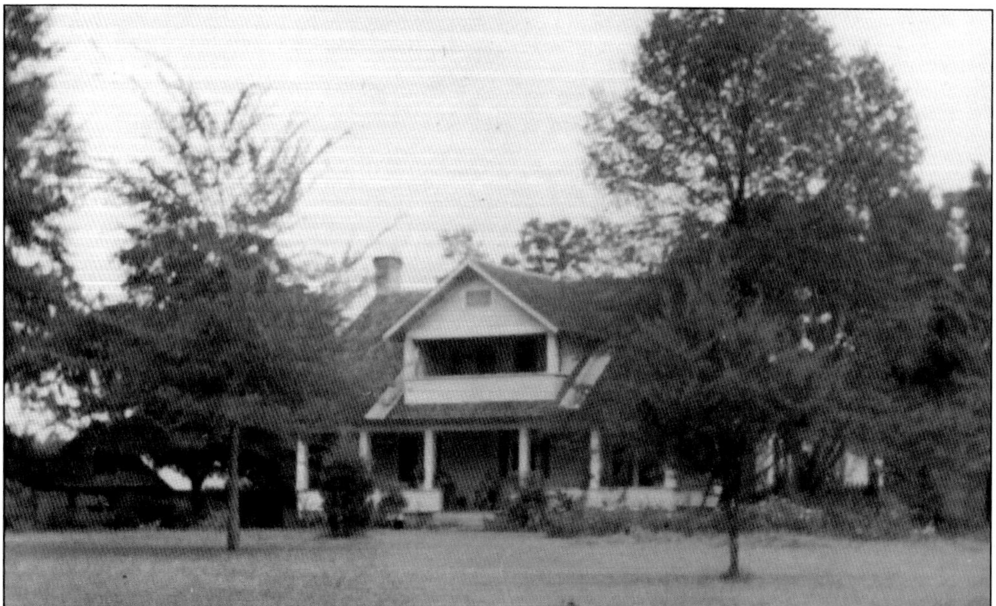

The Rev. John Luther Watts house, flanked with a barn, is seen in this early photograph. The original family home stood on this same spot but burned on Christmas night in 1915. Construction on the house pictured began on December 26, and the family moved in before it was completed. (Courtesy of Peggy Bell.)

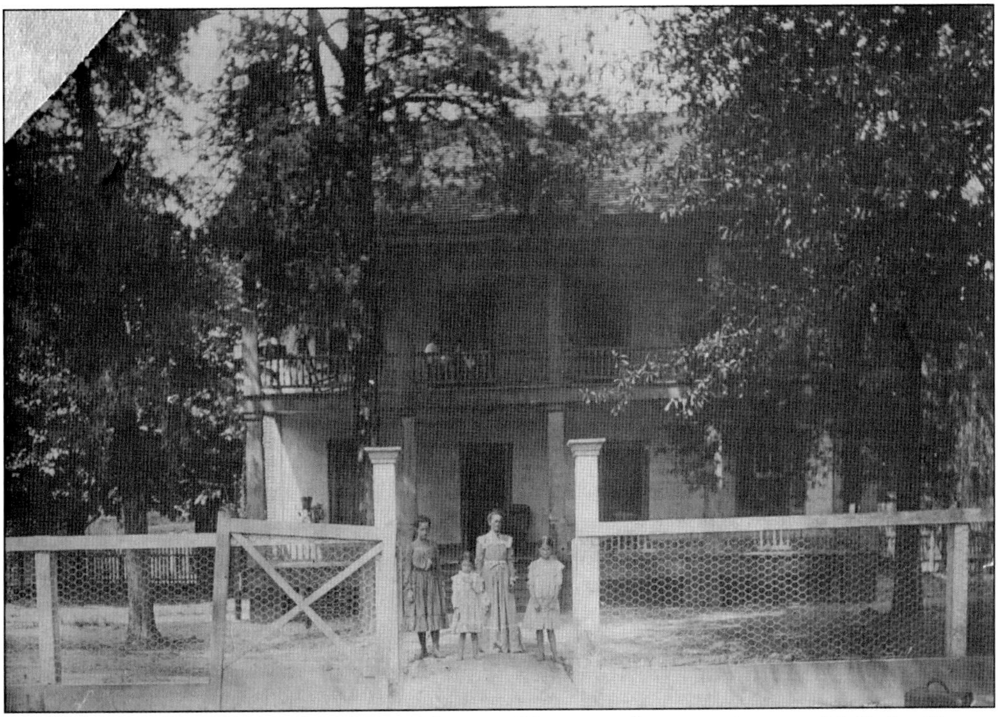

Surrounded by a wire fence, the two-story home of Benjamin Lampton is seen with Esther Patten and her daughters posed in the walkway. (Courtesy of Marion County Historical Society.)

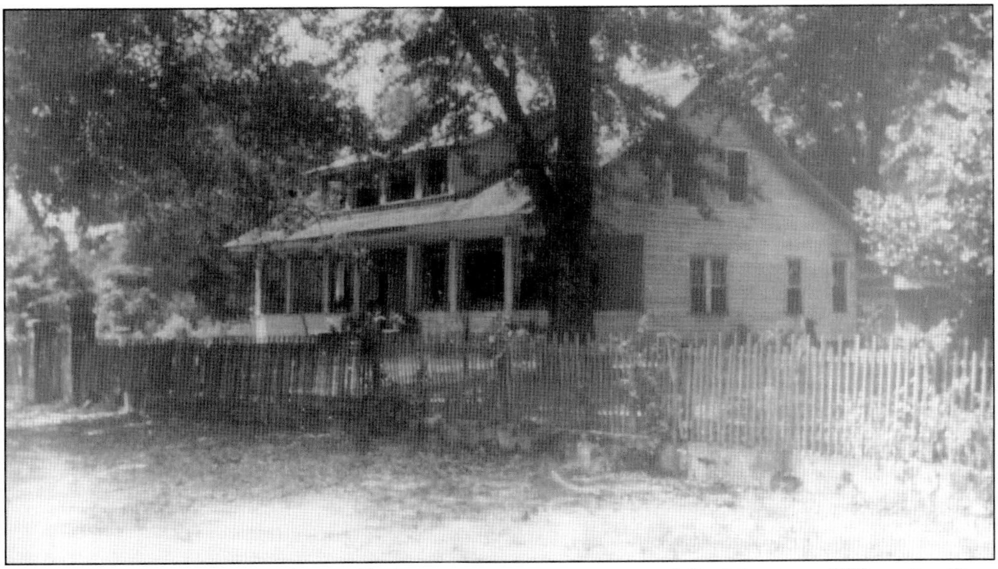

The Watts home has been the cradle for numerous generations of the Morris and Watts families. Seaborn Morris constructed the original portions of this house in 1843. Prior to 1915, the second floor was added, duplicating the lower-floor plan of a large center hallway with five rooms. A later resident, Morris's son-in-law John Lott Watts also lived here and served as the early postmaster for the community. In naming the new post office, Watts gave the community its modern name, Improve. The home is today one of the four oldest standing in the county. (Courtesy of Charlotte Watts Pennell.)

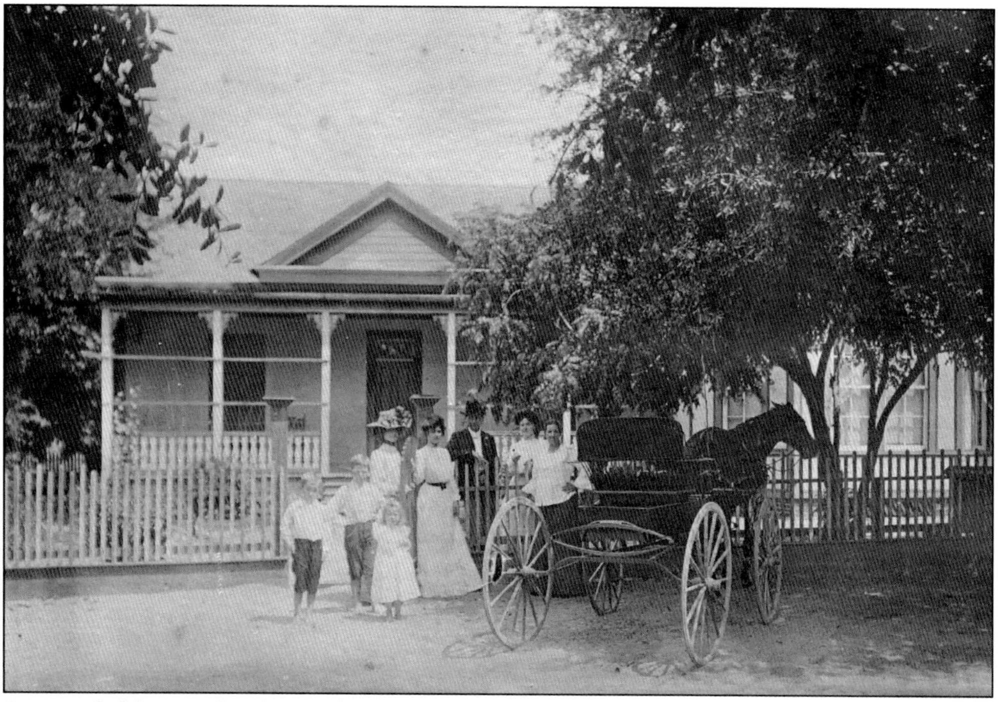

Surrounded by a picket fence, the family home of Dr. Theodore Ford stood on the corner of High School Avenue and Church Street. Along with the horse and buggy that Dr. Ford made his rounds on are members of his family. This photograph is dated August 27, 1902. (Courtesy of Marion County Public Library.)

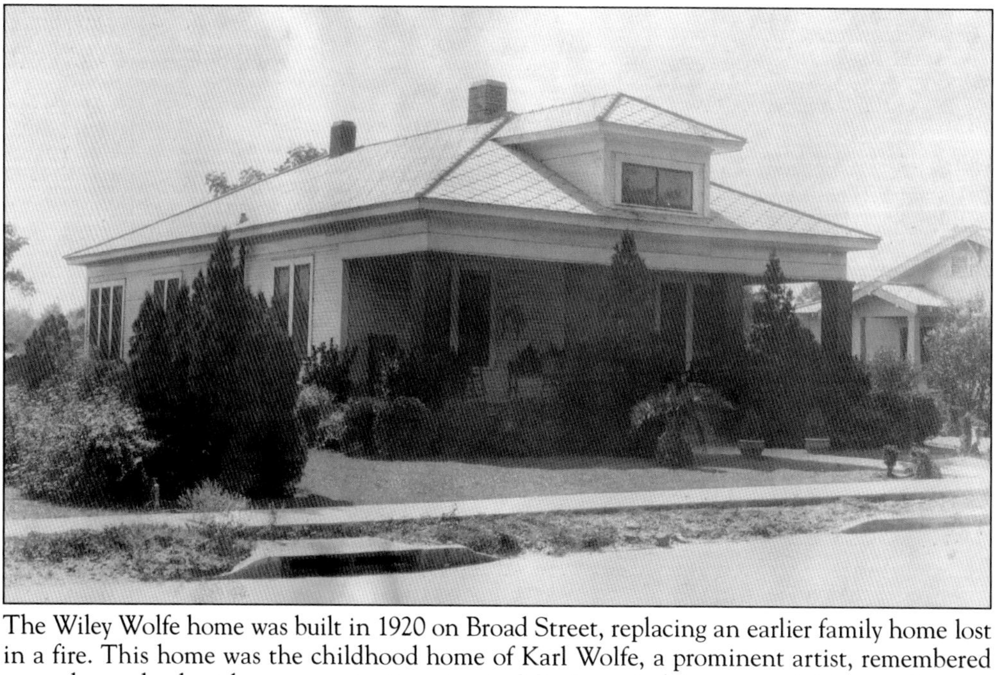

The Wiley Wolfe home was built in 1920 on Broad Street, replacing an earlier family home lost in a fire. This home was the childhood home of Karl Wolfe, a prominent artist, remembered as perhaps the best-known portrait artist in Mississippi. (Courtesy of Marion County Development Partnership.)

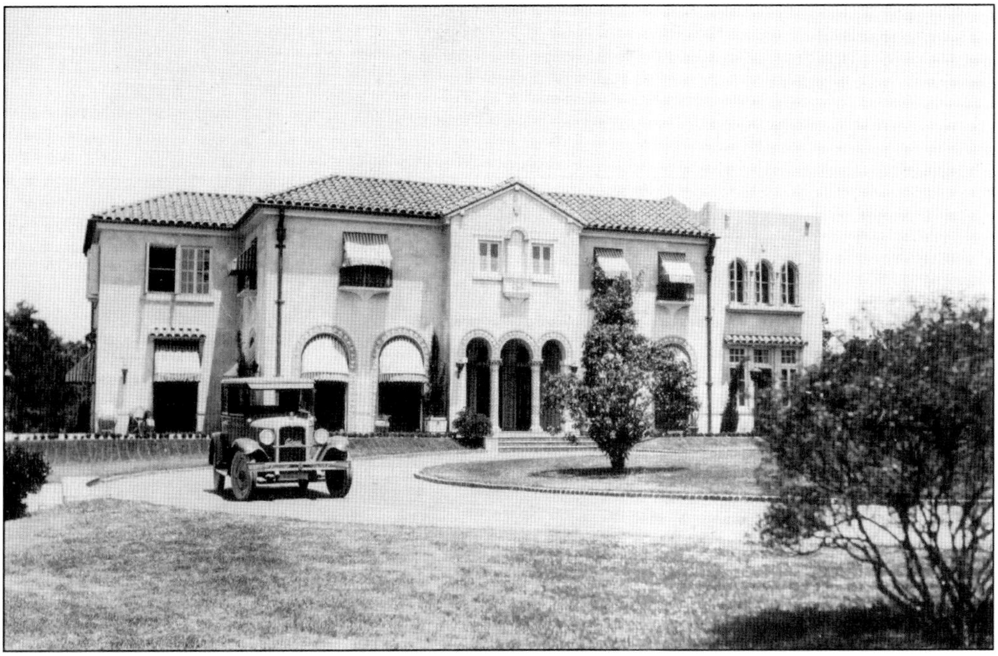

Built in 1925, designed by Claude H. Lindsley and furnished by Marshall Fields, the home of Hugh White on Key's Hill is known throughout Mississippi and has often been described as the finest example of Spanish Colonial Revival style to be found in the state. (Courtesy of Marion County Development Partnership.)

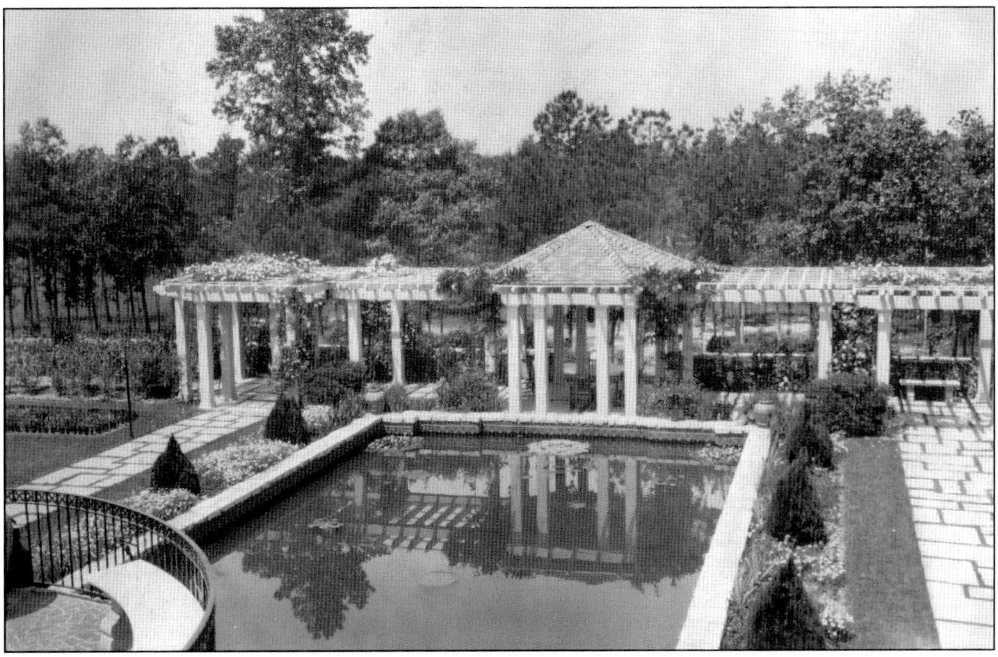

The famous sunken gardens of Hugh White have long been a garden spot in Marion County, consisting of arbors and a reflecting pool lighted from beneath the water's surface. At one time, Governor White employed two full-time gardeners who kept the grounds in bloom year round. (Courtesy of Marion County Development Partnership.)

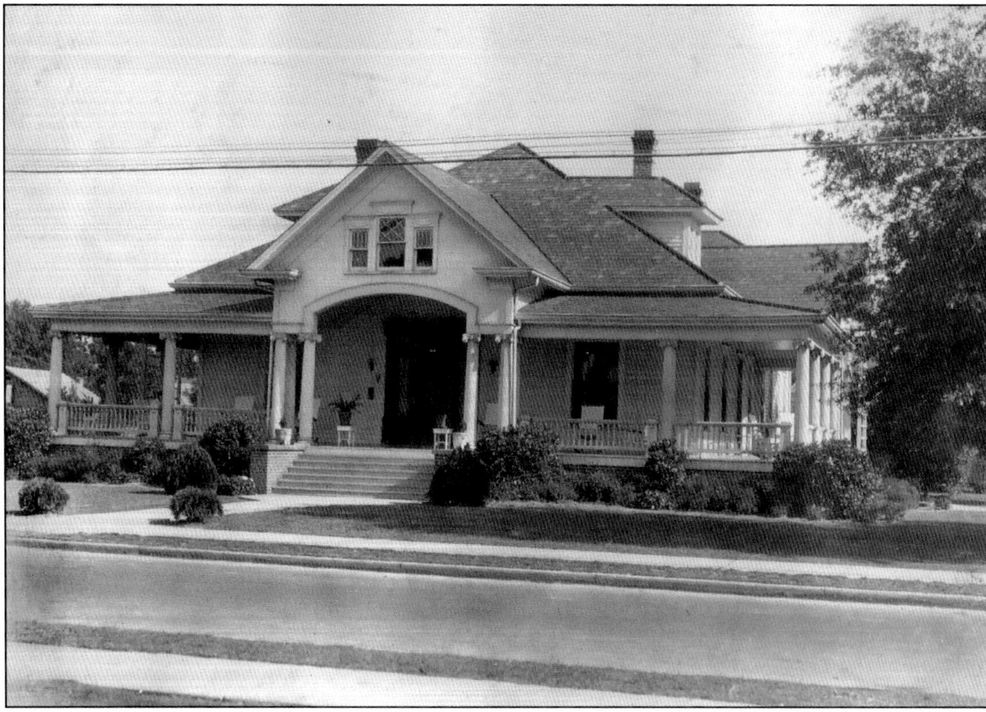

Henry Mounger built this Southern Colonial-style residence on Church Street in 1910. (Courtesy of Marion County Development Partnership.)

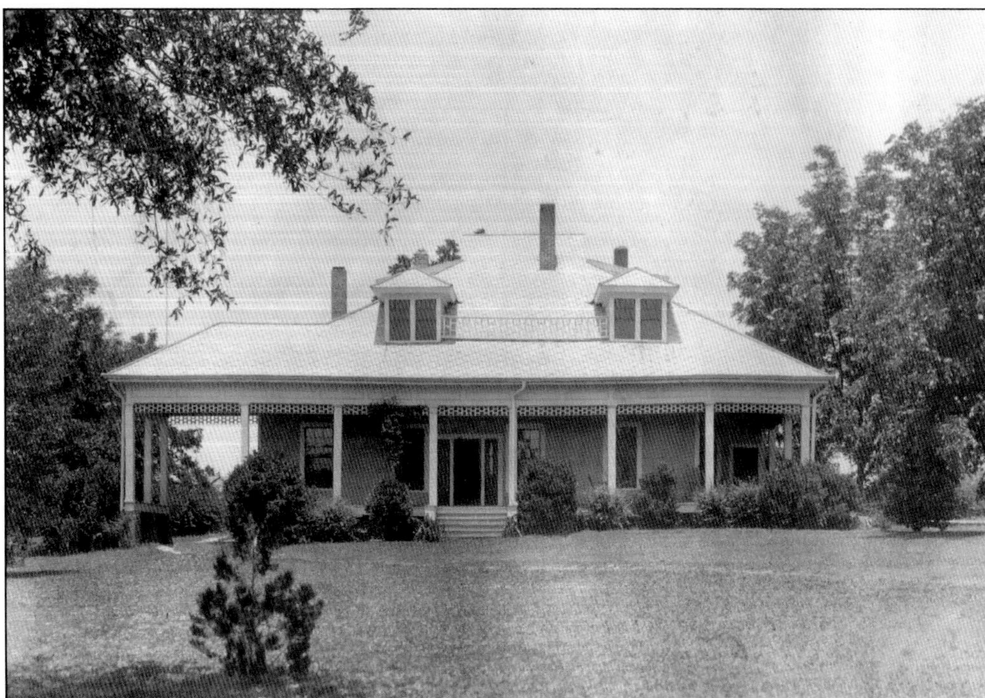

This home on Keys Hill was originally built by Miles Berry in late 1911. (Courtesy of Marion County Development Partnership.)

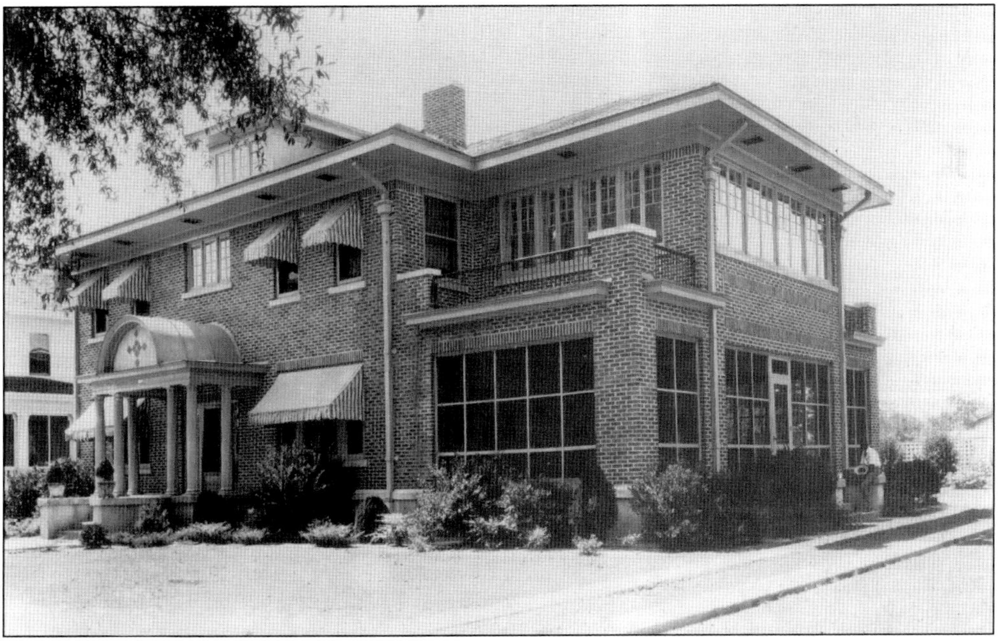

The handsome home of J.T. Rankin, located on Church Street in Columbia, was constructed around 1917. Note the man with his hat in hand waiting at the side entrance. (Courtesy of Marion County Development Partnership.)

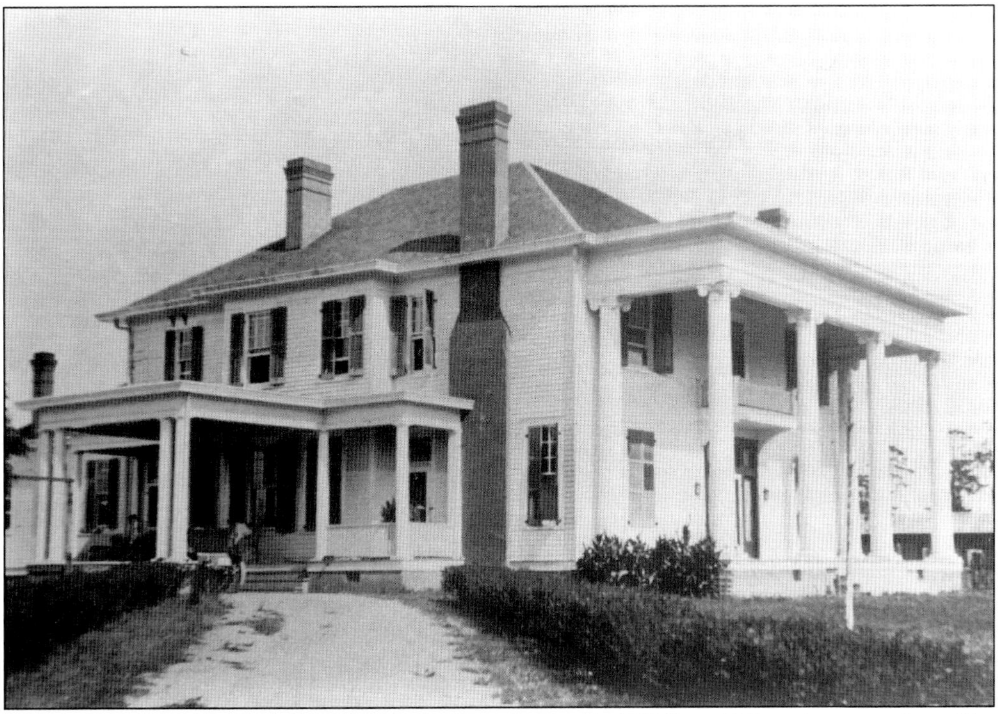

This grand home was built by Edward W. Lampton on Key's Hill in 1910 and was purchased by the Newsom family in 1951. (Courtesy of Marion County Development Partnership.)

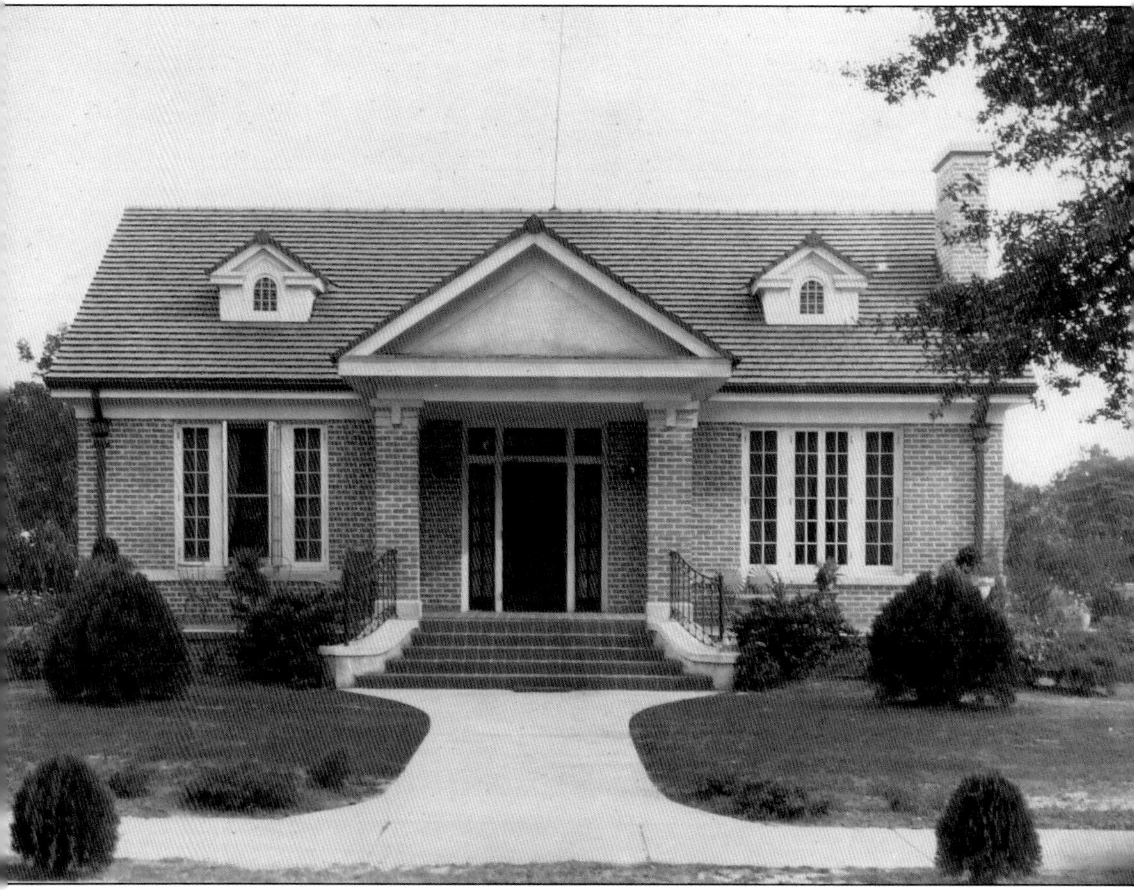

Dr. David A. Ratliff, who, at one time, was the sawmill doctor for J.J. White Lumber Company, built this brick home on Church Street. Dr. Ratliff practiced medicine for some 63 years. (Courtesy of Marion County Development Partnership.)

Nine

NATURAL DISASTERS

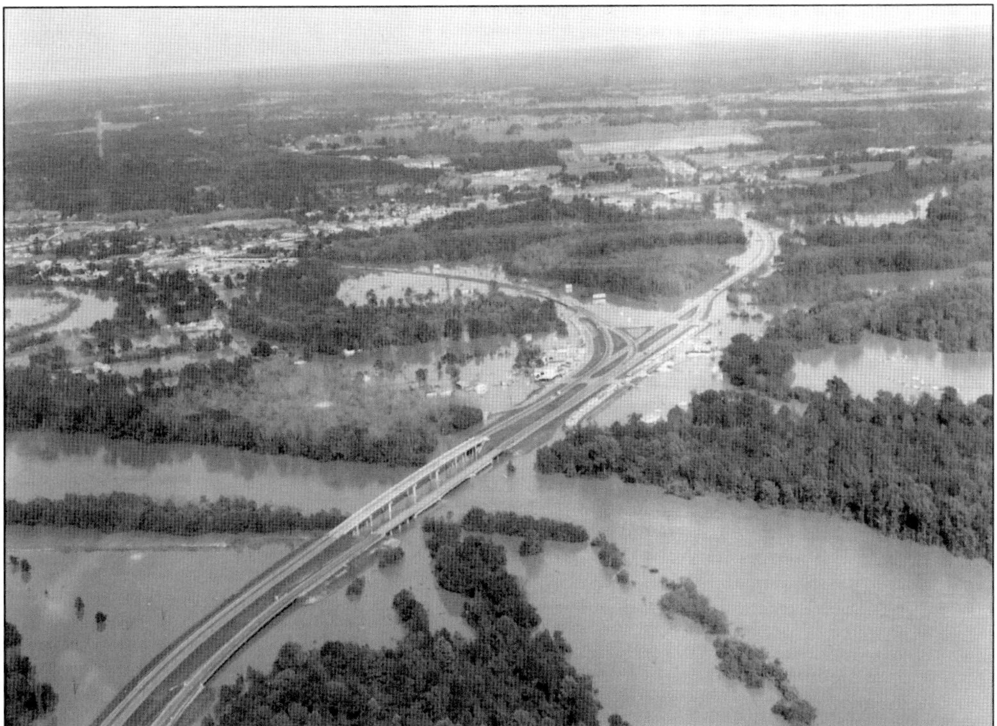

The great flood of 1974 lasted for about two weeks in April of that year. This aerial photograph of Highway 98 and the Pearl River Bridge illustrates the extent of the floodwaters. This photograph was taken by James A. Thornhill, meteorologist and director of civil defense at the time. (Courtesy of Marion County Public Library.)

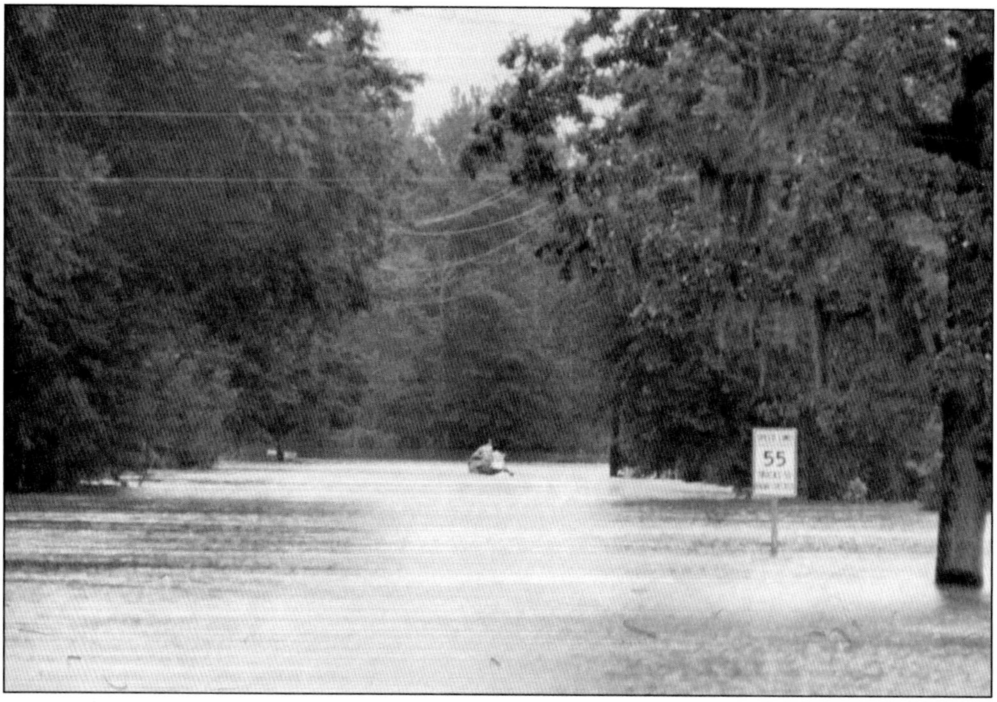

Trees and a speed limit sign are all that is visible of Highway 587 between Foxworth and Morgantown during the flood of 1974. Below, Radio station WCJU and Adam's Furniture are pictured during the flood of 1974. (Both, courtesy of Marion County Public Library.)

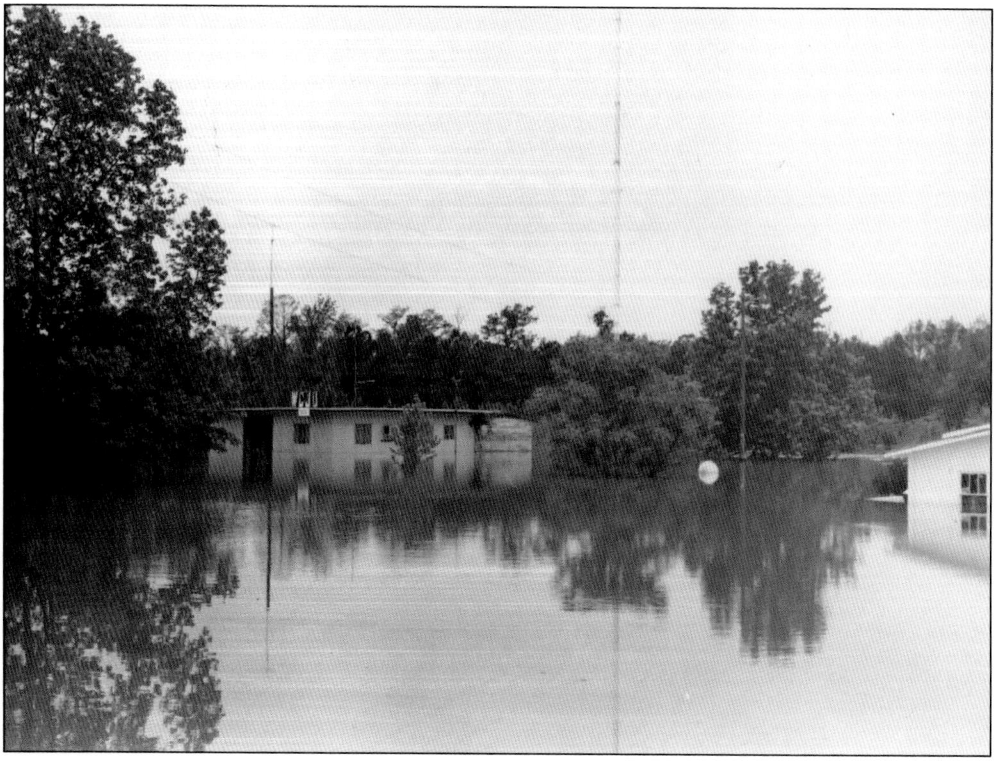

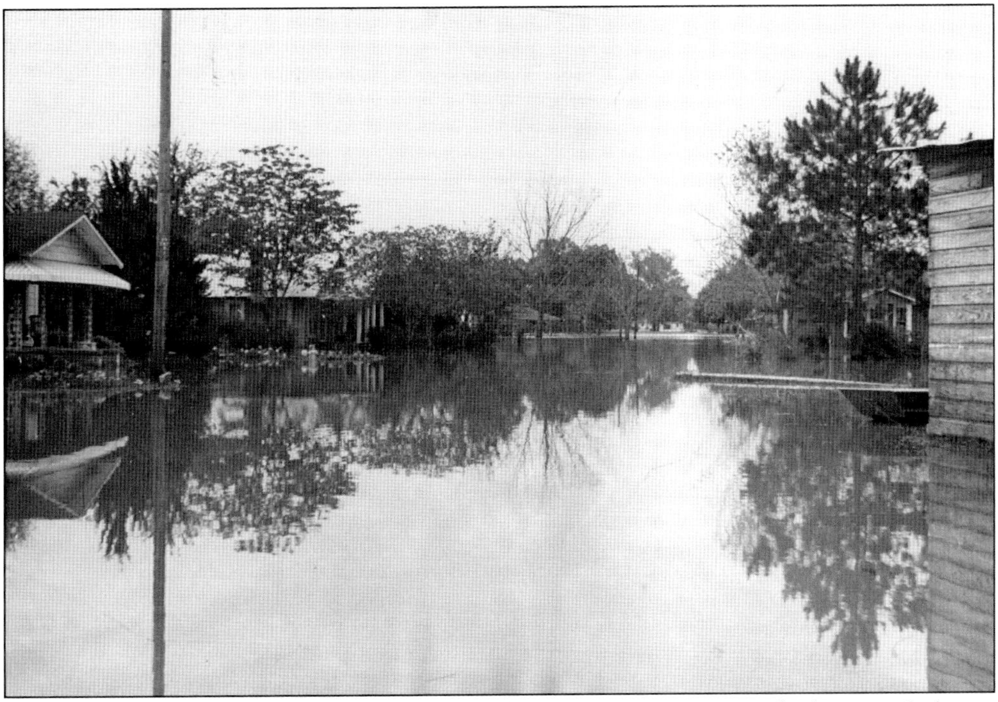

The effects of the floodwaters are evident on Highway 587 at Morgantown looking north during the flood of 1974. (Courtesy of Marion County Public Library.)

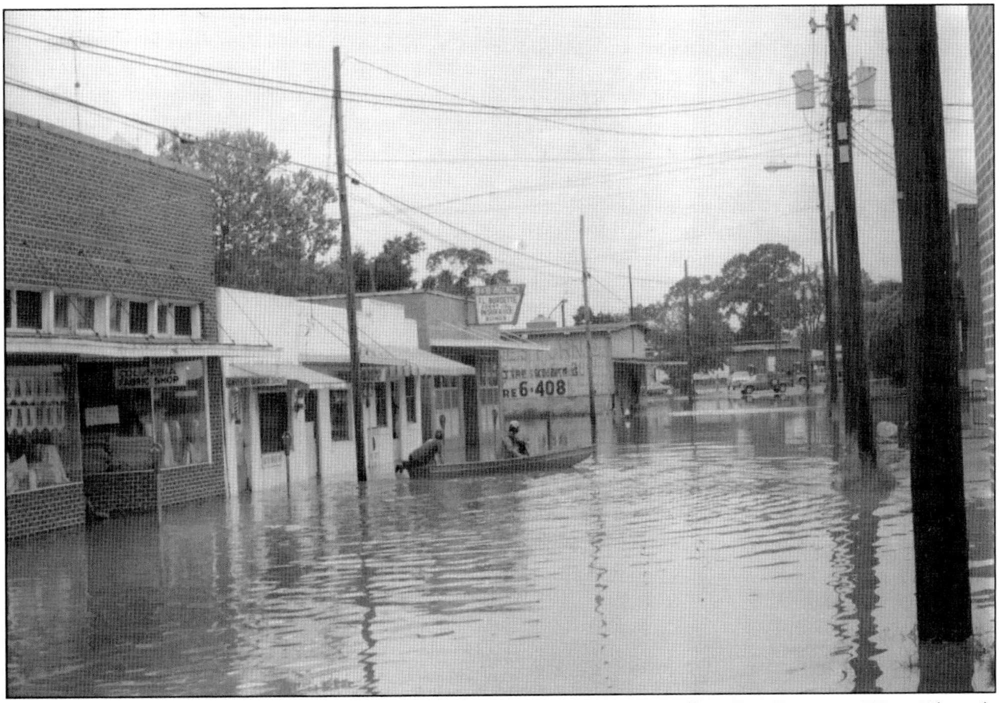

Columbia Fabrics, Carter's Barbershop, and the B&B Agency suffer flooding on West Church Street during the flood of 1974. Note the parking meters along the street during this period. (Courtesy of Marion County Public Library.)

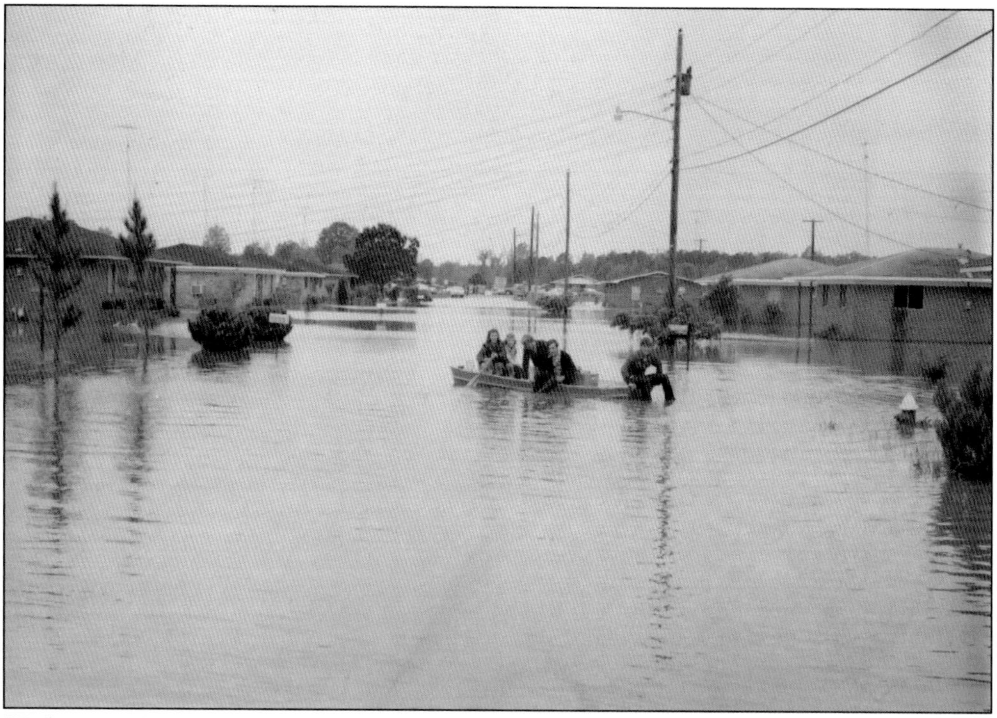

Washington Street in Popetown was temporarily hidden from view by floodwaters in this 1974 image. (Courtesy of Marion County Public Library.)

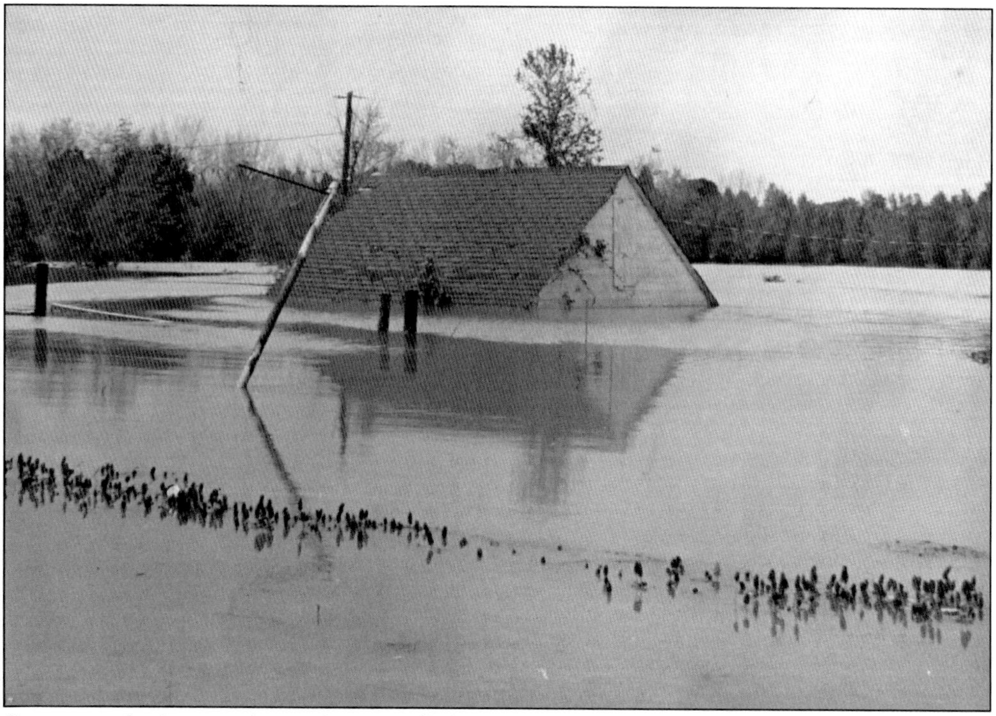

Segments of a fence and a rooftop are all that is visible in this 1974 photograph. (Courtesy of Marion County Public Library.)

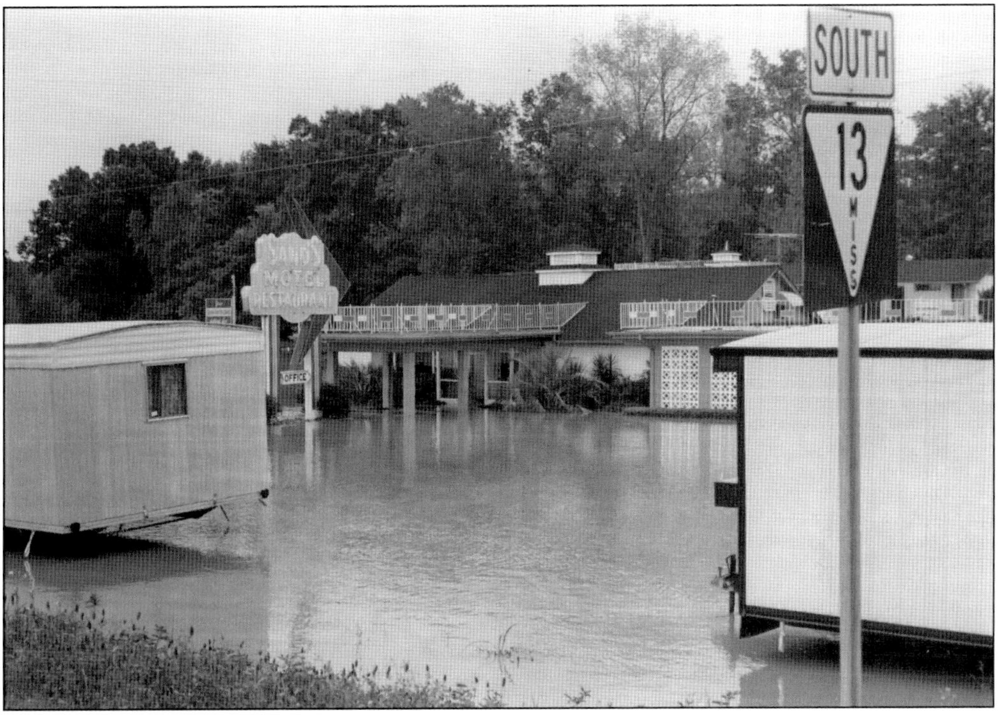

In this view, Sand's Motel and Restaurant is seen in the severe flooding of 1974. Then–civil defense director Jim Thornhill took this photograph. (Courtesy of Marion County Public Library.)

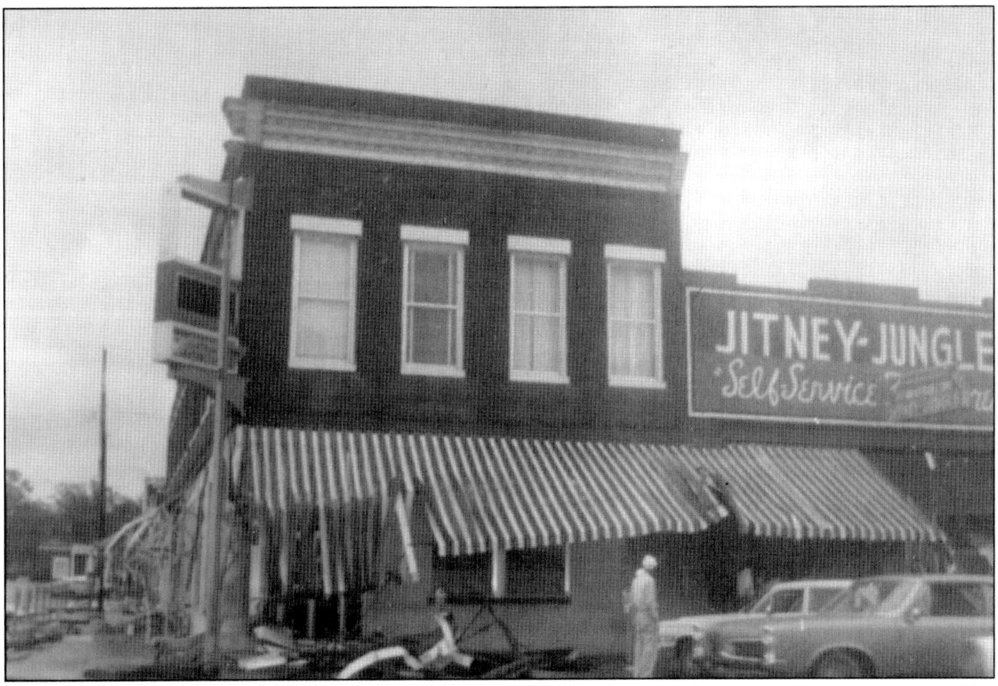

The awning of the Citizen's Bank building was totally destroyed during Hurricane Camille. Similar damage could be found throughout Columbia. This picture was taken in August 1969. (Courtesy of Marion County Public Library.)

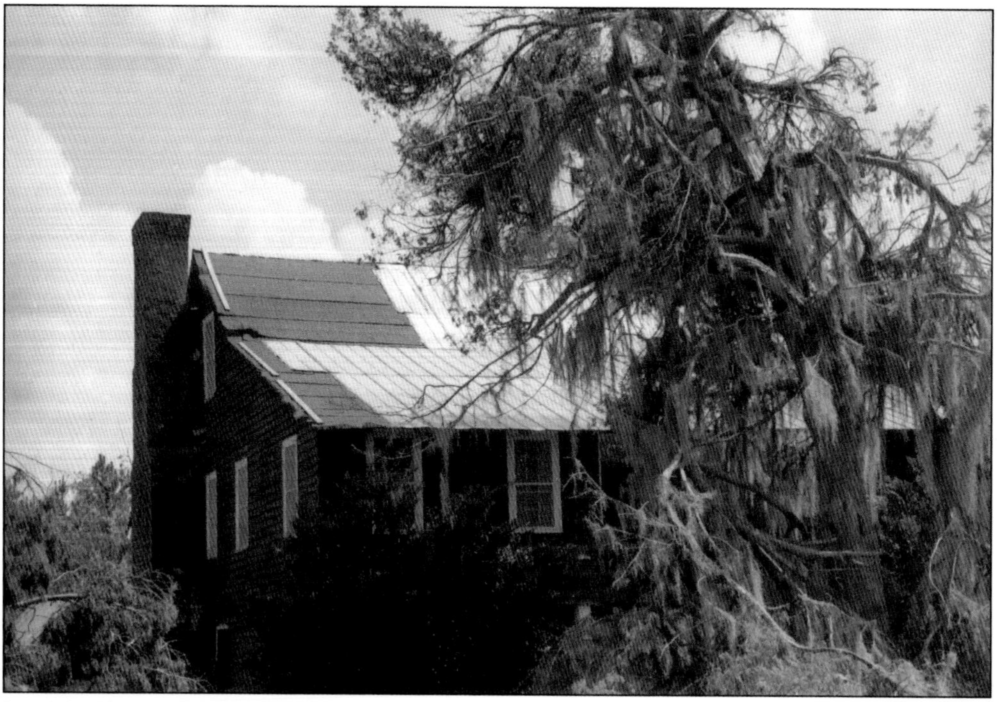

In 1969, Hurricane Camille damaged numerous structures throughout the county. This 1969 photograph documents roof damage to the historic John Ford home in the aftermath of the historic storm. The resilient old home has survived over two centuries of hurricanes, most recently the onslaught of Hurricane Katrina in 2005. (Courtesy of Marion County Development Partnership.)

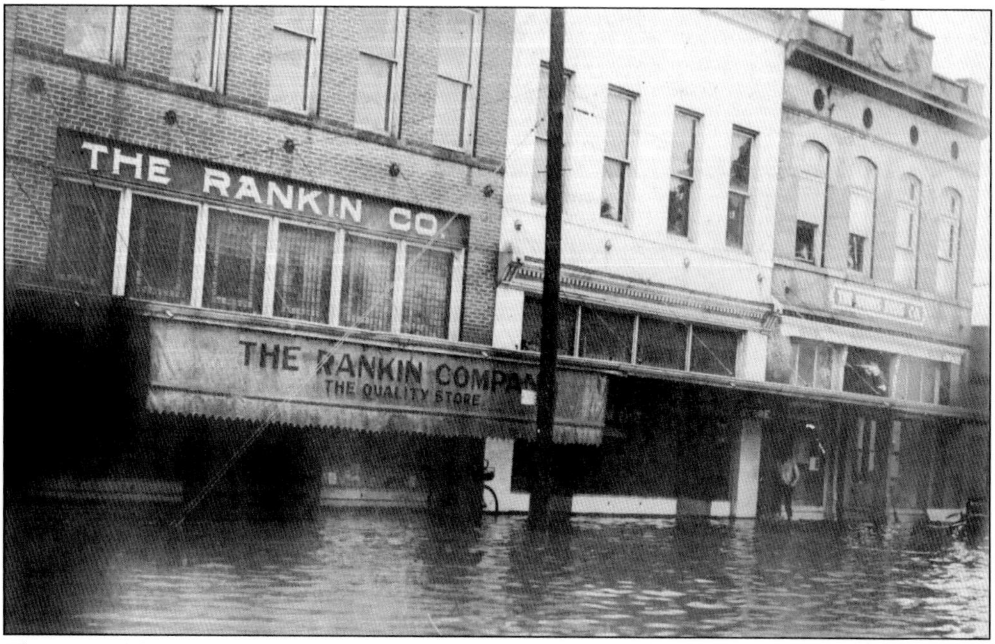

This view of the Rankin Company, Ford's, and Harris Drugs probably shows the buildings already flooded. Note the water up to the front wheel hubs of the car at right. This photograph was taken around 1921. (Courtesy of Fran Ginn.)

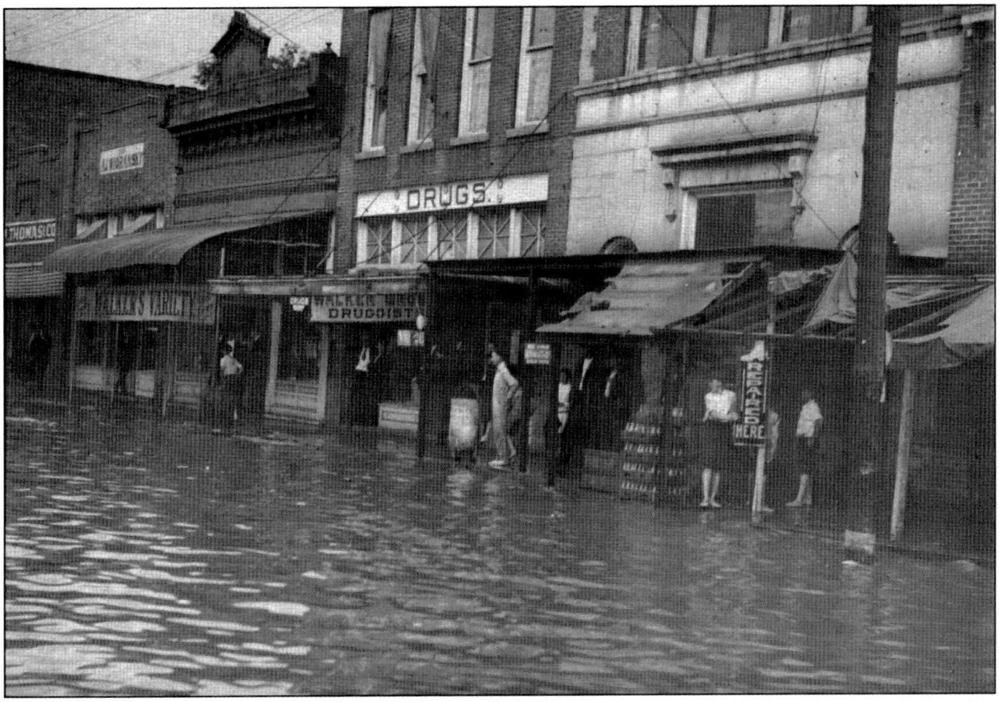

On the east side of Main Street, the floodwaters do not seem to be quite as threatening to the Walker Bros. Drugstore or the shoe repair shop. (Courtesy of Fran Ginn.)

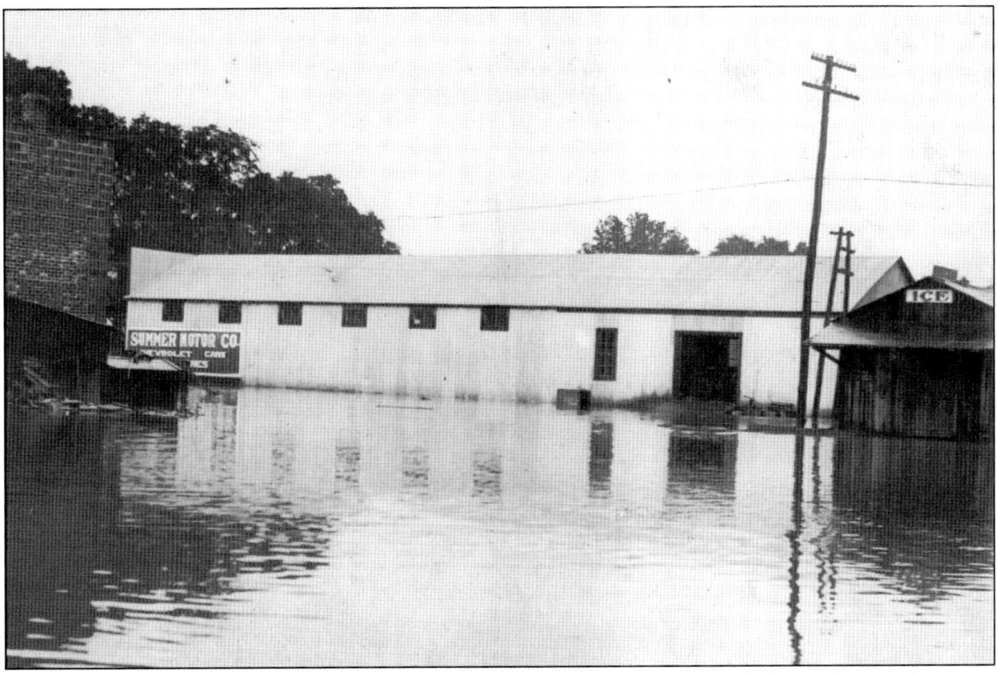

West of Main Street, the waters rise at Summer Motor Company and the icehouse. Summer Brothers was an early Chevrolet dealership that offered various services. The icehouse, fed by an artesian well, can be seen at right. (Courtesy of Bates Bullock.)

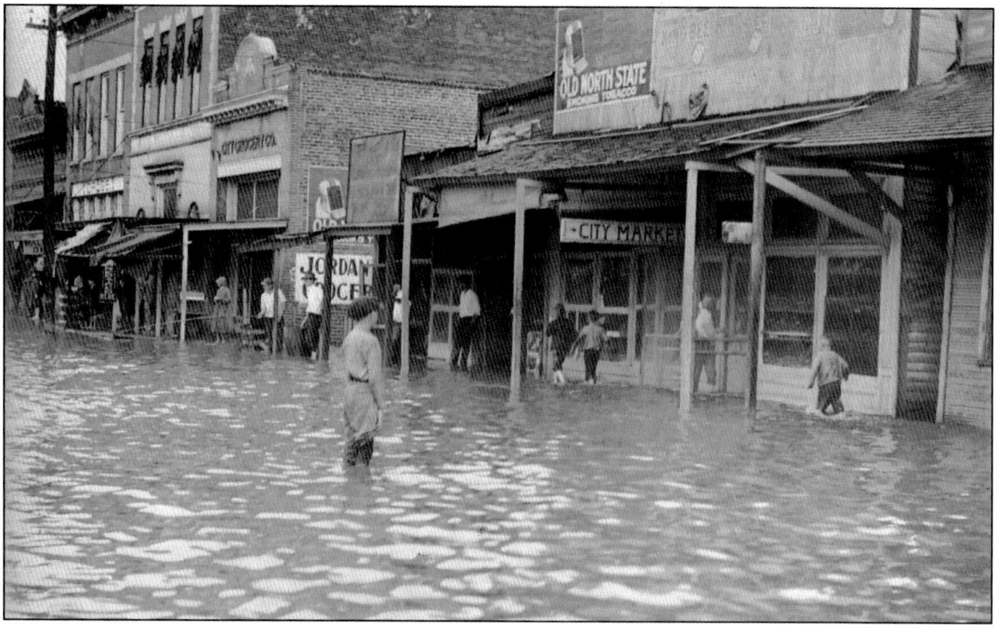

Townspeople slosh their way down the east side of Main Street where the City Market can be seen, as well as City Grocery Company. Note the distinctive Old North State tobacco advertisement in this c. 1921 photograph. (Courtesy of Fran Ginn.)

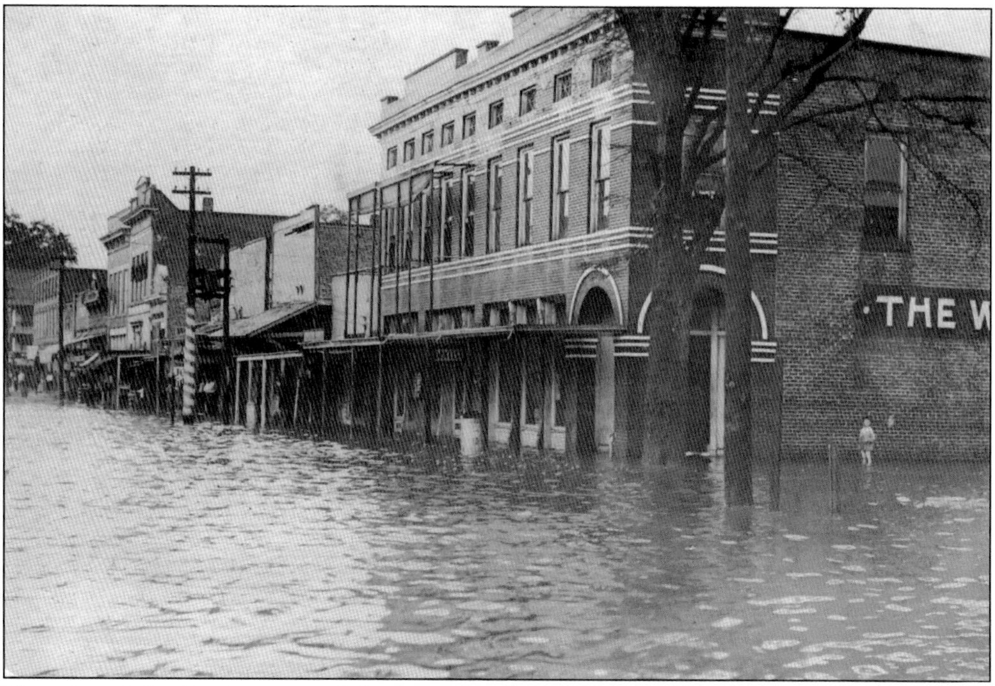

This view of the floodwaters is of the east side of Main Street; the Watts Company can be seen at right. The striped pole farther down the street indicates the establishment of a local barber. Note the child at right playing in the water. (Courtesy of Bates Bullock.)

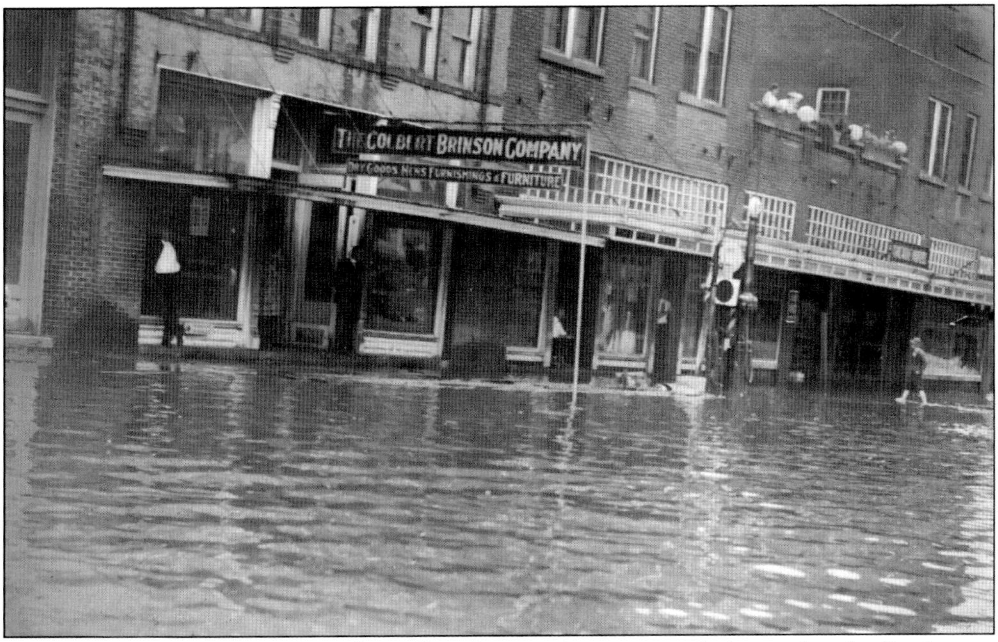

Shoppers loiter on the sidewalk at the Colbert-Brinson Company in the hopes that the floodwaters do not continue to rise along Main Street. The Colbert-Brinson Company was located on the west side of Main Street down from Hill Hardware. Note the gathering on the roof farther down the street. Sources do not agree as to the year of this flood; it is either 1919 or 1921. (Courtesy of Bates Bullock.)

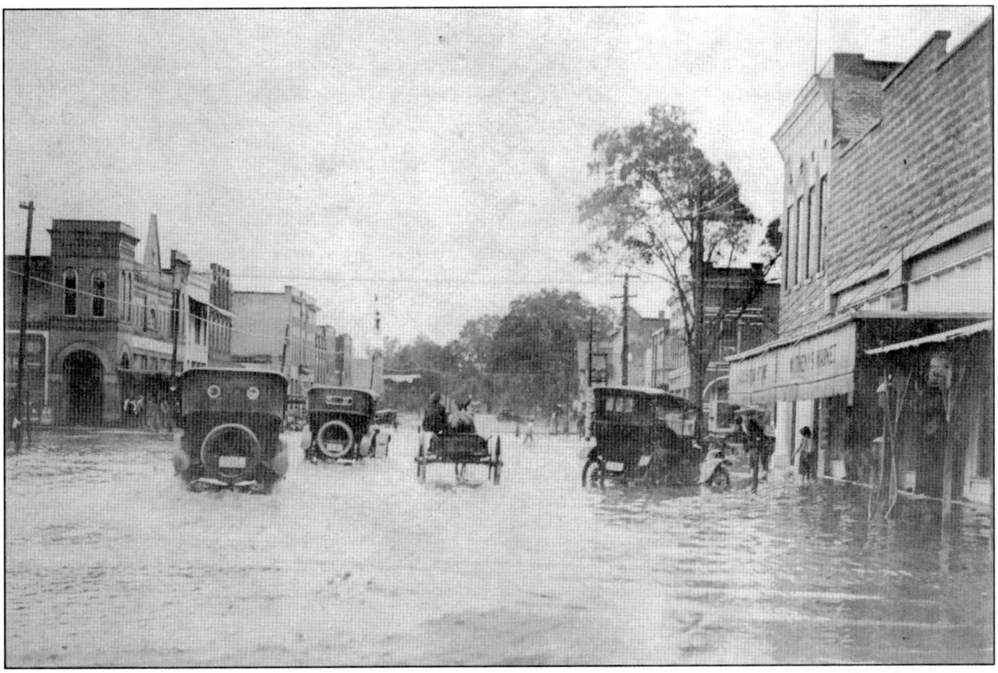

Looking north, Kalil's Fair Store and Matheny's Market can be seen at right with floodwaters up to the store entrances. Clearly, the times were rapidly changing as modern cars impatiently pass a horse-drawn buggy, making their way north through Columbia. (Courtesy of Bates Bullock.)

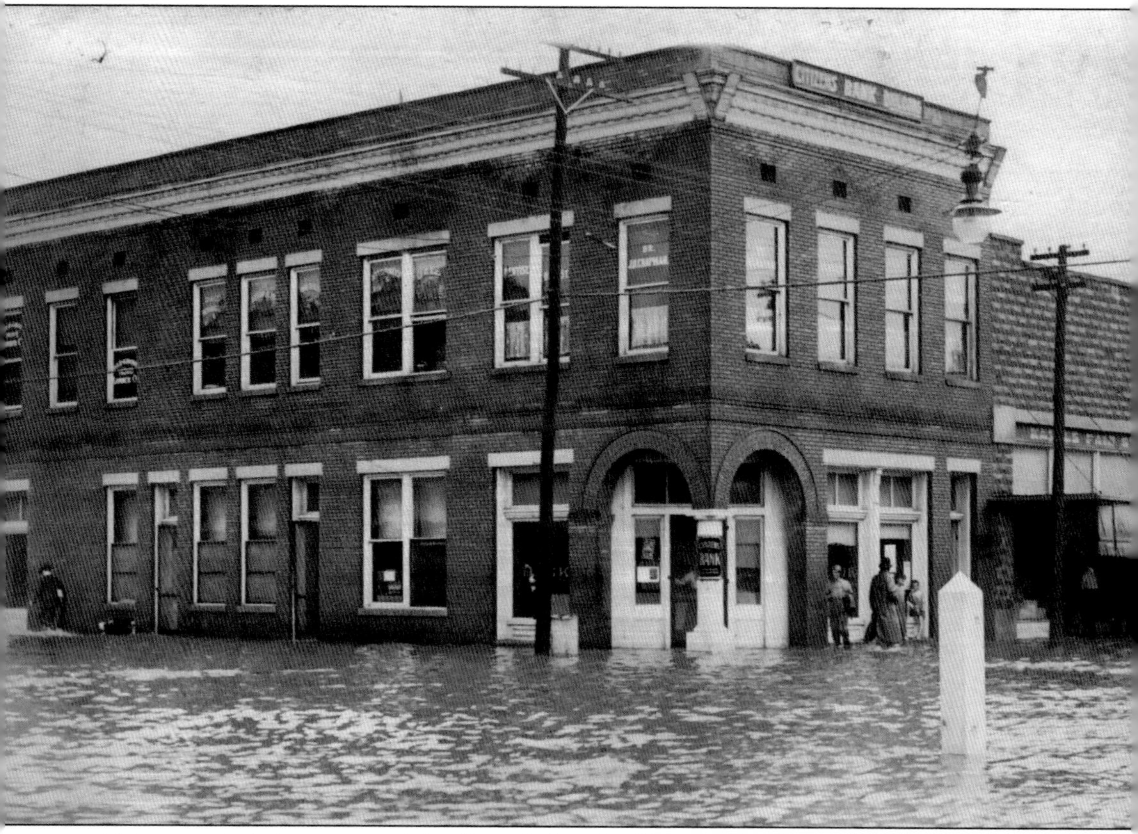

Citizens wade their way around the Citizen's Bank building during the flood. Note the rudimentary lamp suspended over the street in the upper right. The white pike seen at right stood in the middle of the intersection until the streets were bricked over in the late 1920s, and another stood at the intersection of Main and Church Streets. (Courtesy of Bates Bullock.)

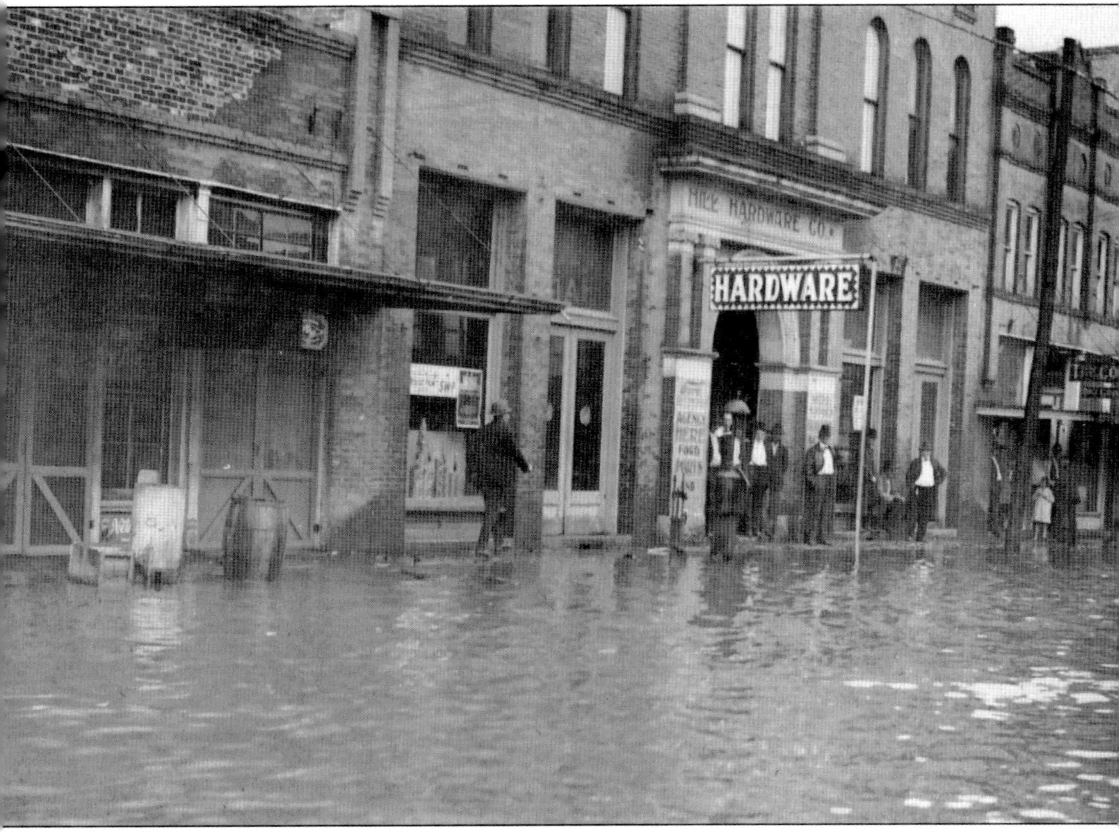

In this view, floodwaters threaten Hill Hardware, a longtime business landmark in downtown Columbia since 1901. The sign on the left of the entrance reads, "Ford agency, Ford parts," while on the curb a gasoline pump, the first in Marion County, can be seen. (Courtesy of Bates Bullock.)

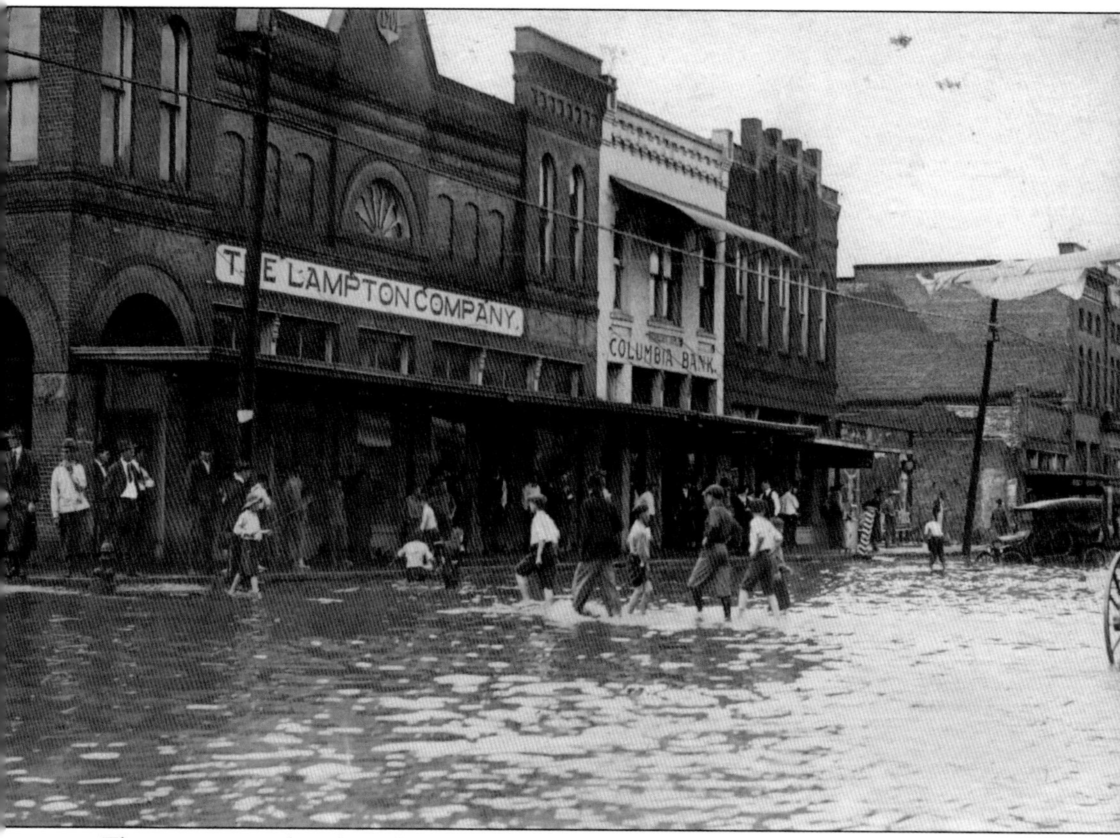

This image was taken from the vantage point of the center of Main and Second Streets. While some loiter on the sidewalks of the Lampton Company, the more adventurous cannot help but get their feet wet and attempt to cross the street. Note the Huckleberry Finn look-alike that appears to be fishing on Main Street! (Courtesy of Bates Bullock.)

INDEX